WHITE SANDS

Mark,
Enjoy the book
& the monument.
Pleasure to meet you
in Albuquerque. 23 Oct 94
Dietmar Schneider-Hett

Solace of the Sands by M. Kath Macaulay 18 x 24 Alkyd

WHITE SANDS

The History of a National Monument

Dietmar Schneider-Hector

The University of New Mexico Press
Albuquerque

Library of Congress Cataloging-in-Publication Data

Schneider-Hector, Dietmar, 1949-
White sands: the history of a national monument by Dietmar
Schneider-Hector—1st ed.
p. cm.
Includes bibliographical references and index.
ISBN 0-8263-1415-5
1. White Sands National Monument (N.M.)–History. I. Title.
F802.W45S35 1993
978.965—dc20   92–33665
CIP

To Gayle—desert sojourner—for all the right reasons. And for all those who venture beyond Rainbow's End.

Contents

LIST OF MAPS

PREFACE

The concept of preserving landscapes has developed relatively recently. As people and their technological advances overwhelm those remaining unspoiled environments, it has become urgent that lands be preserved before they are lost. Even as Americans as individuals agree that each of us must make sacrifices to save our environment, the real story of such protection reveals a struggle between development companies, state and federal agencies, and environmentalists. At times the intensity of their feuds overshadows the landscapes that lie at the heart of the debates. The ongoing battles to preserve America's lands become more intense as the number of available landscapes decline. One very special natural landscape is White Sands, a gypsum dune field in south-central New Mexico. This book is the story of how it has survived exploiters' schemes to become a part of the National Park system and how this national monument endeavors to maintain its integrity.

I first encountered White Sands National Monument (WSNM) during a family outing in the summer months of 1962. Little did I realize that my initial impression of the monument as a gypsum sandbox would be decidedly altered within three decades. The passage of time revealed that White Sands was "more than beautiful—fascinating!"[1] For me the gypsum dunes as a historical subject evolved into a historian's passion that would consume considerable time, money, and energy. As with any such undertaking, the toll inflicted upon personal relationships is incalculable. Optimistically, the positive reasons for researching and writing this book outweigh the short-term personal sacrifices.

I owe the success of this work to many professionals. This project would have been impossible without the direction, encouragement, and sound advice offered by Dan L. Flores, professor of history at Texas Tech University. Additionally, I am grateful to the many people who helped me in my research: the late Ralph Charles; Louise Charles Rutz of Placitas, New Mexico; Lillian Bagwell of Alamogordo, New Mexico; the late Murray Morgan; J. Marion Bell of Alamogordo; Austin Hoover, Lynda Blazer, Marie Peiñado, and Patricia McCann at the Rio Grande Historical Collections/Hobson-Huntsinger University Archives, New Mexico State University, Las Cruces, New Mexico; National Park Service associate director Jerry Rogers; National Park Service Bureau historian Barry Mackintosh; former Southwest Regional historian Melody Webb; historian Richard Sellars at National Park Service, Southwest Regional Office, Santa Fe, New Mexico; WSNM Superintendent Dennis Ditmanson and WSNM Chief of Interpretation John Mangimeli; retired WSNM superintendents Donald Harper and John Turney; retired chief ranger Robert Schumerth; former WSNM naturalist Dennis Vasquez; former WSNM rangers Dave Evans, Jane Tate, and Cindy Ott-Jones; Superintendents Robert Heier, Mesa Verde National Park, and William Wellman, Great Sand Dunes National Monument; and Richard Salazar at New Mexico Records Center and Archives, Santa Fe, New Mexico. Also acknowledged are the many librarians at New Mexico Tech, University of New Mexico, University of Texas at El Paso, Texas Tech University, New Mexico State University, Alamogordo Public library, Las Cruces Branigan Memorial library, New Mexico Records Center and Archives, and the National Archives in Washington, D.C., who provided invaluable assistance in

Preface

locating research materials. Also recognition goes to Barbara Guth and her editorial staff of University of New Mexico Press for their editorial skills, constructive criticisms, and support.

Special thanks are extended to James and Hahn Fenton of Lubbock, Texas, for their social courtesies and countless inspirational talks. And to my parents, Gilbert and Monika Hector; and family members: Hans Georg and Martina Schneider, Chris and Annette Matthews, Barbara Hector, Jim and Patty Mason, Mark Hector, and Sedly-Gayle Barnwell for their encouragement and interest in this project. I must also acknowledge the late Bill Stocks, Sonny Ramirez of McAllen, Texas, and the rest of the "Regulars" (1st Battalion, 6th Infantry, 198th Light Infantry Brigade, Americal Division, 1967–1969), who collectively acted as the impetus for the academic studies all those years ago. A special thanks to John Kyle Thomas of Bristol, Tennessee, who encouraged me to go beyond "the next bend." Not forgotten are professors Preston Hubbard, Richard Gildrie, and Malcolm Muir at Austin Peay State University, Tennessee; and Judy Allen, Pam Sheridan, Knox Long, and Jerry Fecht at Moorpark College, California.

I wish to express my sincere appreciation to Faith Heather Barnwell of Lompoc, California, for her typing skills, personal insights, and encouraging words. Also, a note of thanks to Connie E. Hopper of Las Cruces, New Mexico, Roy E. Gould of El Paso, Texas, and Robert A. Lebsock of Las Cruces, New Mexico, for lending their technical expertise during the computer crises. And finally, thank you to Gayle Pendleton Barnwell Hector, who endured the trials that accompanied this endeavor. Her patience, dedication, persistence, and lengthy hours at the computer ensured the successful completion of this book.

To all of you my heartfelt thanks.

THE GREAT WHITE SANDS
Genesis of a Gypsiferous Sea

Climb to the highest ridge in a dune field and muse on the hills and hol-
lows below. Watch the rising and falling waves of sand and remember
that for everything there is a season, and for life on sand dunes it is the
season of the wind.—Janice Emily Bowers, *Seasons of the Wind*

The White Sands country is an area of environmental di-
versity; it holds lava beds in its northern region, conspic-
uous mountains overshadow it, and a gypsum sea lies on
the floor of the sweeping semidesert plain. The white horizon
cutting across the width of the expansive Tularosa Basin appears
out of place, as if nature had played a trick on itself. At first the
dune field evokes the notion of a mirage or a product of a vivid
imagination or an improbable snowfield. But on approaching the
overpowering whiteness, it becomes evident that, in a syntaxic
fashion, one is "in" the desert as well as "on" a dune. Sitting or
lying on top of a dune in the cool of evening, the senses are overwhelmed by the vast celestial panorama, amazed by the basin's
spaciousness, and captivated by the gypsum dunescape—an
image other than an immense gypsum sandbox. A human being
is dwarfed by the magnificence of this environment. Thus, while
the winds stir the dunes, your mind's eye captures a momentary
reawakening of being, a rejuvenation of the spirit.   White Sands
is one of New Mexico's geological wonders, and, since 1933, a national monument managed by the National Park Service. It attracts more than half a million tourists each year. Countless
American and foreign visitors have asked questions concerning

1

the dunes' genesis and development. This economic gypsum magnet in the land of the turquoise sky is much more than a playground for vacationers; it is a place where any person can enjoy the aesthetic qualities of a unique environment, a place for contemplation, a laboratory for the scientific community, and an area that entices hikers and picnickers. Geophysiographic knowledge of the captivating Great White Sands helps to explain why the area is one of the Southwest's premier pristine natural attractions and why the National Park Service eventually earmarked it for preservation. White Sands' geological significance lies in its gypsum composition; dunes, especially gypsum dunes, occur in few regions of the North American deserts. The four major North American deserts—the Great Basin and the Sonoran, the Mojave, and the Chihuahuan deserts—are distributed within the rugged Basin and Range Province. The Chihuahuan Desert lies in New Mexico, Arizona, Texas, the Mexican states of Chihuahua, San Luis Potosi, Zacatecas, Coahuila, Nuevo Leon, and Durango. Approximately half of the valleys of the Mexican Highlands are known as *bolsons*, valleys without an external drainage outlet. Many of these bolsons range from 4,000 to 5,000 feet above sea level.[1]

Situated on the eastern fringe of the Mexican Highland Section lies an area designated as the Bolson Subsection, which is where the White Sands gypsum dunes are found. The Chihuahuan Desert, like other desert regions, includes basins or bolsons; one of these basins is the Tularosa Basin. This basin comprises the second of four northern projections of the Chihuahuan Desert in the United States. According to geologists the basin evolved nearly 25 million years ago.[2]

The physical features that enclose the Tularosa Basin are natural wonders in their own right. In *Fire on the Mountain*, Edward Abbey described the mountains surrounding the Tularosa Basin as "chains of islands" and a "convoy of purple ships."[3] The lofty Sacramento Mountains are presently protected as Lincoln National Forest; east of White Sands is the prominent Sierra Blanca (12,003 feet)—home of the Mescalero Apaches' winter tourist resort, Ski Apache—and the U.S. Forest Service's White Mountain Wilderness. To the west stretch three sets of mountains: the San Andres Mountains, where San Andres National Wildlife Refuge is found today; the abbreviated San Augustin Mountains with their guardian peak overlooking the historical pass of that name; and the Organ Mountains with their imposing needle-shaped peaks (Organ Needle is 9,012 feet).[4] Sierra Oscura and Chupadera Plateau border the Tularosa Basin in its northern region. The basin's southern boundary is marked by the Jarilla, Franklin, and Hueco mountains and the Hueco Bolson. In sum the expansive basin measures 150 miles in length, 60 miles in width, while encompassing 6,000 square miles (see Map 1).[5]

The tremendous mountain-making movement—known as the Laramide Revolution—produced the Rocky Mountains chain and raised the land elevation throughout the Southwest.[6] The Rio Grande Rift, in which the Tularosa Basin lies, includes twenty-two basins and embraces approximately 70,000 square miles.[7] Sixty million years ago south-central New Mexico experienced a gradual uplift. Volcanic activity and regional uplifts occurred 38 through 140 million years ago. Perhaps as long as 40 million years ago, various erosional forces gradually lowered the region, producing down-dropped basins throughout the Rio Grande Rift region. The principal mountain ranges and intermontane basins evolved with the severe earth movements that were the result of the shifting of the continental plates, interspersed with periodic volcanic activity. These erosive processes deposited in the basin great amounts of gypsum and alluvial sediments from the adjacent mountains.[8] The alluvial fill coincided with the faulting that

3

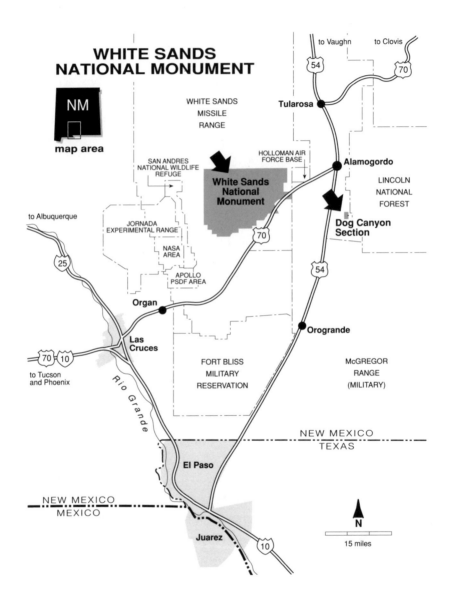

Map 1. Area Map, White Sands National Monument. (Courtesty of National Park Service)

exposed ancient rocks along the escarpments enclosing the basin. Distinct topographical features emerged as a result of various deposits in the basin: for example, lava beds known as *el malpais* (Spanish for badlands), currently protected by the Bureau of Land Management as Valley of Fires Recreation Area (463 acres) and Carrizozo Lava Flow Wilderness Study Area (10,240 acres); the alkali flats or salt beds; and the vast gypsum dune field.

In their quest to explain the origins of White Sands, at the turn of the twentieth century scientists discovered evidence indicating that the Tularosa Basin contained an ancient lakebed known as Lake Otero. One geologist calculated that ancient Lake Otero had once engulfed between 1,600 and 1,800 square miles.[9]

Accompanying Lake Otero's disappearance, a playa or alkali marsh remained at the southwestern portion of White Sands. The alkali flats encompass the western vicinity of the White Sands region and progress southward to the sometimes filled Lake Lucero. At the base of the San Andres Mountains, mountain water runoff is channeled by arroyos into the alkali flats and the lake. A section of the playa floods periodically during the rainy months, usually during July and August, leaving a small accumulation of water within Lake Lucero. Ground water is never more than three or four feet below the playa, leaving the surface generally damp.

The existence of White Sands was known to the prehistoric Jornada Mogollon Culture, the Warm Springs, the Chiricahua, and the Mescalero Apache bands, and to Spanish, Mexican, and American settlers and ranchers. American interest in the area occurred in September 1849, when Capt. Randolph B. Marcy entered the Tularosa Basin by way of the San Augustine Pass and headed southward to Franklin (El Paso), thereby missing White Sands.[10] Several weeks later Lt. William F. Smith departed El Paso to reconnoiter the Sacramento Mountains. During Smith's survey the "white sands hills" were reported for the first time by an explorer representing the U.S. government, but no further investigation followed.[11] Twenty years later Bvt. Gen. August V. Kautz, commanding general at Fort Stanton, New Mexico Territory, sent a gypsum sample to professor George Gibbs in New York with a letter describing "salt plains" in the Tularosa Basin. An amazed Kautz reported that the sand was "so white and the plain so extensive as to give the effect of snowy scenery."[12] Generally, the Tularosa Basin's topography was of little interest to the American government during the mid-1800s. It was a remote location in an undeveloped territory at a time when the government concerned itself with surveying a southern railroad route to California, encouraging trade and settlement of the "New West," and defending and surveying the new Mexican-United States border.

But international interest in dune studies began during the 1880s and 1890s, and results were published principally by Europeans who examined the great sand seas of Asia and northern Africa.[13] The U.S. Geological Survey initiated its examination of the Tularosa Basin and its gypsum dunes in the early twentieth century, after the science had advanced considerably. Academic reports of the gypsum dunes and the Tularosa Basin were first published by 1891. Early authors inconsistently labeled the Tularosa Basin with a variety of designations such as the Tularosa Desert; the Lanoria Mesa, the San Andre(a)s Valley, and the White Sands Plain; the Otero Basin; the Gran Quivira Valley; the Hueco-Organ Basin; the Alamogordo Desert; the Sacramento Valley; and the Jarilla Bolson. O. E. Meinzer's and R. F. Hare's 1915 Geological Survey study, "Geology and Water Resources of Tularosa Basin, New Mexico," eventually contributed to the standardization of the name Tularosa Basin.[14]

6

THE GREAT WHITE SANDS

Today, geologists believe that the gypsum and valley fill arrived in the basin because of hydraulic erosive forces. One scientist contends that the principal agent responsible for transporting and depositing the gypsum of Lake Lucero is water pressure, in fact 33 percent of the gypsum arrived at Lake Lucero as a result of this process.[15] Modern geologists agree that intense rains washed great quantities of gypsum from the mountains into the basin. Without an external drainage outlet, the rain collected in the basin resulting in the water's slow evaporation. The gypsum sediments in the water settled on the lakebed as the water evaporated. These cycles of evaporation and redeposition of gypsum occurred for many centuries. The water that had not evaporated settled as ground water with a subsurface depth of only a few feet. As the ground water saturated the basin floor, the water became permeated with gypsum, which is why it remains undrinkable.[16]

The dune is one of the principal wind-blown or aeolian deposits. Most scientists and tourists consider dunes one of the outstanding landscape features in a desert environment. While single, isolated dunes do exist, they generally occur as groups or colonies—also called sand seas or ergs. They vary in size and shape depending upon the wind speed, the available quantity of gypsum or other particles, and the nature of the vegetative cover. The composition of dunes may also vary; both quartz and gypsum form dunes. Additionally, the physics of dune migration applies to all dune varieties.

The shape of the dunes depends mainly upon the winds' speed and direction. But other agents can influence a dune's development. For example, water, vegetation, surrounding topography, and man-made structures can hinder or impede a dune's progression.[17]

Because of the sparsity of vegetation and intensity of the erosional agents, erosional processes in the desert can alter the landscape dramatically. In arid regions the most immediate and effective erosional forces are running streams, cloudbursts, or high winds. While generally not as dramatic an erosive force as cloudbursts, winds are a constant weathering force.

At White Sands four principal dune formations are prevalent (see Map 2). The first type of dune is the dome-shaped (embryonic) dune, which is found in the region east of Lake Lucero where the dunes initiate their movement to the northeast.[18] Embryonic dunes are formed rapidly; therefore the wind's speed is an important factor in the rate of their evolution. The height of the dunes is predictable because it is limited by strong, unidirectional winds. The embryonic dunes are transitory, migrating continuously; some embryonic dunes have traveled as much as 40 feet per year. A typical embryonic dune measures 450 feet wide, 420 feet across in the direction of the prevailing wind, and 18 feet high.[19] Generally, the embryonic dunes travel twice as fast as other White Sands dunes.

High winds transform the embryonic dunes into transverse dunes, that is, dunes that are characterized by extensive ridges. The transverse dunes attain the greatest height of the four types of dunes. They form long, almost parallel ridges at right angles to the dominant wind direction. A selected transverse dune measures 400 feet in the direction of the wind with a crest at right angles to wind direction 800 feet across. The height of the dune was 40 feet.[20]

High effective winds create barchan dunes, that is, dunes that are crescent or quarter-moon shaped with the horn tips facing forward. Barchan dunes are transitional in the region that separates them from another type, the forward-positioned parabolic dune. A typical barchan dune measures 170 feet wide in the field

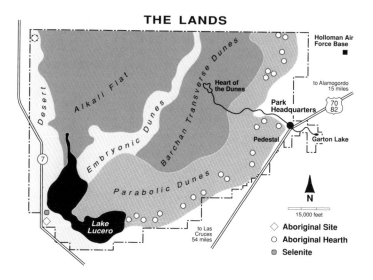

Map 2. *The Lands, White Sands National Monument, "White Sands National Monument Master Plan, March 1976." (Courtesy of National Park Service)*

direction of the prevailing wind, 290 feet from tip to tip, and 18 feet high.[21]

The migration of a barchan dune toward the eastern area of the dune field transforms the dune into a parabolic dune. A parabolic dune presents a U-shaped or V-shaped appearance as it migrates toward the margins of the dune field. The arms of the parabolic dunes generally remain stationary when they reach some obstacle such as vegetation; therefore, the center advances well ahead of its extended limbs. One parabolic dune measured 265 feet wide with arms 900 feet long. These dunes migrate less than 10 feet annually,[22] and in contrast to the other types of dunes in an established dune field, the parabolic dunes are the first dunes to encounter vegetation.

Generally, gypsum dune deposits occur during windstorms. The prevailing winds at White Sands originate from the southwest or the west-southwest. The southwest winds effect the dune

9

field because only winds with velocities of fifteen knots or more influence the development of the gypsum dune. The prevailing winds are effective principally during March and April. During January and February, however, sporadic northern winds sweep across the gypsum field. The relatively brief change in the dominant wind direction alters the dune development because the gypsum particles are redeposited counter to the dune's migration direction.[23]

Reverse winds turn the crests of the dunes back upon themselves, causing blowouts in the loose sand on the downward sides and forming small dunes on the tops of the large ones. The new crest dunes form toward the southwest but are short-lived and are soon erased by the reappearance of the prevailing southwesterly winds. Studies utilizing aerial photographs and plotting measuring stakes, which were taken during six-month intervals for two years, revealed great variation in dune migrations.[24]

Recent studies document that the prevailing southwesterly winds occur principally during February, March, April, and May, while those originating from the south and the east occur during the summer thunderstorms. High winds do not contribute to the dunes' migration to any appreciable degree during rainstorms because the rains inhibit the gypsum grains' movement.[25]

To appreciate the dynamics of a White Sands storm, I experienced one on 10 March 1988. The relationship with the dune storm began by my first viewing the White Sands storm as it was occurring within the Tularosa Basin. I began with a three-mile hike along a trail that wound up on the east side of the Organ Mountains. A quiet, restful, and remote spot was located in the middle of Texas Canyon providing a panoramic view. The observation position was bordered by a swift-running stream, narrowleaf and Rio Grande cottonwood trees (*Populus fremontii* and

P. wislizeni), and immense boulders. The Tularosa Basin's expansiveness was ringed by mountains, and the distant gypsum on the horizon was slightly overshadowed by Sierra Blanca.

From this position I watched the effects of the winds. A continuous white cloud swirled eastward from Lake Lucero and upward into a dark hued sky. The wind speed measured 35 to 45 miles per hour throughout the basin, and even in Texas Canyon the mountain gusts were strong and steady. On a clear day snow-capped Sierra Blanca can be seen with the naked eye from almost any direction within the basin; however, because of the strong gypsum-permeated winds, even this prominent feature on the horizon remained hidden from view. As I gazed upon the distant storm I recalled John C. Van Dyke's feelings in *The Desert,* as he viewed a similar occurrence in Arizona. Van Dyke wrote, "Fifty miles away one could see the desert sand-whirls moving slowly over the beds (gypsum) in tall columns two thousand feet high and shining like shafts of marble in the sunlight." Van Dyke's response to the gypsum storm was one of romantic amazement. I could fully corroborate his exclamation, "Ah! what a stifling sulphureous air!"[26]

After an hour of observation I descended to the base of Texas Canyon and drove approximately half an hour by car to reach the Point of the Sands, located on the southeastern margin of the gypsum dune field and another five minutes to arrive at the White Sands National Monument Visitors Center. A quick two-mile hike along the southeastern dunes brought me to an attractive parabolic dune. Here I began to experience the gypsum storm firsthand. Its intensity forced me to take shelter beneath my blanket. An immense white cloud engulfed me, bombarding my protective cover with billions of gypsum grains. The high winds made it difficult to grasp the blanket firmly, and a gust of airborne gypsum pelted me every time I had to readjust the blanket.

11

I abandoned the encounter after approximately an hour, even though the gypsum storm continued unabated for the next several days. The tremendous intensity of the winds and the sound of the billions of gypsum particles colliding against each other are vivid memory.

In addition to the dunes, an important topographical feature is the interdune areas. These zones equal or exceed the area of the dunes in the eastern, downward portion of the dune field. In the west these areas are narrower and occupy less surface area than the contiguous transverse dunes. Interdune areas are transitory, and their life span is dependent upon the time an encroaching dune requires to engulf the area. The dunes' migration determines the size of each interdune area.[27]

In contrast to the adjacent dunes, the interdune areas are composed of different sediments and hold various plants and materials.[28] The wind deposits the dark-colored particles, thus explaining the high concentration of clay and silt in the interdune areas. The depth of an interdune area is dependent upon the time required for it to be submerged by a dune and the quantity of sediments that collect during the submersion period. In some areas sands are 1–4 feet deep, and as a result you will notice that the gypsum's whiteness contrasts sharply with the tan color.[29]

The sparkling gypsum dunescape may appear sterile, but it is a habitat for a variety of plants and animals. Further study will reveal that the earth's most extensive gypsum deposit holds a wealth of life forms, and for these reasons the National Park Service supported the recommendation to have a portion of the region preserved as a national monument.

The gypsum dunes are young, in geologic terms. By comparison the region's human occupants have been here for only a moment, or an *Augenblick*. The basin has experienced human interaction, even though few people have lived there. As each group engaged in trading, hunting, or warring, the White Sands' interior generally remained untouched but not unnoticed. For the most part human occupation occurred only on the periphery of the dune field. The principal dune area remained inhospitable to humans. Only when early Hispanic New Mexicans followed by American miners and entrepreneurs realized the dunes' commercial potential was any interest shown in the interior areas.

White Sands held little promise except as an environment ripe for commercial ventures that never seemed to live up to expectations. Oddly enough, in spite of successive commercial failures, local residents persisted in their attempts to make the gypsum dune field profitable. It is at this juncture and as a result of this paradox, that the current fate of White Sands began to unfold. This book is the story of the individuals and organizations who desired to exploit White Sands and of those who were determined to preserve it. It is an account of the area—its significance as a geologic formation, as a biological community, as an economic entity. I offer answers to a number of questions that occur to anyone familiar with the area: What contributed to White Sands' attraction? Why has it been designated a national monument? What makes this monument unique in the National Park Service system? If this book encourages you to go out into the Heart of the Dunes and experience for yourself the qualities that prompted the U.S. government to set aside this dune field diamond as a national monument, then it will have served its purpose.[30]

A FLORA AND
FAUNA TO MATCH
White Sands as a Vibrant Ecosystem

The life of the desert lives only by virtue of adapting itself to the conditions of the desert.—John C. Van Dyke, *The Desert*

N early one hundred years ago, naturalist John Burroughs, in *Pepacton*, wrote, "Nature is of course universal, but in the same sense she is local and particular—cuts every suit to fit the weaver, gives every land an earth and sky of its own, and a flora and fauna to match."[1] Seventy years later, essayist Joseph Wood Krutch, in *The Voice of the Desert*, descriptively characterized his adopted Southwestern environment as a "consistent world with a special landscape, a special geography, and to go with them, a special flora and fauna."[2] Even though neither writer specifically described White Sands, both assessments appropriately reflect the complexities of nature in general and the desert in particular. Each offered a unique portrayal of the gypsum dune field's vibrant ecosystem. The White Sands region, about half of which is White Sands National Monument (WSNM), includes a variety of flora and fauna that remains unfamiliar to many visitors.[3] While the geologic and economic significance of White Sands was the primary motivation for its declaration as a national monument by President Herbert Hoover in 1933, zoologists and botanists had for some time been attracted to the indigenous and exotic flora and fauna in this unique habitat. It was an ideal laboratory for studying the wildlife and plant life in a gypsum dune environment. Even though their reports had been published before 1933, they did not

15

contribute significantly to the national monument cause.

Within the American Southwest four principal North American deserts are found: the Mojave, the Sonoran, the Great Basin, and the Chihuahuan. They represent two types of desert: the cold desert as characterized by the Great Basin Desert, and the hot desert associated with the Mojave, Sonoran, and Chihuahuan. A cold desert has low average annual temperatures and considerable precipitation in the form of snow; a hot desert has warmer annual temperatures, and rainfall is the principal source of moisture. Regardless of the type of desert, heavy precipitation occurs mainly during July, August, and September, but the amount of rainfall can vary dramatically from one year to the next.[4] The common denominator for all deserts is aridity, an environment in which evaporation exceeds the annual precipitation.[5]

The Chihuahuan Desert is the largest of the North American deserts but the smallest of the U.S. deserts. Characterized as a warm-temperate desert associated with high elevations, it is bounded by the Rocky Mountains to the north, the Sierra Madre Occidental to the west, the Sierra Madre Oriental to the east, and the Mexican Plateau to the south. Similar to other deserts the Chihuahuan possesses expansive alluvial plains and bajadas (alluvial fans), mountains, and enclosed basins.[6] Approximately 60 percent of the annual precipitation occurs from July to October in the Tularosa Basin. Heavy thunderstorms account for most of this moisture. The summer and fall precipitation originates from the moist air pushing westward over the Gulf of Mexico. The winter and early spring moisture arrives as a result of eastward storms forming over the Pacific Ocean. In contrast to the summer and fall rains, much of the moisture from the Pacific Ocean does not reach central New Mexico because of the mountain ranges west of the Tularosa Basin.[7]

A Flora and Fauna to Match

Historian C. L. Sonnichsen portrays the Tularosa Basin as the harshest area within the Southwest.[8] While there are other candidates for that distinction, earlier chroniclers had also warned of the adverse traveling conditions in the region. John Wesley Powell, the Grand Canyon's explorer, inaccurately described Southern New Mexico as a true desert mostly "naked of vegetation." He believed there were areas "composed of incoherent sands and clays" and remnants of ancient lakes and seas. While he described these areas as the "bad lands of the Rocky Mountain Region," he actually never visited Southern New Mexico.[9] For centuries the Tularosa Basin, like the adjacent Jornada del Muerto (Journey of Death), was an arduous experience for the traveler. Without adequate provisions and water, the journey could prove fatal. Despite the hardships of the trip, the "remarkable purity and transparency of the atmosphere" were astonishing to Capt. Randolph B. Marcy, as he commented in his journal in 1849.[10]

Challenging the idea that Southern New Mexico contained little vegetation, contemporary botanists have concluded that grama grass covered much of the area up until the 1850s. These researchers have pinpointed grazing as the principal force that has effected the change from grasslands to sparsely vegetated areas containing mesquite (*Prosopis glandulosa*) and creosote (*larrea tridentata*). They maintain that the area's classification as a desert grassland is inaccurate and suggest that what exists today is an area (biome) identified as a warm-temperate desertland interspersed with grama grass (*Boutelova spp.*).[11] Other factors responsible for altering the region's flora are building construction and increasing erosion. Subsequently, desert shrubs such as creosote, and mesquite have replaced previously grass areas. Eventually, overgrazing accompanied by droughts reduced or eliminated the dominant grasses.[12]

Black grama grass dominated the desert flora surrounding White Sands 100 years ago, until overwhelmed by invading mesquite and the severe drought of 1851–56.[13] Experts believe that while domestic grazing has usually been cited as the decisive force in grama grass depletion, most ranges (including those without grazers) have not experienced a regenerating grassland. The mesquite's domination continues, proving the complexities of the accelerated transition from grassland to shrubland.[14]

The recent proliferation of environmental studies has educated many people that all deserts, and specifically dune fields, are not barren. Animal and plant species are dispersed principally along the dune fringes and interdune areas. And like all arid land ecosystems, White Sands is a fragile environment. Desert ecosystems are fragile because they support relatively few life-forms. Any disturbance of habitat is likely to result in the erosion of the sparse moisture-retentive soil, preventing or greatly retarding regeneration, so these life-forms are especially vulnerable.

Surrounded by a thriving ecoregion, the White Sands dune field is habitat for plants and animals that are migrants from other areas, as well as for species that are endemic to the dunes themselves. Contemporary botanists have researched many species of flora there, especially rare cacti. Of particular interest is the claret cup hedgehog cactus (*Echinocereus triglochidiatus* var. *gonacanthus*), growing mainly in hard, gypsum-packed soil in the interdune areas.[15] Of equal importance was the recording of the desert night-blooming cereus (*Peniocereus greggi*). The cacti's distribution is in the far western section of WSNM, principally on the alluvial slopes of the San Andres Mountains.[16] Another discovery was the grama grass cactus (*Toumeya papyracantha*), thriving along the eastern margins of the dunes.[17] The last finding was the mulee (*Coryphantha scheeri var. valida*), located primarily in the interdune area northeast of Lake Lucero.[18] Currently the cacti

18

are threatened by encroaching off-road vehicles (military and civilian), illegal collecting, and the browsing oryx.[19] Alerting the National Park Service to the potential loss of these cacti, botanists have recommended fencing WSNM to keep out the oryx, increasing the number of boundary patrols, and encouraging drivers to comply with monument regulations to remain on established roads. However, the greatest threat to the cacti is the result of the introduction of oryx, which not only jeopardize the rare cacti but also endanger WSNM's entire ecosystem.[20]

Botanist Janice E. Bowers has likened the biogeography of the dunes to that of islands because of their isolation. Unlike islands that are surrounded by water, though, dune islands maintain direct land bridges with the surrounding mainland desert. Dune islands like oceanic islands receive their seeds from mainland sources. Studying earlier island hypotheses and observing the flora on several dune fields, it was found that endemic floras are noticeably greater in dune fields than on duneless desert habitats of similar size, and dune flora habitats contain fewer species per similar area than duneless areas.[21] Bowers observes that because they receive 75–95 percent of their flora from the nondune areas, strictly speaking, dune fields do not qualify as "floristic islands."[22] Dunes maintain and retain isolated flora as well as nondunal characteristics.[23]

While the geological and recreational attributes dominated the monument staff's early advertising efforts, the importance of the monument's flora and fauna remained the exclusive domain of the botanists and zoologists. Recognizing a need to educate the public about the monument's biological communities, the WSNM staff prepared its master plan in 1965. It stressed the need for updating studies of flora and fauna so visitors would become "aware of the unique natural values" through interpretive programs.[24] In 1968, the National Park Service introduced the

National Environmental Study Area programs to instill a "lasting Environmental Conscience" in America's youth. Underlying the National Park Service's theme to educate Americans about the earth's geological and ecological complexities was the urgency to alert the public to a person's capabilities to alter the environment. The educational efforts were directed principally toward the public school systems.

In 1970, WSNM Superintendent John F. Turney initiated his National Environmental Study Area program by establishing two study areas: the first area at Garton Lake, an aquatic environment, and the second area at the Big Pedestal, a marginal dune area. The local public schools participated by conducting classes and touring the two National Environmental Study Areas during the spring of 1970. Because of the program's success, the Alamogordo Public Schools added the nature study to its curriculum.[25]

White Sands' environment contains a variety of life-forms. Situated along the eastern and southern monument boundaries are dunes interspersed with grasslands. Among the flora found here are the squaw-bush sumac or skunkbush sumac (*Rhus aromatica*), hoary rosemarymint (*Poliomintha incana*), soaptree yucca (*Yucca elata*), wooly paperflower (*Psilostrophe tagentia*), soft orange globemallow (*Sphaeralcea incana*), and Rio Grande cottonwood (*Populus wislizenia*). In these areas enough species have survived to contribute to the slowing of the dunes' eastward migration.[26]

Those plants that survive until they are overwhelmed by migrating dunes in the interdune spaces are mint shrub or hoary rosemarymint, rabbitbush (*Chrysothamnus nauseosus*), frankenia, snakeweed (*Gutierrezia sarothae*), Mormon Tea (*Ephedra torreyana*), prairie beadgrass or little bluestem (*Schizachyrium scoparium*), Alkali Sacaton (*Sporobolus airoides*), and soaptree yucca. Indian ricegrass (*Oryzopsis hymenoides*) and sand verbena (*Abronia angustifolia*) are situated on the adjacent rising dunes. Located on nearby dunes measuring 15–25 feet high, only mint shrub, rabbit-bush, snakeweed, and Mormon Tea thrive.[27]

Located along the northern boundary of WSNM is a temporary stream known as Lost River. The stream is ecologically important for the following reasons: it attracts a variety of animal life, it develops as a potential staging area for new flora species, and it acts instrumentally in potential dispersion of saltcedars in WSNM.[28] The U.S. Department of Agriculture introduced colonies of salt cedars into the Southwest between 1899 and 1915. First noticed in WSNM in 1939 by Park Service officials, the exotic saltcedar (*Tamarix gallica*) has important significance for the White Sands ecosystem. As with the oryx, the WSNM's saltcedar invasion poses continuous managerial problems for the National Park Service. Saltcedar is found in several areas; for example, in the western section dense saltcedar patches grow quickly, crowding out native vegetation. The equally exotic and unmanageable oryx utilize the saltcedar as shade covering.[29]

In conjunction with the flora, the fauna have also generated biological studies. In 1907, Alexander G. Ruthven examined and catalogued the habitat of the region's amphibians and reptiles. He was the first biologist to observe that the lesser earless lizard (*Holbrookia maculata ruthveni*) in White Sands was lighter in color than adjacent lizard species in the nongypsum areas.[30]

Twenty years later, Lee R. Dice visited White Sands and enumerated the species of animals distributed within various communities. For example, he listed the fauna of the alkali meadow, desert plain, alkali marsh and pool, and White Sands communities. Dice listed the following fauna for the White Sands community: Coyote (*Canis latrans*), Merriam kangaroo rat (*Dipodomys merriami*), Ruidoso (Mearn's) grasshopper mouse (*Onychomys leucogaster*), Chihuahua deer mouse (*Peromyscus maniculatus*), blacktail jackrabbit (*Lepus californicus*), pronghorned antelope (*Antilocapra americana*), and the White Sands pocket mouse (*Perognathus flavescens gypsi*).[31] He was pleasantly surprised by his discovery of the previously unrecorded pocket mouse.[32] Dice's mouse discovery encouraged other biologists, such as John E. Hill and W. B. Buchanan of the American Museum of Natural History in New York City, to visit the White Sands region to study the relationship of the mouse's protective coloring with its environment.[33]

Spurred on by Dice's work zoologist Seth B. Benson studied the light-colored rodents in White Sands and the dark-colored rodents in the nearby Valley of Fires lava beds. He reasoned that the color difference was the rodents' natural adaptation to their respective environments because of predators.[34]

National Park Service associate biologist Adrey E. Borell examined Garton Lake in 1935 for its value as a bird sanctuary. Borell's intermittent research commenced on 19 March 1935 and concluded on 13 January 1938, revealing that the area did attract numerous birds. Limiting his study to the dunes and the lake, Borell's findings disclosed, as expected, that the largest bird populations are present during the spring and fall migrations. Four areas within WSNM were studied: the Garton Lake or marsh area, the Alkali Flats, interdune and fringe gypsum dune areas, and the center or Heart of the Dunes. In the Garton Lake vicinity Borell noted that the marsh was four feet deep and contained warm mineralized water surrounded by widgeon grass (*Ruppia maritima*), muskgrass (*Nitella* sp.), narrowleaf cattail (*Typha angustifolia*), salt grass (*Distichlis tricta*), and bulrush (*Scirpus brittonianus*). He also noted a few exotic saltcedars. Hiking in the Alkali Flats, he observed only four-wing saltbush (*Atriplex canescens*) and a few birds such as desert horned larks (*Otocoris alpestris leucolaema*), sage thrashers (*Oreoscoptes montanus*),

American pipits (*Anthus spinoletta rubescens*), and black-chinned sparrows (*Spizella atrogularis*). Investigating the fringe areas, Borell encountered Rio Grande cottonwoods, squaw-bush sumac, yucca, rabbitbush, and joint fir (*Ephedra*), and in the interdune areas he located crucifixion bush (*Holocantha*) and mesquite that attracted flycatchers, warblers, thrashers, sage (*Amphispiza nevadensis*) and desert sparrows (*Amphispiza bilineata*), and western mourning doves (*Zenaidura macroura marginella*). Scanning the Heart of the Dunes, Borell remarked that there "is but little plant life."[35] Despite the absence of vegetation he spotted infrequent visits to the area by shrikes (*Laniidae*), ravens (*Corvinae*), desert horned larks, and sage sparrows.

In 1935, National Park Service Director Arno B. Cammerer proposed to Acting Interior Secretary T. A. Walters that WSNM's boundaries be extended to include approximately 1,300 acres encompassing Garton Lake and the adjacent artesian spring known locally as Dobie Well. In his letter Cammerer referred to the report by Jay N. Darling, chief of the Biological Survey, as support for the idea of a migratory waterfowl sanctuary and proposed that because of the limited size of the addition the WSNM staff could administer the proposed refuge.[36]

In 1939, while removing cattails from Garton Lake in order to maintain open water, W. B. McDougall, regional wildlife technician, discovered one hundred bass and one carp. During the cleanup of Garton Lake, Emergency Relief Administration workers were also restoring the spring at Dobie Well because it had served as a water source for numerous birds and wildlife.[37] Prior to McDougall's departure from WSNM, rangers asked him to respond to two of their proposals to enrich WSNM's wildlife. The rangers suggested introducing Gambel's quail (*Lophortyx gambeli gambeli*) and a herd of pronghorned antelope (*Antilocapra americana*) into the eastern portion of WSNM. McDougall recommended that the rangers ask New Mexico State Game Warden Elliot Barker about such an introduction. Seizing the opportunity McDougall asked Barker personally about the idea. Barker told McDougall that the introductions sounded reasonable but informed him that any such request must originate with Southwestern National Monuments Superintendent Frank Pinkley. Barker favored introducing the wildlife; however, he wondered if there were sufficient land to sustain the antelope herd. McDougall relayed Barker's response to WSNM, adding that he would endorse the plan based upon Barker's concurrence.[38] The National Park Service refused to act on the plans.

During the first years of the twentieth century, the arrival of the livestock industry, city development, and local bounty hunters contributed to the rapid decline of large wildlife.[39] While there are no large wildlife native to White Sands, wildlife in the region does cross the dune field and inhabits portions of the dunes intermittently. But bounty hunters have systematically eliminated most of the region's larger predators such as the mountain lion (*Felis concolor*) and the Mexican gray wolf (*Canis lupus baileyi*) because of the animals' real or potential threat to livestock.[40]

As recently as 1991, there have been proposals to reintroduce the Mexican gray wolf. The New Mexico Department of Game and Fish has supported the proposals, but military officials at White Sands Missile Range have prevented the reintroduction, believing that the missile range would be overrun by biologists who would draw too much notoriety to the site.[41] However, the reintroduction is tentatively scheduled for 1994. It remains to be seen whether the military will cooperate with the plan. These reasons for nonintroduction are untenable. The University of New Mexico's Wildlife Research Institute's scientists researched mountain lion behavior in the adjacent San Andres Mountains during the 1980s.[42] However, during the summer of 1990 the military notified the biologists that it was proposing to halt or at least to suspend indefinitely the mountain lion research project. As of this writing, the military has granted the University of New Mexico researchers a brief extension, but no final decision has been made. While the officials at the military base claim that its policy derives from a concern that publicity and the visitors it brings threaten national security, those same officials have proudly announced that approximately 40,000 space shuttle enthusiasts witnessed the landing of Columbia at Northrup landing strip on 30 March 1982.[43]

Of all of the species of animals in WSNM, the oryx has had the most impact on the landscape during the last twenty years. Between 1969 and 1973, the New Mexico Department of Game and Fish introduced ninety-three African oryx or gemsbok (*Oryx gazella*) into the Tularosa Basin (within the White Sands Missile Range and Holloman Air Force Base). This project was perceived as a resurrection of earlier plans to reestablish big game populations in the area, such as Elliot Barker's 1930s proposal for pronghorned antelopes and the 1950s introduction of bighorn sheep (*Ovis canadensis*). Unlike the pronghorned antelope, the oryx were exotic animals. A rapidly increasing oryx herd expanded its range, and within three years the oryx were spotted within the boundaries of the unfenced WSNM. National Park Service regulations prohibit exotic animals from parks and monuments, so as the number of oryx sightings increased, the National Park Service initiated a program to prevent the animals from entering WSNM. Fencing that cost more than $400,000 was erected along nineteen miles of the western and southern boundaries. The ambitious project has only slowed the oryx's inroads into the national monument, as verified by rangers' observations of oryx tracks and visual sightings.[44]

In 1979, the Southwest regional director asked the Interior Department which agency was responsible for oryx trespassing into WSNM. Gayle E. Manges, Interior Department field solicitor, responded that the New Mexico legislature regarded the oryx as game animals and that the state agencies were responsible for transporting and introducing the animals into the Tularosa Basin. White Sands National Monument could erect fences to prevent incursions by the oryx, but the state did not have to control game animals by building fences. Manges warned that any attempt by the National Park Service to begin legal action against New Mexico could prove unfavorable.[45] The field solicitor concluded that if the state refused to cooperate with WSNM, the National Park Service should protect its monument by fencing or even killing the animals.[46]

National Park Service studies reveal that the oryx that trespass into WSNM damage the ecosystem by eating and trampling plant species, many of them fragile and rare. As a result, the oryx intrusions were considered as damaging as military trespassing when the National Park Service compiled its 1981 resolution or complaint list.[47] The National Park Service recommended fencing for two purposes: keeping both the oryx and unauthorized military personnel out of WSNM. Unintentionally the oryx introduction resulted in management policy nightmares for the WSNM staff as well as for their superiors in Santa Fe.

In 1983, biologists William H. Reid and Gail R. Patrick reported some discouraging news for the National Park Service. The scientists concluded that these exotic animals could breed and subsist within the monument despite the absence of fresh water. They hinted that one solution might be to relocate the oryx in a similar environment outside the grounds of the monument, where the animals could develop as an "economic asset."[48]

A Flora and Fauna to Match

To control what it considered undesirable native animals, the U.S. Army informed WSNM of its plan to limit an expanding coyote population. Cooperating with the military, the U.S. Fish and Wildlife Service-Animal Damage Control teams engaged in trapping and aerial shooting of the area's two principal predators, mountain lions and coyotes. According to law, whenever the military, state, and federal game officials engage in predator control programs with the possibility of any WSNM impact, they must notify the WSNM superintendent. However, while aerial shootings are confined principally to the remote northwestern White Sands Missile Range section, killings with M-44 (also known as cyanide coyote killer) occur along the eastern foothills of the San Andres Mountains. The predator control teams place the M-44 sets no closer than 100 yards from WSNM's western boundary. The military claims that these killings should not affect WSNM resident animals.[49]

Numerous mammals reside within the White Sands region or are transient foragers. Among the more prominent interior monument residents are kit fox (*Vulpes marcrotis*), bannertail kangaroo rat (*Dipodomys spectabilis*), porcupine (*Erethizon dorsatum*), coyote, gray fox (*Urocyon cinereoargenteus*), striped skunk (*Mephitis mephitis*), and hog-nosed skunk (*Conepatus mesoleucus*).[50] While most native animals are welcomed by the National Park Service, the oryx is not. A rapidly increasing oryx population threatens many native flora within the monument. While both flora and fauna survive in an extreme ecological environment each group endures the continuous processes of adaptation and natural selection required to live in such a severe habitat. This remarkable ecoregion reveals an intricate life-support system in that each element is dependent upon all other life-forms and upon the dunes for survival.

WHITE SANDS

Studies of the flora and fauna in White Sands National Monument have revealed the area's unique ecosystem and its important role in the environmental history of the White Sands gypsum dunes. These recent studies have encouraged the National Park Service to examine and preserve the monument's ecosystem with the same fervor as the gypsum dunes. Studying the area's natural history as an integrated biological and botanical community assists in comprehending the complexities of this environment. The National Park Service, the New Mexico Department of Game and Fish, the U.S. Fish and Wildlife Service, and the military all help to preserve and protect the White Sands ecosystem; however, each agency does so within the framework of its own management or mission directives.

Pasó Por Aquí

Passing Through Tough Country

To live there, has always been risky business —a matter of long
chances and short shrifts; of privation and danger.—C. L.
Sonnichsen, *Tularosa*

The Southwest has experienced an exceptionally long and
diverse human procession. Divergent peoples such as
the Mogollon, the Mimbres, the Mescalero Apaches, the
Spaniards, the Mexicans, and the numerous hyphenated
Americans successively displaced or overwhelmed former
inhabitants throughout most of the Southwestern regions. Each
group differed from the other groups in a variety of ways:
ethnically, linguistically, culturally, and politically. The
discoveries of scientists and scholars in the Tularosa Basin
contribute to the history of White Sands, Western American
history, and the study of human occupation in semiarid deserts
of the Southwest.

Edgar L. Hewett called the Southwest "a vast laboratory of
nature and man."[1] He added that the archaeological remains of
the Southwestern Indians reveal "how they met and tried to
solve the problems that all humanity had confronted."[2] There
has been continuous human presence in the Tularosa Basin for
approximately 1,100–1,200 years, and the Tularosa and
neighboring Hueco basins contain prominent archaeological
sites.[3]

White Sands

The Tularosa Basin is, in fact, an ideal archaeological laboratory. In contrast to developing urban areas where surface sites are disappearing rapidly, the basin generally has remained unscathed by humans. The White Sands region contains numerous surface sites dotted with ecofacts and artifacts lying exposed on the ground.

Among the first humans to inhabit the general region were the Southwestern Clovis groups, known also as plains-based big-game hunters, who relied upon large fur-bearing animals such as mammoths for their subsistence. Between 9000 and 7500 b.c., desiccation or aridity forced the larger animals to abandon the low-lying areas for the wooded mountain areas that could support their needs. As climatic changes affected the ecology of the Tularosa Basin, the evolution of desert biotic communities altered the hunters' lifeways from large-game hunting to small-game hunting and plant gathering.[4] Archaic peoples utilized Indian ricegrass and yucca as food sources and left behind remnants such as hearths, tools, and potsherds, primarily along the marginal dune areas of White Sands.[5]

The next people, known as Mogollon, reached their peak during the 1100s, and the combination of living in a precarious desert environment and by a corresponding decline in food sources sealed their fate.[6] Generally, the Mogollon Culture encompassed most of south-central and western New Mexico and eastern Arizona. The Mogollon peoples actively traded and culturally interacted with their neighbors, the Hohokam and Anasazi. Sites and artifacts reveal that these early Southwesterners cultivated corn and gathered mesquite beans for their subsistence. By 1250–1300, population centers throughout the Southwest were abandoned. Additionally, a major drought occurred from a.d. 1276 to 1299, contributing to the region's general evacuation by a.d. 1350.[7]

Relatively little information is available concerning the human cultures that used the Tularosa Basin and White Sands between 1350 and 1530. A new people migrated into the region following the dispersal of the Mogollon-Mimbres. The new immigrants belonged to the Southern Athabascan linguistic family. The Mescalero Apache, like their predecessors, were mountain people ranging over an expansive domain that included most of south-central New Mexico, West Texas, and sections of Chihuahua, Mexico. The Mescalero camped on the banks of the Rio Grande in the winter months and relocated to the mountains during the summer months. Throughout their excursions, the Mescalero certainly passed White Sands. Because the Apache preferred mountain retreats to exposed camps on the plains, any Mescalero camps adjacent to or in White Sands were probably temporary.[8]

The principal economic item proffered by White Sands was gypsum in large and pure quantities. While Pueblo Indians may have utilized gypsum for ornamental purposes and whitewash to protect their houses from the intense summer sun, and the Chiricahua Apache may have given gypsum as a gift to the shaman during healing ceremonies,[9] there is no evidence that Apache bands used gypsum for any other purposes.

While the numerous Southwest Indian bands went about their daily lifeways, considerable political activity occurred in central Mexico. The Spanish conquistadors, led by the indefatigable Hernan Cortés, conquered the Aztec Empire in 1521. Subalterns of Cortés led expeditions northward in the hope of locating the reputed Seven Cities of Cibola. Among the first non-Native Americans to enter New Mexico's current boundaries was a small party consisting of three Spaniards and a Moorish slave led by Cabeza de Vaca. De Vaca's purpose for traveling across what is now Southern New Mexico was to return to Mexico City following his ill-fated expedition's shipwreck along the Texas coast in 1528. As the surviving members wandered across Texas and New Mexico, they received reports from Indians of wealthy cities located to the distant north. Upon his arrival in Mexico City in 1536, de Vaca informed his superior, Viceroy Antonio de Mendoza, of the Cibola stories, and when these accounts reached other prominent Spaniards, there was a rush to locate the cities.[10] The subsequent Francisco Vazquez de Coronado expedition of 1540 resulted in some of the most important European discoveries of the interior of North America. While Coronado conquered only the gold-less pueblos and not the gold-lined cities of Cibola, he more than doubled the territory of New Spain. Coronado's greatest achievement was recording the geographical features of the new Spanish lands.[11]

Spanish colonization of New Mexico began on 30 April 1598, with Juan de Oñate claiming New Mexico for King Felipe II of Spain. Oñate's expedition, numbering 129 Spaniards and an unknown number of Mexican Indian allies and slaves, entered New Mexico's northern pueblos. The initial Spanish settlements were established adjacent to the various pueblos such as Acoma, Isleta, Jemez, Socorro, and Santo Domingo. The first exclusively Spanish villages were Española, Santa Fe, and Bernalillo.[12] The territory between the Organ Mountains and the Sacramento Mountains remained untraveled and removed from the Royal Highway (El Camino Real) that connected Mexico City and the far northern frontier. Mescalero threats against the Rio Grande villages of Robledo (1598), Doña Ana (1682), and Brazito (1776) precluded any expeditions by the Spanish villagers into the Tularosa Basin and nearby mountains. Spain was unable or unwilling to protect its subjects in the Mesilla Valley from Mescalero attacks. Thus from 1610 until 1821, in spite of the Spanish presence, the White Sands country remained an Apache domain.[13]

Mexico inherited Spain's royal provinces after the revolution in 1821. The villages concentrated along the Rio Grande remained isolated from the principal settlements of Santa Fe and El Paso del Norte and from one another. The small settlements received communiqués from merchants, travelers, government officials, and soldiers who journeyed the El Camino Real. Mexican military protection for the citizens of a far-flung frontier was no better than that usually provided by a struggling young nation, and incessant Apache raiding parties caused New Mexico to become known as the land of war. Heavily guarded caravans were necessary to deter Apache raiders. Reliable geographical information was available only for well-traveled roads, while the regions beyond the principal highways remained isolated and received scant attention from Mexican officials.[14] Mexican pragmatism dictated that it was dangerous as well as foolish to venture toward the periphery of Apacheria, formed by the Organ Mountains (Sierra de los Organos) east of Doña Ana. Selective Mescalero and Chiricahua raids against undefended Doña Ana thwarted any federal or local government attempts to follow the Apaches east of the Organ Mountains. Trader Josiah Gregg remarked in *Commerce of the Prairies* (1844) that as the members of his party passed through the Mesilla Valley, they noticed several villages that were abandoned because "of the marauding incursions of the Apaches."[15] Because of the relative isolation of the New Mexican villages from one another as well as the fear of entering Apacheria, there was a general lack of familiarity with Mexico's northern interior regions such as the Tularosa Basin.

While Spain and later Mexico held official political and limited military control of New Mexico, a new invader emerged from the east—English-speaking Americans. Spaniards and Mexicans had encountered Americans engaged in trading and fur trapping actively involved in military reconnaissances for the United States.[16]

Southern New Mexico received little attention during the early American westward venture. The principal business enterprises were concentrated in the Santa Fe area. During the 1830s, Josiah Gregg implied that he knew of salt lakes located near the Manzano Mountains, adding that situated approximately one hundred miles south "there is another Salina (salt lake) of the same character."[17] The Tularosa Basin and White Sands remained an uncharted region until American military forces captured and occupied New Mexico during the Mexican War. On 18 August 1846, Gen. Stephen W. Kearny and his Army of the West captured and occupied Santa Fe. Four days later Kearny formally proclaimed New Mexico as a United States territory.[18] Approximately two years later, as the Americans debated in Washington, D.C., and in Mexico City concerning how much of Mexico would serve as compensation for the war, the Treaty of Guadalupe Hidalgo resolved the dispute. Article V of the treaty stated:

> The boundary line between the two republics shall commence in the Gulf of Mexico, three leagues from land, opposite the mouth of its deepest branch ... to the point where it strikes the southern boundary of New Mexico; thence westwardly, along the whole southern boundary of New Mexico (which runs north of the town called El Paso) to its western termination.[19]

One of the initial exigencies for the U.S. Government was to survey its new acquisitions. The treaty brought Apacheria under American jurisdiction. Article XI of the treaty revealed that "a great part of the territories ... now occupied by savage tribes, ... will hereafter be under the exclusive control of the government of the United States."[20]

The acquisition and incorporation of half of Mexico placed new demands upon the American government. The Treaty of Guadalupe Hidalgo initiated an American frontier policy that included developing trade and settlement in the West, surveying the West for railroads, developing a strategy for frontier defense, and establishing the international boundary line with Mexico.[21] The urgency to initiate a comprehensive policy for the West was also caused by the California Gold Rush of 1848 and 1849. While the major requirement for the West was railroad construction, the news of gold discoveries and President James K. Polk's annual message to Congress in December 1848 inflamed the imaginations of hundreds of thousands of Americans and foreigners. Individuals ventured to the American West by themselves, in pairs, or in groups such as New York's Fremont Association. The American emigrants followed old Indian trails as well as Spanish, Mexican, and American military roads leading to the California goldfields. The establishment of a large English-speaking population in the midst of an even greater population that primarily spoke Spanish, as well as Native American languages, necessitated the creation of communication links from coast to coast.[22]

Historian William H. Goetzmann proposes that America's westward movement during the 1800s progressed through three critical periods. The first period, "an era of imperial rivalry," was highlighted by the Lewis and Clark, Freeman and Custis, Stephen H. Long, and Pike explorations lasting from the early 1800s until the eve of the Mexican War. The second period, or the westering era (1845–60), included America's military conquest and annexation of half of Mexico and the settling and investing in the new West. The roles played by the Topographical Corps, the Pacific Railroad surveys, and the United States Mexican Boundary Commission surveys are important during this era. The third period (1860–1900), or era of "incipient conservation and planning in the national interest," was the era of the Great Surveys, that is, the geological and geographical explorations led by the "Big Four": Ferdinand V. Hayden, George M. Wheeler, Clarence King, and John Wesley Powell.[23]

In addition to the Big Four, numerous junior officers from the Topographical Corps were assigned to explore the Southwest during and subsequent to the Mexican War. While the principal survey figures achieved some degree of fame, there were many junior officers, ignored by popular history, who played principal roles in the exploration and survey of the Southwest.

In 1848, Col. J. J. Abert, Corps of Topographical Engineers, ordered Lt. William H. Emory to examine New Mexico's uncharted regions and to collect "data which would give the government some idea of the regions traversed."[24] Emory and his party recorded the area's flora and fauna, geological composition, and social conditions of the native New Mexicans. Emory followed the Rio Grande southward until he almost reached San Pedro on 15 October 1846. Approximately three miles above the village, Emory turned west toward the Black Range and California, missing his opportunity to see the White Sands country.[25]

Lt. James W. Abert, another well-traveled but relatively unknown explorer, embarked upon his survey that would delight "the soldier, the archaeologist, the historian, and the naturalist," on 29 September 1846.[26] Accompanied by Lt. William G. Peck, Abert received orders from Gen. Stephen Kearny to survey New Mexico. Abert's and Peck's immediate superior, Lt. William H. Emory, stated in his *Notes of a Military Reconnoissance* [sic] that the two officers would "make a map of New Mexico, based upon the astronomical points and measurements determined by myself

(Emory), and to furnish from the best statistical sources, an account of the population and resources, military and civil, of the province."[27]

Abert and Peck surveyed the pueblos, Fort Marcy, and numerous settlements in northern New Mexico. On 8 October 1846, Abert, Peck, and three men departed Santa Fe to begin the "regular tour" of New Mexico.[28] Abert and his small party traveled slowly southward along the Rio Grande and halted at every village or settlement along the way. Abert noted the flora and fauna of the Rio Grande Valley and provided commentary about the local inhabitants. It is uncertain how far south Abert was ordered to go. Abert visited and sketched the "hoary monuments," as he referred to the Spanish ruins at Abo, Quarai, and Gran Quivira, which are known collectively today as Salinas Pueblo Missions National Monument.[29] The lieutenant also encamped at Bosque del Apache, which currently is a national wildlife refuge, and recorded some of the diverse birds of the future sanctuary. He also captured and killed several birds for scientific purposes. On 12 December 1846, Abert camped at Valverde, located approximately thirty miles south of Socorro. He remained at Valverde until the morning of December 15, when he returned to Santa Fe.[30] Emory and Abert wrote excellent narratives of their New Mexican experiences. They surveyed vast regions of New Mexico but only encountered the Tularosa Basin from a distance. The Mexican War prevented either officer from completing his investigation of the southern regions.

At the conclusion of the Mexican War, the War Department shifted its western military priorities to a policy of assisting in the survey projects to determine the best wagon routes to California. The military designed the roads to link western forts to each other and to provide accessible routes for westward-bound emigrants. Four officers would play decisive roles in the

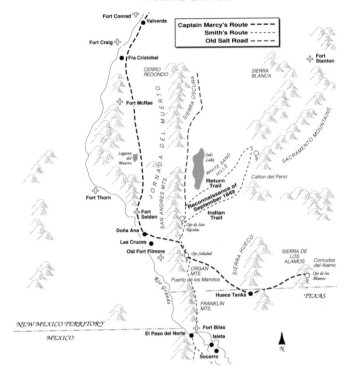

Map 3. Early American Military Routes (Report of Secretary of War, July 1850)

Americans' discovery of White Sands: Captains Samuel G. French and Randolph B. Marcy, Lt. William F. Smith, and Maj. Gen. August V. Kautz (see Map 3). Captain French, who surveyed the road
from San Antonio to El Paso during May 1849, reported that he was aware of "extensive salt flats" adjacent to the Sacramento Mountains north of El Paso. French relied upon secondhand information to describe the territory. In his official military report, French discussed the Sacramento Mountains and stated that this was "where timber is said to be found."[31] French added that the "testimony is concurrent" about the wealth associated with silver mines situated in the "neighborhood," referring to the mines of the Organ Mountains.[32] While French did not reach

38

White Sands, he was aware of the salt lakes and he was astute enough to record information about the Tularosa Basin that had been substantiated by El Pasoans familiar with the region.

On 4 April 1849, Captain Marcy received orders from Brig. Gen. Matthew Arbuckle, commander of the Seventh Military Department at Fort Smith, Arkansas. One of the principal directives ordered Marcy to "ascertain and establish the best route" from Fort Smith to New Mexico and California.[33] Marcy departed Fort Smith with 479 emigrants and reached Santa Fe on 28 June 1849. Marcy reported that during the course of the trip his party encountered few obstacles that would discourage caravan travel or preclude railway construction along the route. The captain prepared for his return to Fort Smith following a six-week respite. He decided to examine the feasibility of locating a southern route from Santa Fe that would allow him to strike an eastward course to the headwaters of the Red River and finally to Fort Smith. An initial problem for Marcy was his inability to find any "Mexicans who knew anything about the country," and the few individuals familiar with the Llano Estacado or Staked Plains of eastern New Mexico and west Texas refused to serve as guides because they would have to return unaccompanied through Apacheria and Comancheria.[34] Marcy finally located a Comanche in San Miguel who volunteered to guide the Americans southward to El Paso. Marcy's new guide informed him that the route originating from Doña Ana eastward to the Llano Estacado would be the advantageous course to travel. The availability of water determined Marcy's decision to follow his guide's directions.[35]

Marcy reached Doña Ana on 29 August 1849 and promptly questioned local residents about the feasibility of crossing the San Augustine Pass and striking toward the east. Town residents hesitated in assisting or volunteering to guide Marcy into

Mescalero Apacheria. Marcy learned that the Apache, or "brigands of the mountains" as he labeled them, had so terrorized the local community that few villagers dared to venture too far from Doña Ana. Marcy believed that the Tularosa Basin remained "wholly unknown" to the residents because of their fear of Apache reprisals.[36] Marcy's patience and persistence in finding a local guide paid dividends when a courageous villager revealed that he knew the territory lying eastward beyond the Organ Mountains.

On the morning of 1 September 1849, Marcy and his caravan completed their preparations for the journey and departed Doña Ana. Marcy crossed the San Augustine Pass and descended into the expansive basin. As Marcy wound his way along the eastern side of the Organ Mountains, he took time to observe the distant skyline. He noted that Sierra Blanca and the Sacramento Mountains "do not appear to be greater distance than eight to ten miles from us"; however, the guide from Doña Ana corrected Marcy's error by informing him that the mountains were more than forty miles away (Sierra Blanca is approximately eighty miles from the Organ Mountain foothills). This illusion, as Marcy referred to it, "is often experienced in New Mexico, and I can only account for it by the remarkable purity and transparency of the atmosphere, which enables the eye to penetrate far, and to discern objects distinctly."[37] Marcy's assessment of the Tularosa Basin remains appropriate to this day, at least on certain clear days! While Marcy was able to view clearly the distant mountains from his position along the base of the Organ Mountains, he was unable to detect the gypsum dune field. On the morning of 2 September 1849, Marcy reached the Salt Road that connected El Paso and what were known as the salt marshes and lakes (Lake Lucero). Turning southeast toward Hueco Tanks, he missed the opportunity to view and record

White Sands. However, Marcy's narrative does reveal that he had examined several salt samples from White Sands and remarked that he believed that the "Salt Lake north of El Paso" provided salt for all of New Mexico, Texas, and sections of Mexico.[38]

As Marcy traveled across the Llano Estacado toward Fort Smith, Lt. William F. Smith, accompanied by a small escort, embarked upon his reconnaissance of the Tularosa Basin. Smith's orders directed him to survey specifically the Sacramento Mountains in order to locate a passage conducive for wagon travel. The lieutenant departed El Paso on 21 September 1849, along the Salt Road. Smith followed the northward road that paralleled the Organ Mountains on the eastern side until he arrived at a water stop called Ojo de San Nicolas and then turned eastward in the direction of Dog Canyon, or Cañon de Perro. Smith and his party examined the western slope of the Sacramento Mountains. In spite of high hopes, the area's ruggedness proved impractical for wagon trains.[39] Smith recorded his findings and "struck for the southern point of an extensive range of white sand hills."[40] Smith may have been amazed at the vast gypsum dune field, but if so he did not record his thoughts in his journal.

Lt. William Smith's report of his Tularosa Basin reconnaissance reveals sketchy information about White Sands and the adjacent region. Smith concluded that the Sacramento Mountains and the "rough terrain" (perhaps he is referring to the lava flow known as the malpais, of which a small portion is preserved as Valley of Fires Recreation Area and Carrizozo Lava Flow Wilderness Study Area) precluded a safe passage for wagon travel. The lieutenant's description of White Sands is disappointing for the modern reader because of his apparent lack of inquisitiveness. Unlike other topographical engineers, Smith missed the opportunity to associate himself with a particular region by becoming the first American to view, examine, and record the survey's conclusions. And Smith, in contrast to French and Marcy, was the only American officer to see White Sands firsthand.

For more than a decade after Smith's reconnaissance, the White Sands region drew no more government attention. Only a handful of private entrepreneurs from El Paso risked their lives to secure salt from White Sands. In 1862 the Salt Road from El Paso to White Sands was discontinued in favor of the salt beds located beneath Guadalupe Peak in Texas. Southwestern historian C. L. Sonnichsen believes that the reasons for the change of location were that the salt was a better quality and that "private owners" threatened to close the White Sands region.[41] It is unclear who the private owners were or why they would end such a lucrative business. I believe that a major reason for the change of location was that the New Mexicans who drove their slow-moving wagons or carretas were less vulnerable to potential Mescalero, Warm Springs, or Chiricahua Apache attacks in the Guadalupe Mountains location.

The first non-Indian attempt to settle in the Tularosa Basin may have taken place in 1858 or 1860. Historian Hubert H. Bancroft wrote that a group of New Mexicans attempted to settle near the Tularosa River in 1861, but Apache attacks forced the settlers to flee southward.[42] The first successful settlement was established at Tularosa in about 1862. La Luz followed the next year, located fifteen miles south of Tularosa.[43] These early New Mexicans had left their homes in the Mesilla Valley because of numerous floods along the Rio Grande. Once settled in Tularosa or La Luz, the pioneers ventured onto the open plain to gather gypsum from White Sands for their houses. After the practice of the Indians, the New Mexicans used the gypsum as alabaster for plastering the interiors of their dwellings. There is no indication that the local villagers utilized White Sands for any other purpose. The Apache no doubt prevented very much leisure or recreational use of the gypsum dunes.

The U.S. Government established a number of military posts to protect its citizens from Apache attacks: Camp Doña Ana (1849), Forts Fillmore (1852), Thorn (1853), Craig (1854), Conrad (1854), Stanton (1855), McRae (1863), and Selden (1865).[44] Historian Francis Paul Prucha, referred to America's frontier army as "agents of empire" who helped in the Americanization of the Southwest.[45] The military tried its best to protect the principal roads and to defend settlers within the territory. The only link from Doña Ana eastward across the Tularosa Basin was an overland stage route that passed the southeastern portion of White Sands known as the Point of Sands. The Point of Sands was a wayside stop to water the stage horses and refresh the travellers at the shallow well. While most passersby paid little attention to White Sands, Maj. Gen. August Kautz in 1869 thought it worthwhile to inform geology professor George Gibbs about White Sands. Kautz described the gypsum dunes as "so extensive as to give the effect of snowy scenery."[46] This statement is the first written record of the geological implications of White Sands.

No major military action occurred in the Tularosa Basin during the last half of the nineteenth century. Minor skirmishes and pursuits between the Apache and Regular Army, particularly the Sixth and Ninth cavalries, were prevalent throughout the period. On 23 July 1881, U.S. Army Apache Scouts pursued Chief Nana's band from the Sacramento Mountains southward, as the elderly chief headed west along the edge of White Sands toward the San Andres Mountains.[47] The only officially recorded military action at White Sands occurred on 25 July 1881, when Lt. John F. Guilfoyle and a Ninth Cavalry detachment attacked Nana's band. There were no fatalities in the fight, and subsequently the cavalry pursued the Apaches into the San Andres Mountains.[48]

While the military and Apache clashed throughout the Southwest, a new group arrived in the Tularosa Basin. C. L. Sonnichsen identifies these newcomers as the "invading Gringos."[49] They were mainly transplanted Texans of Irish or English extraction. Men like W. W. Cox, Perry Altman, Oliver Lee, Pat Coghlan, W. H. McNew, Jim Gililland, John Good(e), John Chisum, and John Slaughter entered Southern New Mexico "with a craze for cattle and cattle ranches."[50] These Texas ranchers composed a portion of the expansion of the western cattle empire throughout the American West.

Eastern New Mexico ranchers such as John Slaughter and John Chisum drove their cattle to various northern markets in Kansas, Colorado, and Missouri. To reach the western beef markets, Chisum pushed his herds westward from the Hondo River along the Ruidoso River, over the Sacramento Mountains, down into the Tularosa Basin, past the Point of Sands, through the San Augustine Pass, and into the Jornada del Muerto for the railhead in Engle. In 1875, Chisum drove more than ten thousand head of cattle past White Sands.[51] Slaughter also drove his cattle westward along the same route and in 1879 this cattle route became known as the Slaughter Cattle Trail.

After the ranchers' arrival, there were several conflicts over water and range rights and cattle rustling. The most noted feud culminated in the Lincoln County War of 1878. White Sands served as a stage for one of the altercations. A faction led by ranchers Perry Altman and Oliver Lee fought sporadically for two years with a party led by John Good. The body of John Good's son, Walter, was discovered in White Sands on 20 August 1888. The Good bloc naturally accused the Altman party of the killing and argued that Walter Good had been taken to White Sands so the coyotes and the dunes would conceal the murder. The coyotes performed their natural function with Good's body, but the dunes failed to cover the skeletal remains. The deadly vendetta continued.[52]

The range wars persisted until a celebrated murder trial in 1899. On the morning of 4 February 1896, prominent Las Cruces attorney and politician Albert Jennings Fountain and his son, Henry, were murdered near Chalk Hill beyond White Sands. According to the evidence at the time of the trial, the guilty parties were believed to be Oliver Lee, Jim Gililland, and William McNew, even though the Fountains' bodies were never located.[53] In spite of Lee's and Gililland's acquittal on 13 June 1899, in Hillsboro, Sierra County, residents in Mesilla and Las Cruces believed that the bodies were buried in White Sands by the killers.[54] The Fountain search parties located trails heading toward the Jarilla Mountains and Dog Canyon. The most promising lead indicated that the murderers carried their victims up the steep trail in Dog Canyon; however, a herd of cattle belonging to Lee obliterated the trail. There were no further attempts to find the bodies. The Fountains could have been buried somewhere in the Sacramento Mountains, Jarilla Mountains, or even under the shifting White Sands.[55]

The conclusion of the Lincoln County War in 1878; the capture, betrayal, and deportation of Chiricahua, Warm Springs, and some Mescalero; and the unsolved Fountain murders ushered in important changes in the White Sands region. The arrival of homesteaders into the relatively pacified area allowed the local communities and ranches to flourish. Albert Bacon Fall, a minor Democratic politician (later turned Republican), emerged as a dominant figure. Fall was the successful defense attorney for Lee and his confederates. Fall's emergence as a forceful and successful politician would result in election as one of New Mexico's first U.S. Senators, followed by his appointment by President Warren Harding as secretary of the interior in 1921. Unknowingly, Fall would be instrumental in establishing the concept of setting aside unique lands such as White Sands from private exploitation in Southern New Mexico.

Coinciding with the influx of homesteaders was the construction of the El Paso and Northeastern Railroad from El Paso to White Oaks. It contributed to the population growth in Tularosa and La Luz, as well as the creation of the rail terminal community of Alamogordo.[56] Alamogordo expanded from three tents and only a handful of individuals in June 1898 to a town of one thousand people by March 1899.[57] The numerous ore and coal mines near White Oaks, vast timber resources in the Sacramento Mountains, availability of government lands for homesteaders, large cattle ranches, and a potentially profitable gypsum dune field acted as magnets to attract people. These early settlers would change the Tularosa Basin as it entered the twentieth century. Ross McEwen, a fictional cowboy in Eugene Manlove Rhodes's novel *Paso Por Aqui* expressed poignantly the changes in the White Sands region. As McEwen pauses and considers how to elude a pursuing posse, he knows he will have to traverse White Sands to reach the Guadalupe Mountains. McEwen "knew the country ahead, or had known it ten years before. But there would be changes. There was a new railroad, so he heard, from El Paso to Tularosa . . . There would be other things too—new ranches, and all that."[58]

By 1899, the local citizens witnessed the political reapportionment of the Tularosa Basin. The region encompassing Malpais, White Sands, and the communities of Tularosa, La Luz, and Alamogordo had been included in portions of Sierra, Doña Ana, and Lincoln counties. The territorial legislature decided that sufficient development and settlement demanded the creation of a new administrative unit. Therefore, Sacramento County was promptly renamed Otero County after the territory's governor, Miguel Otero, in order to win gubernatorial support for the new county came into being.[59] Designated as the county seat, Alamogordo emerged as the political, social, commercial, and economic hub of the new county.[60]

Social events in southern New Mexico had changed dramatically during the last three decades of the nineteenth century. The arrival of numerous homesteaders, miners, land speculators, and railroad construction crews brought an end to the turbulent political and social problems plaguing the White Sands country. In spite of the region's urbanization and employment opportunities, attitudes remained inflexible regarding the future for White Sands. The gypsum dune field retained its traditional appeal as an economic asset. But the only actualized commercial value of White Sands had been as an "outback" for the Mogollon peoples and the Apache and later as a playground for fun-seeking picnickers from the nearby towns. It was not until the twentieth century, when the concept of parks and monuments began to mature, that human society took sustained notice of the gypsum dunes.

BEYOND
RAINBOW'S END
*Tom Charles, Arcadian Boosterism, and A. B.
Fall's National Park Idea*

It was a beneficent scheme, selling ozone and novelty, sunshine and
delight. The buyers got far more than the worth of their money, the
company got their money—and every one was happy. Health and
good spirits are a bargain at any price.—Eugene Manlove Rhodes,
Bransford of Rainbow Range

T he story behind the White Sands National Monument
movement is intertwined with the history of a discredit-
ed and defeated national park proposal. Many individuals and associations played prominent roles in securing a national
monument in the Tularosa Basin. Among the numerous White
Sands supporters, two individuals emerge as the principals who
were instrumental in the local White Sands project: Tom Charles
and Albert Bacon Fall.

Prolific western author Eugene Manlove Rhodes, in the 1920
novel *Bransford of Rainbow Range,* wrote, "Arcadia's
[Alamogordo's] assets were the railroad, two large modern
sawmills, the climate and printer's ink." Rhodes's fictional character, Jeff Bransford, remarked that "Arcadia's folks—why
they're mostly newcomers and health seekers."[1] In 1899, the
emerging railroad town of Alamogordo attracted numerous people because of its advertisement as a major health center. The
fledgling *Alamogordo News* ran many columns publicizing
Alamogordo's healthy climate, urging individuals to settle in the
region.[2] Newspaper advertisements describing Alamogordo as

"the prettiest and most progressive town" in the region stimulated interest in the White Sands country.[3] For Tom Charles and his family in Belleville, Kansas, the lure of the Tularosa Basin's "health giving atmosphere" prompted the Charles family to relocate.[4]

Thomas Isaac Charles was born of Welsh immigrants on 15 November 1874, in Republic, Kansas. Charles was the youngest of seven children of William and Lydia Charles.[5] Information concerning his youth is unavailable; however, growing up on any farm or ranch is difficult work. Charles's nephew, Kamp Charles, remarked that the Charles family, like other rural families, survived by building their own farmhouse, planting crops, and killing game. The family endured numerous hardships, such as swarms of locusts, Indian raids, droughts, and scorching hot winds. In 1893, Charles and his parents remained on their homestead near Republic while he worked various jobs to earn enough money to attend college. Following his graduation from the University of Kansas in 1898, Charles returned to Belleville where he purchased the *Republic City News*. He sold the *News* two years later to buy the *Belleville Freeman*, which he managed until late 1907 [6] As an editor Charles honed his skills as a writer and learned to write "simple [sic] but forcefully."[7]

Tom Charles married Rachel Bula Dancy on 24 December 1898. This union produced four children: Perl, Lucile, Ralph, and Louise. In 1906, after Rachel Bula Charles contracted tuberculosis, a friend recommended that her health might improve in a dry climate. So the Charles family left for Alamogordo, New Mexico Territory, on 17 September 1907[8] in a mule-drawn covered wagon.[9] The Charles family arrived in Alamogordo on 13 November 1907.[10] To provide for his family Tom Charles worked at different jobs, such as collecting and delivering laundry between Alamogordo and El Paso. His perseverance to provide for his family eventually led him to work for about one year as the city editor for the *Alamogordo News*.[11]

In April 1908, Tom Charles purchased an eighty-acre tract from Tom Forrester, the town's "pioneer barber," on the outskirts north of Alamogordo;[12] however, because there was no access to water rights, the family relocated. During those difficult years Rachel Bula Charles's health did not improve, and in order to assist the family Mrs. Charles's niece, Bula Laversa Ward, arrived from Belleville, Kansas, on 24 March 1908 to care for her aunt and the two boys,[13] the girls having returned to Kansas with an aunt.[14] After her prolonged illness, Rachel Bula Charles died on 10 August 1908.[15] On 14 October 1908, Charles claimed a 160-acre homestead five miles west of Alamogordo and moved there early the following year. Tom Charles married Bula Laversa Ward on 3 March 1909, and this marriage produced two boys, Ward and Ray.[16] Tom and Bula Charles never homesteaded at the Point of Sands as Bula later claimed.[17] At the time W. H. McNew owned the Point of Sands, and travelers used it as a rest stop along the Las Cruces-Alamogordo stage route.[18] Severe droughts during 1909 and 1910 forced the Charles clan to move again.[19] In 1910, Charles selected the Fite Place, located fifteen miles southeast of Cloudcroft, in the beautiful upper Peñasco Canyon of the Sacramento Mountains, now known as the Bluff Springs Recreation Area.[20] By 1915, Charles relocated to Alamogordo, purchasing a house so his children could attend high school. Within two years Charles sold his Alamogordo house to buy the Sutherland Place in La Luz.[21] The Charles family lived at the Sutherland Place for many years until their later years when the Charleses returned to Alamogordo.[22]

Tom Charles's early days in Alamogordo were his formative years as an emerging personality in the community. His participation in community affairs coincided with Alamogordo's political and economic growth. Initially, the Charles family arrived in Alamogordo not as pioneers but rather as health seekers and as homesteaders adjacent to a thriving railroad and timber community. By 1910, 7,069 people lived in Otero County, while Alamogordo's population numbered approximately 3,000.[23] At the time of Charles's arrival in Alamogordo, local newspapers commented upon the influx of all the newcomers. One editor's comment warned new arrivals that "hundreds are constantly coming to Alamogordo to live and we can offer them nothing in the way of a house to rent,"[24] and another commentary reassured them that "the homesteader going onto his claim in these days has an easy and comfortable time compared to those who located their claims five years ago."[25]

Charles worked for many years as an insurance agent for such companies as the Philadelphia Fire and National Life Insurance Company and Marine Insurance Company. Additionally, he participated actively in the Masonic Lodge, Sacramento Lodge 24 A. F. and A. M., and remained a Mason until his death in 1943.[26] Charles's activities as a Mason helped him establish contacts with well-known community leaders and businessmen with whom he established life-long social and business relationships. These early social contacts would pay dividends for Charles during his struggle for federal recognition of White Sands.

Tom Charles's interest and involvement in the national park movement sprang from two factors: his booster spirit for Alamogordo and his political admiration for Albert Bacon Fall. The idea for establishing a national park of some type in Southern New Mexico did not originate with Tom Charles; in fact there were many proposals for a national park prior to 1933. The national park idea had been promoted as early as 25 August 1898.[27] This early national park promotion coincided with an outrageous proposal for the creation of a new state composed of an area in Southern New Mexico Territory and El Paso, Texas.[28] On 25 August 1898, El Pasoans, led by Allen Blacker, J. D. Ponder, Howard Thompson, and G. H. Higgins, met at the El Paso County Courthouse to "take some action" necessary to acquire land in the Sacramento Mountains in order to create a national park. In the initial proposal Thompson stated that the proposed national park would encompass twelve square miles, including "the extreme northwest corner" of the Mescalero Apache Indian Reservation.[29] However, the acquisition of the Mescalero lands depended upon the federal government opening several tracts to non-Apache settlements. This would have been tantamount to reducing the size of the reservation and eventually placing the Mescalero, Chiricahua, and Lipan into severalty.[30]

Initially the park planners introduced a grandiose plan that would have included a region advertised for its spectacular and diverse landscapes. The proposal excluded hunting in the park and extolled the aesthetic attributes of a national park in the Sacramento Mountains. It concluded that if for no other reasons the fauna, "beauty and grandeur of the scenery" should be protected.[31] The park advocates' scheme unknowingly reflected John Muir's aesthetic or preservationist conservation concept, that is, nature should be protected for its intrinsic values as well as for its scenery. Moreover, as they gained confidence the regional park boosters wanted the Mescalero National Park to become the "greatest game preserve" in the United States, a goal that was inconsistent with preservationist thinking or with Department of the Interior directives.[32] These men envisioned a national park "where the game and wild animals of the west can be preserved, where they can bread [sic] and multiply and overflow into the surrounding country."[33] The park boosters' expectations revealed that they misunderstood the mandate for preservation in the national parks in contrast to the utilitarian conservation employed by Gifford Pinchot's U.S. Forest Service for the national forests.

The principal stated reason for establishing a national park in the Sacramento Mountains was the misconception by the park supporters that a national park would serve as an ideal hunters' game preserve. The secondary reasons reflected concern by the boosters that hunting would be impossible if the region lost its wildlife, its mountain streams, or the mountain forestlands because of logging operations. Following an inspection of the tentative national park area by A. W. Susen, J. P. Dieter, and August Meisel, members of the park committee, revealed that many fishing streams had been dynamited by loggers and subsequently warned of the environmental damage resulting from such reckless timber destruction. Susen remarked that if the forests were not conserved, the Sacramento Mountains "will become as barren as Mount Franklin" overlooking El Paso.[34] The committee recommended a national park for the purpose of conserving the region's natural resources so that it would offer a healthy environment as well as a sportsmen's paradise.[35]

Spurred on by the conservationists' enthusiasm, they met again on 3 September 1898. This time, however, their hopes for a national park would be dashed by unexpected participants at the hearing. Initially the proceedings began earnestly favoring a national park for the region, as J. P. Dieter requested that the delegation expand the border of the proposed park.

Unknown to the park committee, J. D. Bryan, from Las Cruces, instigated the next speech arguing against the park idea. Supporting Bryan behind the scenes were Charles Bishop Eddy, president of the El Paso and Northeastern Railroad, and his brother, John, who played important roles in extending rail lines and bringing a transcontinental railroad across the state. Eddy's railroad expansions and mining and logging interests in the Tularosa Basin and Sacramento Mountains emerged as the major obstacles for the conservationists to overcome.[36] With such powerful allies Bryan directed his arguments toward individuals who would inhibit progress; specifically, by establishing a national park they would "throw a stumbling block" in the way of plans for an El Paso and Northeastern rail spur into White Oaks, as well as "lock up" rich mineral lands.[37] William A. Hawkins, attorney for the El Paso and Northeastern Railroad and Charles Eddy's "indispensable man," emerged as the railroad's spokesman during the heated debates. Hawkins condemned the national park concept because it would represent another attempt by the federal government to remove lands from the public. He added that New Mexico Territory possessed enough reservations, Indian and military, and that one more would deter El Paso's "upbuilding."[38] The park factions divided sharply over self-interests. The sportsmen-minded conservationists reflected a local version of the Boone and Crockett Club, who, like their Eastern contemporaries, desired to establish game preserves while simultaneously fending "off the march of modern progress."[39] Their opponents were the "enemy,"[40] in preservationist John Muir's words, specifically, the El Paso and Northeastern Railroad, with its interests in land speculations. Railroad interests in the Tularosa Basin centered on exploiting its natural resources, not promoting scenic attractions as the railroads did for Yellowstone National Park.[41] Such struggles went on all over the West during the environmentally activist Progressive era.

Astonishingly, after that fateful September meeting, the national park idea disappeared as quickly as it had developed. On 3 September 1898, at a public forum in El Paso, the last Mescalero National Park debate occurred until revived in 1912 by Sen. Albert B. Fall. The railroad interests had prevailed. Only two dissenting views were heard. An unidentified elderly college professor and W. W. Bridgers accused the Eddy Railroad interests of attempting to control the area's natural resources and of packing the conference with Eddy's supporters. The professor poignantly declared that if the railroad magnates had their way they would "monopolize the air." In the final analysis, the corporate special interests prevailed over the conservationists because "it would hurt the railroad, consequently El Paso does not want the park."[42]

While the park meetings were taking place the powerful yet relatively quiet U.S. Forest Service finally voiced its opinion. As a conservation agency the Forest Service naturally desired the creation of a national forest instead of a national park. In 1906, Forest Service personnel W. H. B. Kent and R. V. R. Reynolds conceded that, even though the Sacramento Mountains region held natural attractions, "there is absolutely nothing here of unusual beauty, magnificence or oddity" that demanded the establishment of a national park.[43]

In spite of this early loss, the national park supporters would not surrender their cause. In July 1902, however, President Theodore Roosevelt established the Lincoln Forest Reserve consisting of the Capitan and White mountains.[44] With the failure of a national park scheme the game hunters succeeded in acquiring the appropriate national reservation for their activities. If a national park could not be established, then a national forest reserve of some type would satisfy the sportsmen.

In 1912, New Mexico finally achieved statehood, and on 2 May 1912 one of its new U.S. senators, Albert B. Fall, introduced Senate Bill 6659 calling for Mescalero National Park; it failed to pass the Committee on Indian Affairs.[45] The next day New Mexico Congressman George Curry proposed a similar measure, House Bill 24123, but the Committee on Public Lands rejected it.[46]

Fall emerged as the principal politician responsible for resurrecting the national park concept for Southern New Mexico. His bill would have converted a portion of the Mescalero Apache Indian Reservation into the Mescalero National Park, requiring $150,000 for compensating the Apaches' resettlement program and for their agricultural and ranching enterprises.[47] A particular issue that would haunt Fall was the location of the Fall-Hatchet enterprise totaling one million acres surrounding his Three Rivers Ranch headquarters. The ranch bordered the Mescalero Reservation and the senator would profit financially with the establishment of a national park. Historian David H. Stratton, Fall's biographer, contends that the ranch was the key problem that led to Fall's eventual political and economic demise.[48]

Fall unsuccessfully introduced at least four national park bills during the next ten years. On 26 January 1914, Fall even changed the name to Rio Grande National Park in Senate Bill 4185 in order to gain support for his Mescalero National Park Senate Bill 4187, but this bill failed also.[49] It remains unclear what lands Fall wanted to include in the Rio Grande proposal or if it mirrored the Mescalero National Park. He reintroduced the Rio Grande National Park on 16 December 1915 and again on 4 January 1916.[50] Characteristically, Fall remained persistent in his attempts to push a project until all potential avenues for success failed.

Not to be outdone, New Mexico's other U.S. senator, Thomas B. Catron simultaneously submitted his proposal (Senate Bill 4537, 19 February 1914, and Senate Bill 2542, 16 December 1915) for a New Mexico national park in an attempt to resurrect an earlier proposal, the National Park of the Cliff Cities or Pajarito National Park, currently known as Bandelier National Monument.[51] As was the case during frequent state political squabbles, sectional rivalry played an important role in the state's national park proposals. For example, when Fall endorsed the All-Year National Park plan in 1921, he revealed New Mexico's divisive politics. Confident of success, Fall remarked that after the All-Year National Park was established then northern New Mexico (or the Santa Fe crowd, as he referred to them) should organize for its own park, namely Cliff Cities, in the same manner as the state's southern Southwestern Park Association.[52] While both senators received grass-roots support, neither captured the necessary political endorsements to carry his project through.

Regional support for the numerous national park bills originated with each city's ultra-boosters, notably the chambers of commerce. Urban historian Howard P. Chudacoff characterizes boosters as "profit-minded as well as public-minded," and Alamogordo's boosters were no exception.[53] Alamogordo's chamber of commerce had evolved from two previous organizations, the Businessmen's Club and the Commercial Club. The Businessmen's Club originated with the members of the Alamogordo Improvement Company, a real estate company, which advanced their business interests in conjunction with the city's growth.[54] The Businessmen's Club, formed in 1907, furthered the "business welfare" of Alamogordo.[55] By 1913, the organization stagnated to the point that the Businessmen's Club was "out of business," failing to generate sufficient funds and interest for its continued existence. The resurgence of Alamogordo's boosterism and establishment of the Commercial Club corresponded with the news that the Southern National Highway would pass through the town. The Southern National Highway was an ambitious plan to connect the Atlantic and Pacific coasts with a transcontinental highway. The road originated in Washington, D.C., and terminated in San Diego, California. Regional boosters were delighted because the road would traverse Roswell, Alamogordo, and El Paso.[56] Alamogordo's Commercial Club heartily supported the national highway project because of the potential lucrative tourist revenue.

Beyond the Tularosa Basin two important events were taking place during the 1910s that would have repercussions for the Southwest: the first in Yellowstone National Park and the second in Europe. On 11 and 12 September 1911, the initial National Park Conference convened to discuss the administration of national parks and national monuments.[57] Interior Secretary Walter L. Fisher and sixty-eight prominent Interior Department officials, park superintendents, foresters, and railroad presidents recommended establishing a bureau of national parks and initiating a forceful advertising campaign.[58] Two more conferences were held, one in 1912 and the other in 1915.[59] The resolutions of the three conferences reached fruition on 25 August 1916 when Congress finally passed legislation, which had been introduced in 1911, creating a national park service.[60] Stephen T. Mather, self-made millionaire and assistant to the secretary of the interior, was appointed as the first director.[61] The creation of the National Park Service assisted in establishing uniform administrative policies, improving concession services, and advertising the National Park Service's attractions.

The advent of World War I on 28 July 1914 drew relatively little attention in many sections of the United States. For most Americans the war was a European war with no direct implications for the United States. The war's proximity and the United States' two and a half years of neutrality permitted Americans the luxury to debate the conflict's "ultimate significance."[62] The war forced American tourists to turn inward for recreation. Seizing the opportunity, Mather actively promoted the parks and monuments to attract the thousands of tourists confined to the North American continent. While federal funds were scarce for the maintenance of the parks and monuments during the war, tourist dollars helped offset his administration's financial burdens. Organizations such as the Far Western Travellers

Association and American Automobile Association reflected the "patriotic public-spirited" efforts to spend American dollars in America.[63]

The advent of the age of mass-produced automobiles permitted greater societal mobility. They made regions accessible that once only relatively few people could reach. The dramatic increase of "tin-can" tourists overwhelmed many parks and monuments. During 1918, 451,661 visitors toured the nation's parks and monuments, and the following year the number almost doubled, reaching 811,516. Encouraged by the figures, Mather wrote that Americans subscribed wholeheartedly to the "See America First" crusade.[64] The distant war to end all wars directly contributed to Americans discovering their cultural and geologic treasures on a grand scale.

As the Great War's end altered European politics, an American political changing of the guard occurred on 4 March 1921, as Republican Warren G. Harding succeeded President Woodrow Wilson. The next day Harding's appointee and "natural chum," Sen. Albert B. Fall, reluctantly assumed the office of secretary of the interior.[65] Fall was not the person philosophically suited for the position as the guardian of the nation's national parks and national monuments. He was given the job as a result of the traditional good ol' boy network. As a member of the "western crowd," and like Richard Ballinger before him, Fall was an outspoken critic of federal land withdrawals. In fact, on 11 February 1914, Fall had sarcastically declared that if any more New Mexico lands were removed from open settlement, "we [New Mexicans] shall either be compelled to ask to be included within an Indian reservation or a national park or be created into a national monument."[66] Three years later Fall denounced conservationists by portraying them as individuals who employed conservation measures in order to install a "state socialistic government."[67]

As the "epitomized Westerner," Fall's conservation philosophy reflected neither John Muir's preservationist theme nor Chief Forester Gifford Pinchot's utilitarian conservation policies.[68] Three principal arguments comprised Fall's conservation philosophy: (1) federal land withdrawals prevented people from utilizing their own natural resources (2) establishing national parks, national forests, or any government reservations halted progress, and (3) land withdrawals stifled ambition. [69] Fall's conservation views duplicated those of his constituency, that is, land and its resources should be used for the present generation and not "locked up" for the future.[70] While a senator he once declared to his colleagues in the Senate that he hoped Congress would eventually dissolve the Department of the Interior.[71] He considered himself and his constituents to be true conservationists; while denouncing federal attempts to reserve any lands from settlement, he boasted proudly, "We oppose bureaucracy." For Fall, the federal government monopolized too much land in the West, especially in New Mexico.[72]

During his brief tenure as interior secretary, Albert B. Fall and the National Park Service reviewed listings of several proposed national parks. One of the most grandiose proposals, and, according to one historian, one of the worst, was Fall's recommendation for the All-Year National Park.[73] The scheme, initially called the "Southwestern All-Year National Park," would include 2,000 acres on the Mescalero Apache Indian Reservation, the entire White Sands gypsum dune field, the Malpais lava beds, and the Elephant Butte dam and lake. This double-U-shaped national park, totaling approximately 500,000 acres, would be connected by eighty miles of highway "making it one of the most delightful drives in the Western country."[74] This remarkable park proposal was the result of Fall's persistent demands for a national park based upon his conservation philosophy! Other motives, such as increasing the value of his Three Rivers Ranch holdings, must have motivated Fall to renew his Southern New Mexico park idea during 1921. In fairness to Fall, he tempered his disapproval of national parks' aesthetic qualities, admitting in 1921, in his first *Report of the Secretary of the Interior,* that "parks are stabilizing and inspiring influences" during national strife and praised "those Congresses who set these areas aside."[75]

During one of Alamogordo's town hall meetings in February 1921, there was a discussion of the possibility of acquiring a "municipal recreational camp" in Lincoln National Forest. U.S. Forest Service supervisor O. Fred Arthur told the Commercial Club that other towns were securing recreational areas and that Alamogordo should not be left out. Arthur recommended a site approximately two miles from High Rolls for Alamogordo.[76] This renewed interest by town boosters for their own recreational site in the Sacramento Mountains reflected earlier attempts to establish their playgrounds.

By 20 October 1921, the campaign was under way in the Southwest to resurrect Fall's old national park proposal, modified to include new areas such as White Sands, White Mountain (today identified more readily by its Spanish name, Sierra Blanca), Malpais, and Elephant Butte Dam and Lake B. M. Hall. As early as 13 October 1921, Alamogordo dispatched a committee composed of F. C. Rolland, J. R. Gilbert, and Tom Charles to Three Rivers Ranch to discuss with Secretary Fall "important matters of special concern" for Southern New Mexico. As the dominant personality, Fall dictated his views to the committee as to how they should proceed with the park proposal. Approximately two weeks later, the club appointed an eight-member delegation, including Tom Charles, to meet neighboring commercial clubs to form an organization to promote its national park. According to Clarence W. Morgan, *Alamogordo News* editor and Commercial Club member, the time was ripe for a national park proposal because the Southwest had "an official [Fall] in Washington that can be expected to be in full sympathy with this move" (see Map 4).[77]

At his Three Rivers Ranch, A. B. Fall met with such promi-

PROPOSED SOUTHWESTERN ALL-YEAR NATIONAL PARK SITE

Map 4. *All-Year national Park. (Exerpt from "Southwestern All-Year National Park Association Newsletter," January 1922)*

nent regional figures as Frank T. French, H. H. Brook, Vincent B. May, C. F. Knight, attorney Mark Thompson, and professor H. L. Kent to organize a Southwestern national park association.[78] On 3 December 1921, 500 invited individuals met in Las Cruces to choose the executive committee of the Southwest All-Year National Park Association. The committee's stated goal was to encourage Congress to "create a much-needed National playground in the Southwest."[79] Among the delegates was Alamogordo insurance agent, Tom Charles. Governors and representatives from New Mexico, Texas, Arizona, Oklahoma, and Kansas met formally on 11 January 1922 in El Paso to organize the association. The All-Year National Park campaign had officially begun. Confidently Morgan predicted that the park would become a "reality in the near future."[80]

As the delegates returned home, not all of them shared Morgan's optimism. Much of the discontent originated with the representatives from Albuquerque and Santa Fe, who had not been permitted to question the proceedings. And upon their return home they accused the Southern New Mexico and West Texas delegates of improprieties. D. B. McKee of Albuquerque complained that W. A. Hawkins had proposed that counties north of Socorro be denied admission to the conference and thus "we knew everything was already cut and dried."[81] As 1921 drew to a close, New Mexicans were divided over the park issue. Meanwhile, Tom Charles, Alamogordo's ultra-booster, was emerging as a prominent local personality while Albert B. Fall was reaching the apex of his governmental and political career.

The All-Year National Park supporters advanced their agenda based upon several premises: in contrast to other national parks the park would remain open year-round; the park would attract farmers because planting and harvesting during the traditional national park season permitted little leisure time; and thousands of tourists would stimulate the region's economy.[82] Initially endorsement for the park grew swiftly throughout the Southwest. Officially, Merritt C. Mechem, New Mexico governor and president of the All-Year National Park Association, led the campaign. However, the executive committee, headed by H. H. Brook, and committee members W. A. Hawkins, Mark A. Thompson, Robert Martin, Z. B. Moon, H. M. Dow, J. B. French, and R. F. Burges actually promoted and directed the association's efforts. During early 1922, national park efforts were in full stride, and several members of the Southwest All-Year National Park Association even went to Washington, D.C., to lobby for their cause, but they met with little enthusiasm for the idea.[83]

To the boosters' chagrin not everyone understood the All-Year National Park idea. Myron H. West, president and general manager of the American Park Builders in Chicago, Illinois, wrote Harry L. Kent informing him that he wanted the contract "to properly develop this tract."[84] Kent replied politely to West's inquiry stating that "perhaps you have misunderstood our movement. The proposition is to establish a large National Park."[85]

In Washington, D.C., Stephen T. Mather reluctantly accepted Fall's long-standing invitation to visit him at his Three Rivers Ranch and tour the proposed park sites. In May 1922, Mather spent the first three days inspecting main attractions or "spots" in the region: Cloudcroft, Mescalero Apache Indian Reservation, Elephant Butte Dam, Lake B. M. Hall, Malpais, and White Sands. White Mountain had been deleted because the Forest Service refused to surrender the area to the National Park Service. Southwest All-Year National Park Association executive committee members, William A. Hawkins, Richard F. Burges, Horace B. Stevens, and Mark Thompson, accompanied Mather during his inspection. Upon his return to Three Rivers Ranch, Mather met with Fall and with a delegation from Alamogordo composed of F. C. Rolland, Benson Nowell, and Tom Charles. On 3 May 1922, the Commercial Club held a banquet during which Mather told the gathering that he considered the plan impressive but had reservations, remarking that the sites he had visited lacked scenery generally associated with national parks. Noticing the audience's silence, Mather quickly consoled them by adding that there remained sufficient areas to compensate for the apparent deficiencies.[86] Apparently that soothed the gathering.

In retrospect it is evident that Mather to a certain extent patronized his hosts during his visit. After Mather returned to Washington, D.C., he informed Albright that he had been treated hospitably during his tour, but he decided that Fall's park proposal was unrealistic. The more the director analyzed the proposal, that is, its disjointed boundaries, lack of spectacular scenery, and questionable usage, "the more preposterous it seemed."[87]

Even though R. F. Burges and W. A. Hawkins drafted the All-Year National Park bill, A. B. Fall remained its principal architect.[88] The interior secretary met with the Southwest All-Year National Park Association's executive committee on several occasions to inform the members of the format and content he desired. By the time the bill reached the Senate Committee on Indian Affairs, Fall had rewritten the text to such a degree that it had become his bill. On 28 April 1922, Sen. Holm O. Bursum (New Mexico) introduced Senate Bill 3519 defining the All-Year National Park, subsequently referring the bill to the Committee on Indian Affairs. The preface to the bill reads: "Defining the rights of the Mescalero Apache Indians in the Mescalero Apache Indian Reservation, providing for an allotment of certain lands therein in severalty to the Mescalero Apache Indians, and creating and defining the All Year National Park, and for other purposes." [89]

On 7 July 1922, the Senate Committee on Indian Affairs queried Bursum about the park. Sen. Thomas J. Walsh (Montana) asked Bursum to explain the bill and its affect on the Indian reservation. Bursum answered that it would authorize a national park totaling 2,000 acres within the Mescalero Apache Indian Reservation.[90] He emphasized that 2,000 acres was a small fraction of the 60,000-acre reservation. Secretary Fall would select the site and include only "the most mountainous and picturesque land, and desirable land" for the national park.[91] The bill would permit the interior secretary to purchase approximately three hundred additional acres, in order to "round out" the park. An astonished Walsh responded to Bursum's park description by remarking that "it seems to me a remarkable thing to create a national park inside of an Indian Reservation," and 2,000 acres would be an astonishingly tiny park![92] Throughout the brief exchange the discussion centered only on the Mescaleros' land (2,300 acres), even though the park planners envisioned a total area eventually encompassing 500,000 acres!

Whether it was a simple oversight, failure to read the bill in its entirety, or misunderstanding by the senators of the additional territories to be included, the All-Year National Park bill passed the Senate on 7 July 1922.[93] If the senators had read sections 1 and 2 and questioned Bursum at length, the outcome might have been different. Of significance was the inclusion of "territory surrounding the Elephant Butte Reservoir, the White Sands, and the Malpais lava beds." [94] When asked by the Senate presiding officer if there were any objections to the bill's consideration, not one senator challenged it.

Initial opposition against Fall's park came from the New Mexico Game Commission. In November 1921, New Mexico Game Warden Thomas P. Gable stated that the commission was opposed to the park proposal because Elephant Butte should remain under state control.[95] By the end of July 1922, opposition to Fall's All-Year National Park had gained momentum.

Prior to the creation of the Southwest All-Year National Park Association in December 1921, there had existed the National Park Association of New Mexico.[96] The National Park Association of New Mexico's agenda reflected Sen. Thomas B. Catron's 1914, 1915, and 1917 unsuccessful Cliff Cities National Park proposals.[97] This association, dominated by northern New

Mexicans, argued that if the All-Year National Park passed, it would be the only national park in New Mexico. Editorials in the Santa Fe New Mexican lashed out against Fall's "lame duck of [the] national park system" by denouncing the proposal as an unworthy candidate for status as a national park.[98] In fact, in one commentary, a reader ridiculed the plan, stating that visitors "would die either of heat or laughter" during their tour of the multi-purpose or "chromos" park, as northern New Mexicans labeled it.[99]

The strongest opposition to Fall's park came from the National Parks Association, known today as the National Parks and Conservation Association. The National Parks Association blasted New Mexico's "spotted park" in its bulletin as early as 7 June 1922.[100] It criticized the potential introduction of a host of non-Park Service concerns such as grazing, water, mining, timber-cutting rights, and privileges. The second principal argument against Fall's park was the park's composition, based upon the distance between "spots" or attractions. Managing and protecting such an expansive and disjointed national park would be extremely difficult for the undermanned National Park Service. The third reason was the conflict of interest inherent in the location of Fall's Three Rivers Ranch. Fall's 600,000-acre ranch bordered the Mescalero Apache Reservation; therefore, his holdings would increase in value with the park's creation.

Robert Sterling Yard, executive secretary of the National Parks Association, and Horace McFarland, president of the American Civic Association, the leading critics of the All-Year National Park, vigorously assailed the park bill and its supporters. In the National Parks Association bulletin, Yard demanded that the bill be defeated because "the safety of the entire National Parks System from commercialism" requires it.[101] The National Parks Association concluded that if the park bill passed the House of

Representatives, New Mexico's only park "would be pitiably under-class in the great company" of the National Park Service.[102] Perhaps to ease tensions as well as to offer a compromise, on 19 July 1922, Yard suggested to Fall that he create an alternative organization, modeled on the National Park Service, for regional recreation areas. Fall's response was brief and predictable: only a national park would do.[103]

Despite New Mexico Congressman Nestor Montoya's assurances that he would support the park bill when it reached the House of Representatives, Fall's park died quietly of neglect there.[104] The combination of outspoken park opponents and the initial investigations into Fall's far-flung ranching enterprise ensured the defeat of his All-Year National Park, thereby sealing the fate of "so ignoble a park unit."[105] In disgust a tired and disillusioned A. B. Fall announced his decision to resign his post on 2 January 1923 to be effective 4 March 1923.[106] Fall's resignation ensured that Mather's national park ideals would remain intact and established the independence of the National Park Service from secretarial pressures on any future proposals, including regions removed from "reclamation areas and Indian reservations."[107] One historian commented that in the end the "natural resources of the West made and broke" Albert B. Fall.[108]

To Fall's credit he never pressured the National Park Service to support his plan. Horace M. Albright, Mather's successor, noted Fall's political tact over this potentially explosive issue within the Department of the Interior. Much to the surprise and relief of the National Park Service, Fall fully supported the Service during his brief tenure as secretary of the interior from 1921 to 1923. Many years later, Albright credited Fall for his support of the "pet scheme," he had "always been fair with the National Park Service." [110]

The defeat of the All-Year National Park bill resulted in the dissolution of the Southwest All-Year National Park Association accompanied by a brief period of regional booster inactivity. The boosterism of the Southwest, specifically Southern New Mexico and El Paso, was temporartily curbed. Though disheartened, Tom Charles remained confident that some portion of Fall's park plan could be salvaged. Tom Charles, a longtime admirer of Fall, selected one of the former interior secretary's park "spots." White Sands, to preserve as a "pleasuring ground" for the region. During the next decade Charles championed White Sands as a national park or monument while emerging as its foremost local spokesman.

A. B. Fall's
Gypsum Phoenix
Tom Charles's Drawing Card Evolves as a
National Monument

Like any species evolving in response to its environment, we see in nature what we're conditioned to see, what our cultural experiences have prepared us to believe is worthy of attention, important. So the human perception of nature, of regional landscapes and their significance, changes over time.—Dan L. Flores, *Canyon Visions*

I n the long run, it was not Albert Fall's political rise and fall that directly contributed to establishing White Sands National Monument (WSNM), but it was his All-Year National Park proposal that first drew attention to the gypsum dune field as a potential federally protected area. White Sands, like many other oddities already preserved under the monument system, represented "a dreamland for those with preservation-oriented agendas."[1] The drive to acquire National Park Service status for White Sands succeeded because of the advertising efforts of regional boosters led by Tom Charles, who asked his fellow boosters, "Do we want to sell the Great White Sands at five cents per ton or at $21.50 per inspiration?" and because of National Park Service Director Horace M. Albright's favorable recommendation for the region.[2] White Sands became a national monument so that its unique scientific gypsum features would be protected; however, its scenic, aesthetic qualities were not overlooked by the National Park Service.

In 1931, Tom Charles proudly boasted during the struggle for national recognition, "There is no question in our [Alamogordo

71

Chamber of Commerce] mind but the White Sands ranks with the Carlsbad Caverns National Park and the Lincoln National Forest as a drawing card" for Southern New Mexico and West Texas.[3] By examining Charles's contributions to protect some portion of White Sands and by looking at his environmental philosophy, we uncover the boosters' motives to accomplish their goal. His persistence culminated in President Herbert Hoover's 1933 WSNM proclamation.

Commercial exploitation at White Sands had been continuous from the Spanish-Mexican eras through settlement in the area by American entrepreneurs. As early as 1882, there were regional plans to utilize the gypsum dunes for fertilizer and to extract salt from the salt lake. A railroad proposal revealed that the rail line would run along the old Salt Road eastern slope of the Organ Mountains, connecting the White Sands to Tularosa and Carrizozo Springs, with the railhead terminating in White Oaks. The planners hoped that building a rail line would connect El Paso with the mining and timber resources in New Mexico and that the natural resources in the White Sands country would be accessible to entrepreneurs. Apparently access to New Mexico's mineral and timber resources was vital to the region because the significance "of this road can hardly be overestimated."[4] In 1885, Las Cruces attorney Albert Jennings Fountain predicted that since a projected railroad would pass in close proximity to the dunes the White Sands gypsum would develop as a "valuable fertilizer to [sic] the wheat fields of the East."[5] Several years later territorial officials publicized the commercial potential of White Sands, announcing that in a brief time the gypsum would become valuable as road construction material and attempting to induce individuals to make gypsum "fortunes" in New Mexico Territory.[6]

In 1901, Miguel A. Otero, governor of New Mexico Territory, in his report to the interior secretary, acknowledged not only that the White Sands was one of the "great natural wonders of the Southwest" but also that the region would in the not-too-distant future emerge as "a source of great wealth."[7] Otero added that a cement factory in Alamogordo was processing White Sands gypsum for building uses and that the company planned to increase its processing rate over the next several years.[8] Several years later, geologist Fayette Alexander Jones predicted that gypsum would play a major economic role in New Mexico's development.[9]

Private and commercial mining interests in White Sands and the adjacent playa were active during the early years of the twentieth century. Ranchers valued the salt supply in Lake Lucero for their cattle herds, and for many years residents, in the old Indian and Spanish traditions, collected gypsum to whitewash the interiors of their homes. The gypsum acted as a "cement plaster" for the houses and was valued for its fireproof properties. The gypsum's most attractive quality was the variety of purposes for which it could be used: stucco, dental plaster, fertilizer, and plaster of Paris.[10]

During the early 1900s the Rock Island Cement and Plaster Company, located in Ancho, New Mexico, manufactured gypsum products so successfully that their profits encouraged Alamogordo citizens to draft a plan to develop the White Sands dunes. In order to develop the dune field, though, outside interest and capital were required because local investors did not have the funds to build a gypsum-processing plant. In 1906, J. A. Eddy, owner of the Eddy Claims mining operations, predicted that the region's soda mines would also generate considerable interest by investors. Local boosters were extremely vocal in asserting that the wealth of White Sands gypsum and soda would benefit Alamogordo, thereby bringing in numerous mine proprietors and operators.[11] Arguing that "fortunes lay at our own doors in these mountains of seemingly worthless sands," promoters heartily endorsed and subscribed to every plan for commercializing White Sands.[12] In spite of their optimistic view of the area's mining potential, the town remained without a profitable gypsum plant, even though J. F. Milner, president of a White Sands mining company, had constructed a large calcine furnace at White Sands in 1907.[13]

The following year, Milner sold 25,000 acres of his White Sands property for $100,000 to the White Sands Company, an Arizona-based mining company financed by eastern capitalists. The White Sands Company's purchase of the dune field rekindled enthusiasm for what boosters believed would become "one of the greatest projects in the whole Southwest."[14] Local businessmen envisioned an economic boom for the Tularosa Basin because of the potential financial investments and employment opportunities. The company's plans included laying a railroad spur from Dog Canyon, south of Alamogordo, building a processing plant for $10,000, and creating jobs for 800 employees. Company officials calculated that they could process three tons per hour once the gypsum plant was operational.[15] Their plans, like those of their predecessors, failed because of low market demands and the high cost of transporting the gypsum from the remote Tularosa Basin to distant urban centers.[16]

Although the gypsum processing ventures never reached fruition, the lure of commercialization of the dunes persisted. Official New Mexico publications continued to describe the dunes as "a great natural curiosity and a great resource."[17] In 1916, Otto L. Tinklepaugh, secretary of the Alamogordo Commercial Club, wrote to State Land Commissioner Robert P. Ervien informing him that a fortune could be made at White Sands by anyone "with sufficient capital to develop them [the gypsum dunes]."[18]

A.B. Fall's Gypsum Phoenix

During the late 1920s and early 1930s, anticipation ran high in Alamogordo that a successful commercial enterprise would emerge and curb the area's rising unemployment rate. Companies like the Great Sulphur Company (1921), the Gypsum Products Company (1922), and the United Gypsum Company (1924) boasted of their plans for White Sands, but each company only generated high hopes.[19] Even as late as the WSNM negotiations, a new venture, the Great White Sands Gypsum Company headed by James Orr and T. F. Wyly, proposed to construct a spur railroad line north of the tentative monument boundary to transport the gypsum to Alamogordo. After conferring with Tom Charles and William A. Hawkins, Orr and Wyly concluded that their commercial operation would not interfere with the national monument because of the "abundance of area for both commercial and recreational development."[20] Surprisingly, this venture also failed. On 19 March 1932, Charles informed Gov. Arthur Seligman of local sentiment: "We [the Commercial Club] do believe that the recreational values in the Sands hold out much greater promise to the state than does the commercial. For thirty years the commercial development of White Sands has been one promotion after another."[21] After these disappointments, Charles realized that for many years White Sands had attracted thousands of tourists to the region; slowly local businessmen came to realize that the dunes merely offered a different kind of commercial prospect. With that idea in mind, Charles divided the White Sands gypsum into "Commercial Gypsum and Recreational or Inspirational Gypsum."[22] Rather than addressing and promoting the aesthetic qualities of White Sands, Charles supported the new possibilities for tourism. Charles's comment about the "beauty and splendor" of the gypsum dunes did not entirely represent his principal aims that White Sands should be recognized "as an ideal playground." Charles's "drawing card" promised the elusive "commercial value" that would generate and maintain a healthy local economy.[23]

Following the defeat of the All-Year National Park, the boosters from Southern New Mexico and West Texas had generally maintained silence concerning National Park issues. As a result of the All-Year National Park catastrophe, Fall's resignation as interior secretary on 4 March 1923, and subsequent investigations into possible improprieties (subsequent trials revealed the Teapot Dome affair) while he had been in office, many Southwestern booster projects remained dormant. Contrasting the aggressive boosterism of the early 1920s, the mid-1920s witnessed a decline in coordinated regional promotions. Local community boosters contented themselves with advertising local areas of interest; however, by the end of the decade boosterism's downward trend reversed itself. Among the many civic-spirited citizens, Tom Charles surfaced as the leading individual credited for reviving regional boosterism.

The Carlsbad, Roswell, Las Cruces, El Paso, and Alamogordo commercial clubs acted in concert and independently to promote the WSNM idea. Each chamber sent numerous inquiries and supportive letters to each other and their congressmen and state officials. While advertising White Sands as "one of the Southwest's most alluring playgrounds," the newly proposed road between Las Cruces and Alamogordo was also a principal issue. Charles, a member of the Road Committee for the Alamogordo Commercial Club, urged the state highway board to plan for an Alamogordo–White Sands–Las Cruces route.[24] Consequently, on 16 March 1926, the Alamogordo Commercial Club held a special meeting wherein the members unanimously agreed that any highway between Alamogordo and Las Cruces must pass White Sands. In their plan the highway, known locally as the Old Saint Nicholas Road, would run from Alamogordo to the Point of Sands, past Baird Well and connect with the Old Salt Road at the base of the San Andres Mountains.[25] This suggested link was the same route that Lt. William F. Smith had traveled in 1849.[26] During the next six years the intensive debates for the Las Cruces–White Sands–Alamogordo highway evolved into a cause promoting both the road and WSNM.

Tom Charles's motives for leading the countless attempts to establish WSNM remain complex. Charles cared little for aesthetic preservation but supported utilitarian conservation in the spirit of Gifford Pinchot, the former chief forester of the U.S. Forest Service, rather than that of the conservationists (also known as romantic aesthetics). His conservation philosophy echoed English philosopher Jeremy Bentham's greatest happiness principle—the individual and society should strive to create the greatest happiness for the greatest number.[27] For Charles, conservation implied that a portion of the gypsum field should be protected for people's recreational impulses and removed from the clutches of private industry. However, those gypsum dunes excluded from monument selection would remain open to commercial exploitation. He revealed as early as 1925 that he maintained "no personal interest in the matter of conservation, nor the lack of it except the interest which any citizen should have in the greatest good to the greatest number."[28] He rarely wrote of the natural beauty of White Sands; instead he emphasized the economic benefits Alamogordo would receive from a federal park or monument designation. Only at the end of his career did he stress the aesthetic qualities of White Sands.

Contrary to regional folklore, the idea or concept for establishing a national monument did not originate with Tom Charles. Instead, that honor belongs to Numa C. Frenger of Las Cruces. On 23 March 1926, Frenger wrote Charles describing White Sands as a "beautiful national wonder" of the United States worthy of the country's attention. Frenger insightfully proposed that any road between Las Cruces and Alamogordo should "skirt" White Sands. In his postscript Frenger remarked upon "another idea that I have had for sometime," that is, "I think a large part of it [White Sands] should be saved as a Government monument." This is the first reference to any national monument proposal. Frenger encouraged Charles and the Alamogordo Chamber of Commerce to "go after this" and to solicit the National Park Service for recommendations.[29]

The next day Charles responded to Frenger's ideas, writing that he favored the "idea of setting aside a part of the sands as a national monument." The significant portion of Charles's correspondence is his admission, "I like your idea."[30] Therefore, Charles's local reputation as "Father of the White Sands National Monument" is somewhat misleading. While Charles looked to others for ideas and counsel, to his credit, he was the "tiresome fighter and conscience" for the monument movement, serving as its "source and spring of enthusiasm."[31]

Like many Southern New Mexicans, Charles was a staunch admirer and supporter of Albert Fall, and he remained loyal to Fall during and after the sensational trials uncovering the Teapot Dome Scandal. Following his correspondence with Frenger, Charles wrote to the former interior secretary inquiring about his views regarding the possibility of an effort to reserve a portion of White Sands as a national monument.[32] Fall's immediate response is unknown; however, it can be inferred that Fall favored the idea based upon his eventual acceptance of an invitation to appear as the guest of honor at the WSNM's opening-day ceremony in April 1934.

In 1929, Charles informed U.S. Sen. Sam Bratton that he had received several queries from individuals who wanted to homestead along the dunes. What upset Charles was that the prospective homesteaders wanted to build gas stations and concession stands while charging fees to enter the dunes. On 12 December 1929, Charles requested that the senator investigate the possibilities of having a portion of White Sands withdrawn from public entry. One month later, Bratton asked Park Service Director Horace Albright and Interior Secretary Ray Lyman Wilbur to request that President Hoover withdraw the necessary lands.[33] On 11 February 1930, Sen. Bronson Cutting also wrote Wilbur requesting the National Park Service to inspect White Sands for consideration as a possible monument or park site.[34] Wilbur informed Cutting that on 7 February 1930, President Hoover had already withdrawn the White Sands public lands for national monument purposes.[35] Because of Albright's interest in White Sands and influence with Secretary Wilbur, President Hoover's executive order withdrew the entire White Sands region located in Townships 16, 17, 18, S., Rs 5, 6, and 7 E.[36] Wilbur also referred the letters to Albright, who remarked that certain lands in the dunes might be of "distinctive character" to justify a national monument. The director then solicited the opinion of Thomas Boles, custodian of Carlsbad Caverns National Monument (which became a national park on 14 May 1930), and he in turn surprisingly declared that the gypsum dunes did not constitute an interest for the National Park Service.[37] A cautious Gov. Richard Dillon expressed restraint with the reservation crusade, remarking to Wilbur that "the matter of creating a National Park out of the White Sands" should be delayed until all interested persons could voice their opinions.[38]

Inspired by Frenger and Fall, Charles initiated the White Sands project movement. Writing to Congressman Dennis Chavez in 1931, Charles argued that as little as one-tenth (forty-three sections, or approximately 27,000 acres) of White Sands would be sufficient for a national monument.[39] The proposed monument would include "those two miles facing the road just north of the Motel camp ground . . . and then take a strip two miles wide across the sands and soda lakes (alkali flat)."[40] It remains a mystery why Charles and the Alamogordo Chamber of Commerce contented themselves with such a small recreational area when they believed White Sands to be a major drawing card for the Southwest. Evidently Charles hoped to avoid delays and controversy with the mining community when he wrote, "It would not seem to us [Alamogordo Chamber of Commerce] necessary or even desirable perhaps to withdraw all the White Sands" because of the commercial potential of the dune field.[41]

As early as 22 May 1931, Charles declared that there would be no local opposition to any plan transferring most of White Sands from private holdings to the state as long as Gov. Arthur Seligman agreed to support "a National Playground" for the dune field.[42] Despite Charles's optimistic prediction, William A. Hawkins, Southern Pacific Railroad attorney, emerged as the plan's principal opponent. Hawkins initially opposed federal government efforts to withdraw any dunes. The attorney argued that White Sands should not be considered for park or monument status because it was "a vast valuable state resource and asset."[43]

Ironically, the development issue held sway on both sides of the controversy. On 10 July 1931, Charles sought Hawkins's endorsement for the proposed monument. Taking a noncommittal posture, Hawkins grudgingly admitted that he did not have all the facts about the monument's size and location; therefore, he refused to endorse the project until he had received all the necessary information. He answered that the monument's proximity would be convenient for the people of Alamogordo and that the town would benefit from the tourist influx.[44] Opposition to the monument steadily subsided as the monument supporters reassuringly stressed that only a small portion of the dune field was desired.

The monument proposal presented to the National Park Service by Charles and the boosters reflects their outlook toward conservation. They repeatedly argued for only a "small part" of White Sands as a national monument in contrast to Frenger's suggestion that "a large part of it should be saved" or even "have it all declared a monument."[45] The modest request most likely reflected the desire of the boosters to avoid conflict between developers and recreationalists. Nor was there a local activist preservationist with the stature of, say, John Muir who could publicize other attractions than the commercial. Only a handful of supporters, such as Frenger, spoke in favor of establishing the entire White Sands region as a national monument or park. National Park Service official Arno Cammerer, in a memorandum to Albright, enthusiastically recommended the entire White Sands for conservation purposes because the National Park Service should "get what we consider necessary" and determine "what we consider essential and take it or leave it."[46] Cammerer's proposal reflected a more enlightened view of the debate. In contrast to the regional boosters, Albright, Cammerer, and Toll wrote about White Sands in aesthetic terms, and not merely as a playground. While Charles, Seligman, Hawkins, and H. L. Kent, president of New Mexico Agriculture and Mechanic College (currently New Mexico State University), supported the national monument to varying degrees, not one of these men who were most familiar with the dunes stressed any motive beyond the commercial exploitation of the area's resources.

The Albright-governed National Park Service played its typically cautious role in the movement to declare White Sands a national monument. The Park Service required two reports concerning White Sands, including an evaluation of the status of land rights and a comprehensive evaluation of the distinctive topographical features, by National Park Service officials. The initial submission to Director Albright was Boles's unfavorable letter. Despite the initial setback, Albright had already submitted his own recommendation to the secretary of the interior recommending White Sands for investigation because its "distinctive character" would justify a national monument.[47] Responding to Interior Secretary Wilbur's recommendation, President Hoover withdrew the public lands for inspection in early 1930. In April 1931, Boles, accompanied by Charles, conducted a preliminary inspection trip but was unable to render any decisions about the gypsum field because of high winds.[48] Boles's potential second visit generated considerable booster activity revealed by the numerous inquiries submitted to politicians.

The National Park Service's interest in White Sands excited the chambers of commerce throughout Southern New Mexico and West Texas. On 24 July 1931, J. S. B. Woolford, president of the Roswell Chamber of Commerce, met National Park Service Associate Director Arno B. Cammerer in Roswell. Cammerer was on a whirlwind inspection tour to review approximately 120 sites recommended for park or monument status. During their meeting Woolford asked the director about White Sands, and Cammerer remarked that the dunes would be inspected soon. Woolford relayed the news of Cammerer's visit to Charles, reassuring him that he would "keep hammering away in the hopes of getting some results" for the White Sands project.[49] By late September 1931, Boles wrote E. H. Simons, vice-president of the El Paso Chamber of Commerce, stating that he did not want to "pass an opinion" regarding White Sands without first conducting a thorough two- or three-day inspection. Subsequently, Boles informed Simons that Superintendent Roger Toll of Yellowstone National Park had been directed to survey the region.[50]

A.B. Fall's Gypsum Phoenix

Roger Toll was an instrumental figure in evaluating potential park lands. As the former superintendent of Rocky Mountain National Park and holding his current prestigious position, Toll acted as Albright's eyes and ears while assessing park and monument proposals in the West.[51] During an inspection tour of the Great Sand Dunes situated in the San Luis Valley, Colorado, in early 1931, Toll learned of the importance of dune formations.[52] Toll completed his White Sands inspection in November 1931 and collected his findings for his report to Albright. Toll's White Sands analysis revealed that the monument should include less than half but more than a third of the dune field. Additionally, he desired all of Townships 17 and 18 plus the edge of the dunes approximately one mile away. The northern boundary was established at Township 17 South. Toll wanted an expansive area sufficient for "recreational purposes."[53] Surprisingly, in his own recommendation to Toll, Charles had omitted the southern dunes because vegetation covered the marginal areas, making them "not at all attractive."[54] Toll recommended the inclusion of the southern dunes and Lake Lucero, and Toll subsequently increased the proposed monument boundaries submitted by Charles by approximately 120,000 acres.[55]

After hearing local opinions and chamber of commerce recommendations, Toll determined the acceptable monument size. Almost every prominent citizen favored some limitation of the size of the monument. Two outspoken critics, Hawkins and E. H. Wells, president of New Mexico School of Mines, argued that the commercial potential of the dunes be analyzed before agreeing to settle the monument boundaries. In 1931, Governor Seligman, like his predecessor Richard Dillon, requested the National Park Service to withhold any park or monument study in order to permit the state to review the economic value of White Sands. The commercial potential of the gypsum prompted

Seligman to remark that White Sands was not "such a national curiosity" as to qualify as a national monument.[56] In a letter to Governor Seligman on 7 February 1932, Charles reflected local sentiments when he agreed that the monument should not embrace any land north of Township 17 South in order to leave "two thirds of the sand out for commercial development and take about one third for the national playground."[57] Charles did not request an expansion of the proposed monument even when J. F. Hinkle, New Mexico commissioner of public lands, suggested to him that he would not contest a request for the southern half of Township 18 if Charles desired it. Standing his ground, Toll remarked that White Sands should include "reasonable boundaries," thus revealing that he favored a large monument instead of a small one.[58] Toll informed the boosters that he would advise Albright against establishing a national monument if the region were too limited in size.[59]

After his November 1931 inspection, Toll submitted his review to Albright on 29 January 1932. The superintendent rendered a favorable recommendation for a WSNM; however, there were several unresolved problems. Roger Toll advised state and local officials that if any objections were raised against the establishment of a national monument that could not be resolved by the state the White Sands project should be canceled. Furthermore, any valid mining claims and land exchanges had to be settled before a national monument proclamation.

For the next two years James F. Hinkle, W. R. Eccles, who was state highway engineer, and Albright, Cammerer, Demaray, and Charles exchanged correspondence attempting to establish boundaries and secure an appropriate access road into or adjacent to White Sands. The route of the federal highway leading from Alamogordo to Las Cruces was an important item on the agenda of the Alamogordo Chamber of Commerce. On behalf of the chamber, Charles wrote countless letters imploring state and federal officials to route the projected highway as close to White Sands as possible, preferably by the Point of Sands. Erroneously, Charles believed that the National Park Service's monument or park designation hinged upon the route's proximity to the dunes and the potential number of tourists.[60] Boles, Toll, and Albright repeatedly reminded Charles that they were inspecting White Sands only for national monument consideration.[61]

In distant Washington, D.C., with President Franklin D. Roosevelt's inauguration on 4 March 1933, there was a new era for the National Park Service. Roosevelt's New Deal recovery proposals and budget increases benefitted the money-starved park lands. One of the most important recovery acts for the nation as well as the National Park Service was the National Recovery Act, which created numerous measures to relieve unemployment in America. Among the most successful and beneficial programs were those directed by Robert Fechner, director of the Civilian Conservation Corps, to construct and rebuild the nation's roads and federal highways. The federal government presented New Mexico $5,792,935 in nonmatching funds for highway construction. Surprisingly, New Mexico responded so quickly to the generous federal funds that the major delays in actual construction were caused by lack of appropriate machinery.[62]

Alamogordo's struggle to obtain a major road passing close to or even through the gypsum dunes succeeded after State Route 3's partial completion in late 1928. There had been several attempts to acquire a highway from Alamogordo to Las Cruces. In 1922, one plan had called for the highway to leave Alamogordo due south for Orogrande and then strike west for the San Augustin Pass (also known locally as Organ Pass), but the state highway department shelved this proposal because of the local public protest against the route. The commission then presented a second route originating in Tularosa leading south to Valmont and westward to Las Cruces over the San Augustin Pass. Eventually both of these routes would become portions of Federal Highway 54 connecting Alamogordo with El Paso but without a westward bypass to Las Cruces.

By 1932, the Alamogordo–White Sands–Las Cruces road became a project funded by the Federal Assistance Project and identified as Federal Assistance Project 176. While local boosters were delighted by State Route 3 passing White Sands, they demanded that the road be a federal highway because it would attract national attention, federal dollars, and, of course, more tourists. Three road proposals confronted Charles and state officials: (1) the current road, which left Alamogordo due west for ten or fifteen miles and then turned southward where it struck the White Sands approximately two miles above the Point of Sands; (2) the state highway department's plan for a road that would depart Alamogordo in a southwesterly direction and employ the overpass on the rail line, this road would proceed in a straight line until it reached the Point of Sands and then turn southward, but it would be 350 feet closer to the dunes than the first proposal; and (3) a proposal for a compromise presented by Eccles, whose road followed the same course as the second proposal but reached the dunes similar to the approach route of the first plan. Charles and the boosters supported the first option because this road would permit the best tourist access to the gypsum dunes, while the other two routes would cross major mountain drainage runoffs.[63] Charles repeatedly warned Governor Seligman and Eccles that if they failed to establish a major highway according to the first plan then they would have to answer to "every Chamber of Commerce."[64]

Charles's persistence paid dividends when Eccles met with A. E. Palen of the Bureau of Public Roads to discuss the boosters' determination to gain a federal highway that followed State Route 3. Palen acceded to Alamogordo boosters' wishes and agreed to resurvey the route.[65] Following his visit to White Sands in June 1932, Albright informed Toll that he favored the existing route for the federal highway. The director added that he would agree to a loop road off the highway paralleling the perimeter dune slopes. By August 1932 the National Park Service, state and local officials, and boosters finally reached an agreement concerning the Alamogordo–White Sands–Las Cruces federal highway.[66]

The second major barrier to a National Park Service WSNM endorsement was the question of who actually owned the gypsum dunes, or according to Hawkins, who possessed valid rights. Horace Albright, astonished to learn of the existence of potential mining claims, promptly dispatched letters to John T. Murphy, chief of the Santa Fe Field Division of the General Land Office, to research the situation. After conferring with C. R. Wilkson, his representative in Las Cruces, Murphy informed National Park Service Director Albright that practically the entire gypsum dune field contained valid mining claims.[67] Therefore, any decision had to wait until the mining claims could be verified. Because of the terms of the Mining Law of 1872 that allowed individuals to file mineral claims on federal lands, Hinkle predicted that if the mining claims were valid then the WSNM proposal would be "blown up."[68]

Spurred on by the question of White Sands ownership, Charles interviewed area residents and sent inquiries to the county clerks in Doña Ana and Otero counties. He asked them if they had any knowledge or record of any placer or mining claims in the dunes. Charles's relentless determination in researching the claims question revealed that several individuals had filed placer claims, but none of them had any finalized assessments. The National Park

Service suspended its discussions until the resolution of these claims. Additionally, none of the White Sands townships were leased by the state. The designated monument area initially included school sections; however, commissioner Hinkle suggested that these sections or any other state lands would not hinder or halt the monument project.[69]

In late May 1932, Murphy investigated the mining claims and concluded that the claims were no longer valid. In his report to Albright, Murphy stated that "all of the placer locations herein have been completely abandoned" and that "it would be perfectly safe to consider them abandoned, null and void." [70]Upon receipt of Murphy's report, Demaray wrote Murphy stating that the National Park Service would renew its examination of White Sands.[71] A relieved Tom Charles and anxious local chambers of commerce cheered after receiving news in July 1932 that the National Park Service would renew its negotiations with state officials regarding the boundaries for the proposed national monument.[72]

On 25 July 1932, Hinkle, speaking on behalf of Governor Seligman, informed Albright that he agreed to the monument boundaries proposed by Roger Toll and that no problems would arise with state lands existing in the monument area.[73] Three weeks later Cammerer informed Hinkle that if a boundary agreement could be reached, the National Park Service was ready to draft the WSNM proclamation. Commissioner Hinkle agreed with Toll's boundary recommendations and finally on 7 December 1932, Conrad Wirth, assistant director in charge of the Branch Lands, directed George A. Moskey, assistant director of Branch of Use, Law, and Regulation, to prepare the White Sands proclamation for Interior Secretary Wilbur's review. Secretary Wilbur endorsed the proclamation draft based upon Albright's strong recommendations and his own favorable impressions. On

16 January 1933, Wilbur forwarded the proclamation draft to President Hoover. Writing to President Hoover, Wilbur stated:

> The area covered by this proposed proclamation has been examined by experts of this Department [Interior] to determine its qualifications for a national monument. The reports show the sands to be glistening white and 95% pure gypsum. These sands are highly interesting from a scenic standpoint and have recreational possibilities.[74]

On 27 January 1933, Sen. Bronson Cutting telegraphed Tom Charles informing him that the president had "signed the proclamation establishing White Sands National Monument . . . congratulations."[75] Director Albright sent Charles a congratulatory letter thanking him for his significant contributions to the WSNM efforts.[76] Clarence W. Morgan, the *Alamogordo News* editor, reported that the people of Alamogordo were elated by the news.[77] Morgan appropriately acknowledged that the "greatest measure of

Map 5. National Park Service Area in Region III (Region III Quarterly, January 1940)

NATIONAL PARK SERVICE AREAS IN REGION III

1. Region III Headquarters
2. Bandelier Nat'l. Monument
3. Chaco Canyon Nat'l. Monument
4. El Morro Nat'l. Monument
5. Gran Quivira Nat'l. Monument
6. Carlsbad Caverns Nat'l. Park
7. White Sands Nat'l. Monument
8. Gila Cliff Dwellings Nat'l. Monument
9. Chiricahua Nat'l. Monument
10. Tumacacori Nat'l. Monument
11. Saguaro Nat'l. Monument
12. Casa Grande Nat'l. Monument
13. Organ Pipe Cactus Nat'l. Monument
14. Tonto Nat'l. Monument
15. Petrified Forest Nat'l. Monument
16. Montezuma Castle Nat'l. Monument
17. Walnut Canyon Nat'l. Monument
18. Sunset Crater Nat'l. Monument
19. Wupatki Nat'l. Monument
20. Grand Canyon Nat'l. Park
21. Grand Canyon Nat'l. Monument
22. Pipe Spring Nat'l. Monument
23. Boulder Dam Nat'l. Recreational Area
24. Lehman Caves Nat'l. Monument
25. Rainbow Bridge Nat'l. Monument
26. Navajo Nat'l. Monument
27. Canyon de Chelly Nat'l. Monument
28. Aztec Ruins Nat'l. Monument
29. Mesa Verde Nat'l. Park
30. Yucca House Nat'l. Monument
31. Hovenweep Nat'l. Monument
32. Natural Bridges Nat'l. Monument
33. Arches Nat'l. Monument
34. Colorado Nat'l. Monument
35. Black Canyon of the Gunnison Nat'l. Monument
36. Wheeler Nat'l. Monument
37. Great Sand Dunes Nat'l. Monument
38. Capulin Mountain Nat'l. Monument
39. Platt Nat'l. Park
40. Hot Springs Nat'l. Park
41. Tuzigoot Nat'l. Monument

credit for the results is due Tom Charles" (See Map 5).[78]

In retrospect, White Sands had been one of 103 national monument proposals for fiscal year 1933. The National Park Service had investigated forty-six nominees, and by 30 June 1933, Hoover and his successor had proclaimed nine national monuments, including White Sands.[79]

While Herbert Hoover may be most remembered for his unfortunate identification with the Great Depression, his administration did successfully promote many conservation measures. In fact, conserving the nation's resources was a principal focus of his administration even during economic hard times. One of Hoover's numerous biographers, Harris Gaylord Warren, remarked that even though Hoover was a vigorous supporter of states' rights, he stood against unrestrained rights of the individual "plundering the common heritage of natural resources."[80] Interior Secretary Wilbur characterized Hoover's conservation interests as more than "genuinely zealous" because of his familiarity with the West while working on numerous government surveys as a young engineer.[81] During Hoover's administration the National Park Service increased its holdings by approximately three million acres, or 40 percent.[82] Hoover's receptivity to National Park Service proposals for parks and monuments and two capable conservation leaders, Wilbur and Albright, culminated with the establishment of WSNM.

Interior Secretary Wilbur remarked that Albright's National Park Service philosophy "was very much like my own" and that the National Park Service had his "deep interest."[83] Wilbur's views concerning national monuments revealed that he did not necessarily expect them to possess magnificent scenery, but the national monuments differed from national parks only "in extent of interest and importance."[84] Wilbur's tenure was a productive period for the National Park Service. The Hoover, Wilbur, and

Albright era witnessed four new national parks, ten new national monuments, and the addition of 75,000 acres to existing areas, plus the acquisition of the War Department's national military parks, national parks, battlefield sites, national monuments, memorials, and cemeteries.[85] Announcing his policy, Wilbur insisted, "In making selections it was kept in mind that the National Park system should possess variety, accepting the supreme in each of the various types and subjects of scenic, scientific, and historical importance and of interest to the nation as a whole."[86]

Relying upon Roger Toll's strong recommendations and Horace Albright's endorsement, in addition to their firsthand accounts and Secretary Wilbur's strong support, President Hoover signed the proclamation creating WSNM. The proclamation reads, "Whereas it appears that the public interest would be promoted by including the lands. . . within a national monument for the preservation of the white sands and additional features of scenic, scientific, and educational interest."[87]

The creation of White Sands National Monument remained consistent with the administration's National Park Service land acquisition program. White Sands entered the national monument ranks with 142,987 acres and rightfully received national recognition as a region "of great interest from a scientific and geologic standpoint" as well as a "recreational playground" recognized for its "marvelous splendor and beauty."[88] National Park Service historian John Ise wrote that during Albright's tenure as National Park Service director, from 12 January 1929 to 9 August 1933, the National Park Service witnessed the inclusion of the most "scenic national parks and scenic and archaeological monuments."[89]

The entry of White Sands into the National Park system is to some extent an example of national parks historian Alfred Runte's "worthless lands" thesis—that after lands proved to have no commercial value, local interests began to exploit them for scenery and to attract tourists. While Runte argues that many National Park Service areas had to be proven valueless, in the case of White Sands, the gypsum dunes continuously attracted commercial interests. During Roger Toll's inspection in 1932, Tom Charles reminded him that federal designation of any portion of the dunes would only stimulate added commercial interest. The local boosters' clamor for a limited reservation was intended to pacify the mining companies as well as rekindle hopes that the dunes would become economically beneficial for the region. In contrast to Toll's recommendation that the entire Great Sand Dunes be reserved, it was the potential economic value of White Sands that dictated that only a fraction of the dune field be set aside as a national monument. Offsetting Charles's suggestion concerning the size of the monument, Toll insisted that he would recommend monument status only if it would encompass a sufficient area. Toll advised the local boosters of his decision, emphasizing that if there were any serious opposition to his recommendation, he would reject White Sands as a monument candidate. Because of the numerous mining failures, the only economic potential of White Sands was its attraction for tourists. While regional businessmen viewed White Sands as "useless scenery,"[90] it was that very image that allowed the proclamation of WSNM of a significant portion of the dune field. At its establishment, WSNM posed no threat to competing private mining companies because of the dune field's immense area. But even more significant were the immediate economic benefits that tourism would provide for the region and the state. Accordingly, White Sands always retained the interest of developers, schemers, and recreationalists. Thus the time-consuming and tedious process of securing a White Sands national park or monument came to fruition because of the unswerving dedication exhibited by Tom Charles and those persistent regional boosters, a dedication that was supported by conservation-minded Roger Toll and Horace Albright, Secretary of the Interior Ray Lyman Wilbur, and President Herbert Hoover. Ultimately Fall's failed All-Year National Park scheme resurfaced in diverse forms: Elephant Butte Lake State Park and Recreation Area, Valley of Fires Recreation Area (until recently a state park) and Carrizozo Lava Flow Wilderness Study Area, White Mountain Wilderness, Mescalero Apache Indian Reservation, and WSNM. The date of the proclamation, 18 January 1933, was an important day for Tom Charles, Alamogordo, and the Southwest. Tom Charles's patience and persistence to push his White Sands project for federal designation had evolved into a passion for which he had "never lost his enthusiasm."[91] Eventually his "drawing card" proved to be more than just a regional attraction; its special geological features finally commanded national and international audiences.

Tom Charles certainly had many shortcomings; however, he receives credit for pioneering two WSNM trails: one as its first custodian and the second as the monument's first concessioner. Tom Charles's enthusiasm for Alamogordo and his unrelenting determination to alert state and federal officials to the potential of White Sands for National Park Service status are his legacy. Charles's personal stamp on White Sands led Frank Pinkley affectionately to call the dunes "Tom's Gyp Outfit."[92]

BEING A MONUMENT ISN'T SUCH AN AWFUL FATE
The Formative Years

The evolution of the monument category provides one of the clearest pictures of the changing values of American preservation. Because it could be applied to much more than archaeological sites, the Antiquities Act remained useful as the accepted ideas of what constituted an important part of the American past changed.—Hal Rothman, *Preserving Different Pasts*

The White Sands National Monument (WSNM) proclamation on 18 January 1933 paved the way for what would become an extremely popular tourist attraction. Until its establishment as a national monument, White Sands had been unsupervised and unmanaged. Formerly a relatively unknown area, the National Park Service surveyed White Sands, updating and going far beyond county surveys that had been completed at the turn of the twentieth century. Previously most people had skirted the interior dunes, camping or picnicking along the dunes' eastern boundary. And as the National Park Service made much of the area accessible to the public, management policies called for the preservation of the monument's integrity and resources.

Local historical inaccuracies led many historians and National Park Service administrators to believe that the regional national park movement of 1921–22 pertained only to the White Sands dune field and that somehow in the local boosters' enthusiasm the "project got out of control."[1] They were not aware of the history of Secretary of the Interior Albert B. Fall's All-Year National Park proposal. The National Park Service never considered White Sands as a potential national park in its own right, even though many local residents later regarded national monument status merely as a temporary designation until national park status could be secured. Southwestern National Monuments Superintendent Frank "Boss" Pinkley, angered by the National Park Service's traditional second-class treatment of monuments, and by the general public's perception of national monuments as inferior landscapes or natural curiosities, voiced his displeasure with the remark, "Being a Monument isn't such an awful fate."[2]

White Sands National Monument did not endure financial deprivation in comparison with Southwestern national monuments that had been established earlier.[3] It went without support during its first year only because operating funds were not appropriated until fiscal year 1935, and federal relief measures and forceful centralized leadership altered the status of national monuments during the New Deal. National monuments historian Hal Rothman credits Roosevelt's presidency as being a watershed in National Park Service history because national monuments were granted equal administrative standing with the national parks.[4]

Coinciding with the monuments' administrative elevation was the National Park Service requirement for professional staffs, thereby eliminating the custodian positions generally associated with national monuments and replacing them with superintendent appointments. The role played by the custodians was significant considering the numerous handicaps under which they performed their jobs. Rothman characterizes the custodians as "a mixed batch" who had few common interests.[5] Many of the custodians were not National Park Service professionals, and most performed their duties in conjunction with other jobs. They patrolled the monuments when time permitted. Often they were not familiar with the regulations or the conservationist and administrative philosophies of the Park Service.

Generally the early custodians were ultra-boosters for their particular national monument. Following the establishment of a national monument, they orchestrated the opening-day ceremonies, which highlighted the area's history and identified the individuals responsible for securing the monument. The irony was that the custodians themselves often were not recognized during these events, even though they had given so much of themselves to the monument-making efforts; generally the day belonged to local and state politicians, to boosters who spoke of the monument's potential economic benefits to the region, and to National Park Service dignitaries who welcomed the new monument into the National Park system. The custodians' achievements are even more remarkable in light of their inadequate salaries. Enthusiasm was the common denominator that drove them to remain with their special project through the formative years, and at WSNM Tom Charles was no exception.[6]

Unlike Southwestern archaeological monuments, the geologic monuments—for example, Great Sand Dunes and White Sands—did not demand constant vigilance or prompt attention to protect them from vandals, arsonists, or the natural elements. In fact, for years many custodians "turned a blind eye" to visitors removing gypsum or sand from the areas and actively encouraged tourists to satisfy the "urge for personal inscription . . . upon the sides of the dunes."[7] Ironically, while Tom Charles actively engaged in providing gypsum samples to anyone who asked for them, he requested Frank Pinkley to provide protection for WSNM because of the increasing number of visitors to the dunes.[8] It was one thing for the part-time custodian to remove gypsum for advertising purposes but quite a different matter when the general public engaged in the practice. Charles continued "distributing" the gypsum until he was admonished by Pinkley in 1935. The custodians believed that the National Park Service condoned such activities when practiced by officials, and certainly their actions were well intentioned, if misguided. Of course, the National Park Service did not support or endorse any vandalism.

Officially and realistically, the necessity for immediate guardianship at Great Sand Dunes and White Sands monuments was not a priority issue early on because the National Park Service could not provide full-time positions to prevent boosters and visitors from removing gypsum or sand samples nor were its officials aware of the problem. In spite of the obvious drawback of utilizing local boosters as custodians, without such determined and dedicated individuals the National Park Service's early management and protection policies of its national monuments would have been much more difficult to apply or at the least implementation of those directives would have been dismal failures.

Contrary to local legend, at WSNM there were several individuals interested in the publicized position of dollar-a-year or honorary custodian without pay. According to the National Park Service personnel form for the part-time position, the custodian's principal responsibilities were to "give information to tourists and to prevent vandalism, reporting to the Washington Office, National Park Service and from time to time through superintendent Frank Pinkley" in Coolidge, Arizona.[9] The two main prospects, Tom Charles and Frank L. Ridinger, the latter the owner of the White Sands Motel at the Point of Sands, submitted their inquiries. On 22 May 1933, National Park Service senior biologist Walter P. Taylor remarked that the two most promising applicants were Charles and Ridinger.[10]

The Alamogordo Chamber of Commerce endorsed its former secretary and president for the job to the National Park Service. Local booster and newspaper editor Clarence W. Morgan reflected the area's sentiments with the comment that "the greatest measure of credit" for securing the WSNM belonged to Tom Charles; therefore, the only appropriate choice for custodian should be Charles if he desired the position.[11] Charles did want the job, pointing out his thirty years "of intimate association," his chairmanship of the White Sands Committee, and finally that White Sands "was still my baby."[12] Additionally it was Charles who had repeatedly asked Pinkley about hiring a full-time custodian and permanent park rangers. Certainly the motive behind Charles's request was his desire to become WSNM's first full-time custodian. Having met with Tom Charles in June 1932 at White Sands and believing the dune field to be a potential park area, National Park Service Director Horace M. Albright selected Charles for the position.[13] Later, during Albright's administrative absence, Arthur E. Demaray, acting and senior assistant National Park Service director, also supported Charles because of "very high" endorsements.[14] Shortly after Albright's return to duty, he forwarded the Charles nomination to President Franklin D. Roosevelt, who in turn appointed Charles WSNM custodian on 10 July 1933.[15] The appointment became effective on 1 August 1933.[16]

Charles's appointment was that of temporary or nominal custodian that was renewable every three months. His initial pay was $4 per month increasing to $32 per month on 14 July 1934, and on 16 November 1936 his salary increased again to $45 per month.[17] Throughout Charles's brief National Park Service career as custodian, he frequently publicized his scanty pay and allowances. Charles's pay was increased, but not automatically; he had to request raises in salary. Interestingly, Charles did not utilize the proper administrative channels for his pay requests. He bypassed Pinkley, his immediate supervisor, writing directly to National Park Service Director Arno B. Cammerer. As early as April 1934 Charles requested a $400 to $500 per year increase.[18] Cammerer responded by forwarding Charles's inquiry to Pinkley. At times angered by Charles's insubordinate actions, Pinkley did not raise Charles's pay further because Charles was also a U.S. commissioner. Civil Service regulations precluded individuals who were only part-time employees, such as custodians, from earning more than $540 annually. Additionally, an individual could not earn more than $2,000 collectively from two federal government jobs.[19] It should also be remembered that Charles was requesting pay raises during the height of the Great Depression. Charles's position as WSNM custodian was not as financially unrewarding as he boasted later in his career. Frank Pinkley informed Charles that his salary should help prevent his "losing money running that Monument [WSNM] for us."[20]

In April 1933, Ferris Shelton, president of the Alamogordo Chamber of Commerce, wrote Senator Cutting about the possibilities of receiving Emergency Conservation Act funds and personnel for repairing roads, constructing residences for rangers, and building a headquarters building at WSNM. Shelton, at Charles's urging, desired to acquire federal funds to develop WSNM as an attractive and accessible tourist area. The boosters thought that by acquiring the monies the area's unemployment problem would be solved. Shelton and Charles apparently misunderstood the type of projects authorized in the Civil Works Administration's reforestation program. Cutting forwarded Shelton's letter to Albright, who answered Shelton that the National Park Service budget and national emergency funds would not provide for WSNM construction projects.[21] Additionally, WSNM certainly did not qualify as an area requiring reforestation.

After the establishment of Civilian Conservation Corps camp DG–39–N (the company numbered approximately 200 men and was located at two sites, at La Luz and at Tularosa north of Alamogordo), Charles concluded that WSNM should have a similar camp. Unlike Carlsbad Caverns, Chaco Canyon, and Bandelier, the National Park Service did not acquire a CCC camp at WSNM; however, Pinkley received $26,044 from the Civil Works Administration and a labor force to complete the WSNM work projects.

The WSNM proposal allowed for eight miles of road to the center of the dune field with a turn-around or loop. At the turn-around point a large parking area was cleared in the Crystal Bowl. The Civil Works Administration work force completed the road project and associated survey on 26 April 1934, just in time for the monument's opening-day ceremony three days later. The public could gain access to the Heart of the Dunes for the first time. Pinkley, accompanied by associate engineer, Walter Atwell, landscape architects Charles Richey and Lyle Bennett, and chief clerk Hugh Miller, arrived at WSNM on 4 December 1933 to inspect the road construction and familiarize themselves with WSNM.[22] Charles guided Pinkley's party along the monument's boundaries, and to the horror of the inspection team drove over the dunes at 60 miles per hour. Charles assisted Pinkley's team by directing them to the Heart of the Dunes area and pointing out the vastness of the gypsum dune field.[23]

It is unfair to judge Charles too harshly regarding his conservation behavior while custodian. He acknowledged his shortcomings in his first report to Superintendent Frank Pinkley, when he wrote that "by no stretch of the imagination can I believe that you are as sorely in need of information from the custodian [Charles] as he is in need of information from you."

Charles added that he encouraged Pinkley or members of his staff "to come over soon and set us right on the Park program."[24]

Since the only security initially required at White Sands was to guard against visitors damaging or vandalizing the picnic tables and entrance station, Charles's principal duties upon assuming WSNM custodianship were to count visitors and to submit a monthly status report to White Sands headquarters. In his first monthly report Charles expressed his amazement at Pinkley's requirement that he count visitors.[25] For Charles, tallying the number of cars and tourists was a "nightmare."[26]

Struggling to abide by Pinkley's guidelines Charles attempted to have the visitors register by signing in at the entrance in 1934 but in 1938 relocated the register in the Heart of the Dunes area. The number of visitors counted and visitors registered rarely matched. He estimated the first month's visitor tally at approximately 4,700 cars, and calculating that there were at least four people per car, the first month's visitation totaled 19,000 visitors (see Table 1).[27] Entrance fees were not collected until 1 May 1939 and were set at 25 cents per person. By September 1939, the National Park Service increased the fee to 50 cents per car for the season.[28]

The long-hoped-for opening-day celebration occurred approximately a year after the monument's establishment. Actively involved in the festivities, the Alamogordo Chamber of Commerce scheduled the dedication for 29 April 1934. The well-publicized ceremony was a major occurrence for Southern New Mexico and West Texas boosters. And to show their support approximately 4,700 people (even though only 600 cars had been counted) attended the day's ceremonies.[29] A variety of events were held in the Crystal Bowl: musical concerts by the New Mexico State University and Alamogordo High School bands; a program recognizing the area's pioneers—the Old Timers' Reunion; a base-

Table i. Attendance Figures

Year	Attendance	Year	Atetendance
1933	12,000	1955	279,000
1934	34,000	1956	283,000
1935	34,000	1957	304,000
1936	48,000	1958	320,000
1937	108,000	1959	380,000
1938	91,000	1960	389,000
1939	59,000	1961	377,000
1940	57,000	1962	331,000
1941	73,000	1963	393,000
1942	53,000	1964**	397,000
1943	36,000	1965	524,000
1944	35,000	1966***	402,000
1945	56,000	1967	516,000
1946	75,000		
1947	97,000		
1948	125,000	1977	627,000
1949	154,000	1978	600,000
1950	181,000	1979	586,000
1951	194,000		
1952	219,000		
1953*	93,000	1985	431,000
1954	227,000	1986	667,000

*July – November Statistics missing
**July Statistics Missing.
***April – May Statistics Missing.

Compiled by author from Southwestern National Monuments Monthly Report, 1933-40, and Superintendents' Monthly Narrative, 1941-67, WSNM Library; "National park Service Statistical Abstract," 1979, 19; El Paso Times, 12 Mar 87, New Mexico Section, p,1 col. 1–4.

ball game fielded by two black teams from El Paso and Las Cruces; and most importantly, the dedication services.[30]
An impressive group of speakers addressed the large crowd. Among the distinguished guests were W. A. Sutherland of Las

Cruces; Judge E. L. Medler of Hot Springs (now Truth or Consequences); George Frenger of Las Cruces; Judge E. B. McClintock of El Paso; former New Mexico governors George Curry and Richard Dillon; and W. G. Atwell, who represented the National Park Service. Featured speakers were Oliver M. Lee, a former state senator; A. N. Blazer of Mescalero; George Coe of Glencoe; H. S. Hunter, editor for the *El Paso Times*; and professor H. L. Kent. However, the dominant personality and guest of honor at the dedication was former Secretary of the Interior Albert B. Fall.[31] Eugene Manlove Rhodes, the Tularosa Basin's most famous literary figure, was among the numerous invited personalities unable to attend. Rhodes explained in a letter to his friend Bernard De Voto (who was not present at the ceremony), "I can't go. No strength, money or time." He was quite ill at the time. Rhodes added sardonically, "Coe and Rhodes and Lee and Fall, God have mercy upon us all."[32]

While no transcripts of the addresses exist, the *Alamogordo News* commented that Fall's speech left the audience "spellbound." According to news accounts Judge Fall was "visibly affected" by being among his numerous friends and supporters.[33] Fall's voice was said to be so weak that only those listeners nearest to him heard his address. C. W. Morgan witnessed the event. "It was indeed a pathetic sight," he wrote, "to see that he [Fall] had to be assisted from his car and supported during his talk." Fall mentioned that because of ill health the ceremony would be his last opportunity to meet his friends. Interestingly, the substance of Fall's remarks was that the best use of the gypsum dunes was as a recreational area. A responsive audience gave Fall a "big hand" cheering loudly. It was an emotional experience for everyone in attendance.[34]

The "Big White Sands Dedicatory," as it was known locally, represented the culmination of years of efforts by J. S. B. Woolford of Roswell, Mose Stevens of Las Cruces, and especially Tom Charles, to secure federal designation for White Sands. From Fall's earlier national park proposals through Charles's efforts to salvage one of the landscapes it singled out, the ceremony reflected the full circle of the regional boosters' attempts to establish an all-year playground in Southern New Mexico. It is ironic that Fall and the other speakers neglected to credit Tom Charles or anyone else associated with the monument movement. It remains doubtful whether Fall ever knew of Charles's admiration for him or of Charles's motivation for undertaking the White Sands project. Keenly aware of the speaker's neglect or oversight in complimenting specific monument boosters, Tom Charles's contributions to the White Sands monument movement were acknowledged by Clarence W. Morgan and later by Horace Albright. In his editorial Morgan proudly noted Charles's "noble part" in promoting a national monument for the region and that WSNM would "stand as a monument to him."[35] In 1939, after reading Charles's pamphlet *The Story of the Great White Sands*, Albright thanked Charles for his "marvelous job" in publicizing White Sands as a national attraction.[36] Indeed, Charles had done his part.

The White Sands National Monument's formative years witnessed numerous advertising campaigns. Among the many Alamogordo supporters who offered their services to Tom Charles was Oliver (Jack) M. Voyde, a local photographer and tailor. Voyde produced countless gypsum statuary plaques and bookends depicting gypsum dune scenes. Charles used Voyde's products for souvenirs or gifts to National Park Service officials, state and local politicians, and numerous visitors.[37] During the early 1930s, Charles used Voyde's popular gypsum products selectively, presenting them to individuals who supported the national monument movement.

Once it was established as a national monument, numerous ideas emerged for White Sands projects. On 7 February 1936, R. T. Spence, vice president of the Alamogordo Chamber of Commerce, provided an itinerary for G. M. Wootton, manager for the Rock Island Railroad's Vacation Travel Tours, encouraging him to design side trips for Rock Island passengers to Alamogordo and the nearby attractions such as Cloudcroft and WSNM. Spence informed Wootton that there is "no danger of over-advertising" WSNM. The booster sincerely believed that a "sort of Rock Island-Southern Pacific resort with facilities for sleeping in the Heart of the Dunes" could be developed.[38] Spence's idea reflected a consistent theme that emphasized organized recreation in WSNM.

As happened earlier at Yosemite, Grand Canyon, and Yellowstone national parks, WSNM experienced the folly of unrealistic schemes.[39] Perhaps the most outrageous plan for WSNM was geologist L. M. Richard's vision, later reintroduced by Tom Charles, of "a large steam shovel at work" constructing an artificial lake in the Heart of the Dunes.[40] As with many such projects, Charles quickly assumed the idea as his own. When Pinkley learned of a potential Lake White Sands, he promptly squelched the suggestion and rebuked Charles, informing him that the National Park Service's landscape division would not be "enthusiastic" about such a proposal.[41] Repeatedly, Charles failed to comprehend the preservation responsibility required by his position. On another occasion in 1936, Charles wrote to Pinkley that "the prospects of a beautiful road" winding across the Heart of the Dunes to Lake Lucero delighted him.[42] Again, Pinkley intervened. Charles's narrow expectations of WSNM as merely Alamogordo's playground annex cannot be understated.

In late 1935, the Alamogordo Rotary Club sponsored a White Sands parade float for El Paso's Sun Bowl Carnival scheduled for 1 January 1936. Local businesses contributed supplies, equipment, time, and laborers for the enterprise. The float's theme portrayed a family picnicking at WSNM and provided considerable free advertising for WSNM.[43] Alamogordo's Sun Bowl Carnival entry received a first place award for originality. White Sands National Monument gained additional publicity in regional newspapers and at events such as county fairs. For example, the 1938 Otero County Fair was a White Sands booth that earned a blue ribbon for its creativity.[44]

One of the most pressing problems confronting WSNM during its early years was establishing definitive boundaries. In 1934, Pinkley notified Acting National Park Service Director A. E. Demaray that boundary changes were necessary because New Mexico State Highway 3 had been altered, thereby placing the monument's entrance adjacent to private land. After receiving notice from Charles that several local residents planned to build a gas station and concession stands, Pinkley urged Demaray to extend WSNM's boundary to prevent such encroachment. Charles informed Pinkley that the land was "perfectly worthless," but acquiring the area would protect the WSNM entrance.[45] Demaray agreed with Pinkley's recommendation to expand the boundary, requesting Acting Interior Secretary T. A. Walters to draft a proclamation extending the boundaries for President Franklin D. Roosevelt's approval. On 26 October 1934, Walters approved the request, recognizing the urgency to prevent inappropriate or undesirable buildings bordering the monument headquarters.[46] President Roosevelt signed Proclamation 2108 on 28 November 1934, adding 158.91 acres to the monument[47] and preventing the establishment of commercial enterprises near the monument headquarters. The addition prevented a circuslike atmosphere similar to those that have drawn so much criticism near the entrances to Yellowstone and Yosemite.

In addition to establishing firm boundaries, the National Park Service officials needed to identify and resolve the problem of nonfederal lands within WSNM. During a meeting of area ranchers, they learned that the Lucero family held the deed to 160 acres situated at the extreme western portion of WSNM.[48] After the family moved to Las Cruces, they retained their ranch property mainly as grazing land. Unintentionally, the Lucero property was included in President Herbert Hoover's 1930 White Sands land withdrawal order and subsequently included in WSNM. Jose R. Lucero contacted Tom Charles in June 1939, asking for a grazing permit, and Charles forwarded Lucero's request to Pinkley.[49] Acting Southwestern National Monuments Superintendent Hugh M. Miller advised Charles that it was "contrary to policy" to allow grazing within a national monument because of the need to protect the monument's flora.[50] Therefore, the National Park Service denied a grazing permit for the family. By 1940, the Luceros relinquished their property after realizing that it would be impossible to manage their ranch surrounded by a national monument.[51]

The National Park Service determined that its best interests would be served by eliminating all private ownership of lands within WSNM. It also wished to acquire a water source in Dog Canyon, located fifteen miles east in the Sacramento Mountains. As of January 1937, 14,134 acres valued at $42,295 were privately owned within the monument.[52] By November 1937, the state land office had removed the restriction on the state acquiring lands thereby removing "any serious stumbling block," so that Maier could proceed with the land exchange negotiations (see Map 5).[53]

Monument land exchanges continued for the next thirty years between the Bureau of Land Management, the state of New

Mexico, and the National Park Service. White Sands National Monument's original lands included 129,030.3 acres from the Public Domain and 11,216.7 acres acquired as a result of purchase, donation, or exchange. After examining several National Park Service WSNM "Annual Report of Real Property Owned by United States Government" forms (Government Service Agency Form 58–15317), I realized that none of the final figures matched, explaining the conflicting acreage reports for the monument.[54] Adding to the confusion is the fact that WSNM's "Land Ownership Record" deeds total only 140,299.60 acres.[55]

In 1968, Superintendent Turney reported that WSNM included 145,952.35 federal acres and that Price F. Sanders, Genevieve Sanders, and Simon L. Lucero still claimed 200 acres in the far western portion of the monument. These individuals had leased their acreage to the military by an exclusive use contract in 1950.[56] In 1968, there remained 582.99 nonfederal acres in WSNM; it was unclear if the existing claims were still valid. The acreage discrepancies surfaced because of the uncertainty of who actually held deeds to the lands. The federal government resolved the question by acquiring the lands by quit claim deeds and by presidential proclamation.[57]

While consolidating its holdings, the Interior Department obtained a detached area situated south of WSNM called Garton Lake on 14 November 1936, but the land was not transferred to WSNM until 6 June 1942. In 1909, the area that would be called Garton Lake had drawn the attention of oil speculators because investigations of the artesian well indicated oil sources. Subsequent studies by the U.S. Geological Survey revealed little oil.[58]

Garton Lake became the monument's Recreational Demonstration Area as part of the Resettlement Administration's policy of acquiring submarginal lands. The previous property owner, Lester L. Garton, sold the area to the federal government for $750; because of its homestead status, the land title could only be returned to the federal government. According to Interior Secretary Douglas McKay, the Resettlement Administration never properly acquired the area because Garton Lake assumed "unreserved public domain status."[59] Therefore, Garton Lake did not officially become part of WSNM until President Eisenhower added the area's 478.53 acres in 1953.[60]

Shortly after the military's entry into the Tularosa Basin in 1942, federal officials requested permission to use Garton Lake as a swimming pool and as a general recreational area. Even though the National Park Service approved, the military unexpectedly withdrew its request. Garton's ranch house and adjacent buildings were destroyed by the National Park Service in 1961 in order to restore the area to its natural state.[61]

Another detached WSNM area, Dog Canyon, had also proven to be an administrative headache for the National Park Service. The Recreational Development program permitted the National Park Service to negotiate for the option of acquiring Dog Canyon water rights from its owner, J. L. Lawson. Hugh M. Miller, Pinkley's assistant superintendent, and Tom Charles contacted Lawson on several occasions to acquire the 440-acre tract, but Lawson would only consent to giving up title to 160 acres. Accusing each other of misunderstanding the arrangement, Lawson and the National Park Service arrived at an agreement on 9 September 1938.[62] The federal government paid Lawson $2,820 for 440 acres and water rights in Dog Canyon.[63] Ultimately, problems in securing easement rights and frustrations caused by numerous delays forced the National Park Service to seek another water source in Alamogordo. Fortunately for the National Park Service, in 1948 the air force offered to provide drinking water for the monument. Recognizing the futility of securing water from Dog Canyon, the National Park

Service accepted the air force's offer in 1952, when the National Park Service and officials at Holloman Air Force Base finally signed mutual agreements. The initial understanding limited WSNM to 300,000 gallons per month, but by 1965, Superintendent Donald Dayton asked for an increased allotment totaling 1.5 million gallons. The air force, acting as a good neighbor, agreed to honor the superintendent's request because the increasing number of visitors (approximately 524,000 in 1965), required more sanitation facilities and water fountains.[64] Ironically, while the National Park Service did not make the Dog Canyon stream its water source as originally intended, WSNM issued a special use permit to the air force in 1966 allowing the service to supplement the base's water supply from Dog Canyon.[65]

Throughout the 1960s, the National Park Service regional office submitted boundary status reports recommending that Garton Lake and Dog Canyon be eliminated from WSNM.[66] The National Park Service claimed that the reason for protecting the lands surrounding the lake was inconsistent with WSNM's primary mission of preserving the gypsum dunes.[67] In 1978, the Dog Canyon area reverted to the state, which subsequently designated Dog Canyon and adjacent Oliver Lee ranch house as Oliver Lee State Memorial Park in 1980.[68]

Garton Lake proved inadequate to supply water for the monument's needs, but it became useful in another capacity. Seconded by wildlife technician A. E. Borell, and Tom Charles, Pinkley recommended that the lake become a bird sanctuary.[69] Unlike Dog Canyon, Garton Lake remains a portion of WSNM but is not open to the general public.

After steering the monument through its initial years, Charles prepared to resign as custodian by 1939 because he understood that he could no longer keep pace with the pressing demands of the position. In his final report to Frank Pinkley, Charles acknowledged that it was time to pass the leadership mantel and leave the "technical work at the Great White Sands to men who are trained in the art."[70] His resignation was not "without a pang," but he believed he had done all he could, remarking with a sense of history that "in the totals [WSNM's history] my part may prove important." The new technological and scientific approaches adopted by the National Park Service were beyond the abilities of a custodian like Tom Charles. Reflecting upon his decision to resign, Charles concluded, "I like the old days best."[71]

The importance of Tom Charles's contributions to WSNM cannot be overlooked. He played a crucial role during the monument's genesis. His opinion of how National Park Service lands should be utilized reflected his time and his region and his custodianship of WSNM was similar to other early national monument custodians; he performed his duties according to his own dictates. And like other custodians who lacked professional training or were unschooled in National Park Service management policies, Charles viewed his national monument in local terms, not in the greater contexts of Southwestern National Monuments and the National Park Service. Charles conducted himself in the way he knew best and that was with the interests and welfare of Alamogordo in mind. In the final analysis, Tom Charles "boosted" Alamogordo by advertising WSNM as "America's most perfect playground."[72]

1. Tom Chartles (l) and Lester L Garton (r) sitting in front of Garton's ranch house. (Courtesy of National Park Service.)

THE MAGIC SANDS
A LAND OF MYSTERY

TWO hundred seventy-four square miles of sand appears to have been set down here in a field of grass and vegetation. From a perfectly level surrounding the great white sand dunes rise abruptly one hundred feet high. The scant plant and animal life at the edge of the sands dwindle until in the center of the area it is as complete a desert as the Sahara.

Here the familiar field mouse is white as snow, the hoofs of the antelope grow long and turn and coil like horns, the scant rain fall forms in shallow lakes which, at seasons, are crimson red. Groves of large cottonwood trees are covered beneath the curling drifts of snow white sand and not infrequently there are uncovered for a time, the remains of a prehistoric civilization and then are covered up again.

It is a land of mystery and thrill.

For Information, address

CHAMBER OF COMMERCE
ALAMOGORDO, NEW MEXICO

2. The Great White Sands Brochure. (Found in WSNM Library)

3. *Opening-day crowd on 29 April 1934. (Courtesy of National Park Service)*

4. *Roger Toll's inspection of White Sands on 15 November 1931. (Courtesy of National Park Service)*

5. *Constructing the road into the Heart of the Dunes, 1933–34. (Courtesy of National Park Service)*

6. *Superintendent Johnwill Faris at his desk, early 1940s. (Courtesy of National Park Service)*

7. *Ranger Charlie Steen and Mrs. Frank (Edna Townsley)Pinkley signing the registration book in the heart of the Dunes, late 1930s. (Courtesy of National Park Service)*

8. *Tom Charles and his wife Bula standing by their house located at 1115 Vermont St., Alamogordo, New Mexico, ca. 1941–42. (Courtesy of National Park Service)*

9. *Garton Lake with Sierra Blanca looming in the Background. (Photo by Author)*

10. *Postcard depicting the White Sands Service Company car negotiating the dunes. (Courtesy of National Park Service)*

11. *Early postcard showing the headquarters complex.* *(Courstesy of National Park Service)*

12. *Yucca Surviving on a pedestal.* *(Photo by author)*

13. White Sands National Monument's original hoped-for water source, Dog Canyon. It is now part of Oliver Lee State Memorial park. (Photo by author)

14. Looking from the Southeastern portion of White Sands with the San Andres and Organ mountains in the distance. (Photo by author)

15. *Ranger Cindy Ott-Jones and author at Lake Lucero, April 1987. (Photo by Gayle P. Hector)*

16. *Cottonwood tree surrounded by dunes near the Big Pedestal area. (Photo by author)*

17. *An archaeological site within the monument. (Photo by author)*

18. *Vistors enjoying the Lake Lucero Caravan and interpretive information provid-ed by the ranger. (Photo by author)*

19. Pool of water in Big Pedestal area. (Photo by author)

20. White Sands, yucca, and clouds. (Photo by author)

21. Yucca losing ground in the shifting dunes. (Photo by author)

22. *Rubber rabbitbush holding its own on pedestal. (Photo by author)*

23. *Horned owl resting under shade of cottonwoods. (Photo by author)*

24. *Albert B. Fall and Eugene Manlove Rhodes, about 1928. (Courtesy of the Rio Grande Historical Collections (ms. 8), NMSU Library.)*

GOOD MEN AND TRUE
Managing a Monument in a Precarious Environment

The hectic life of a National Monument.—
Robert W. Righter, *Crucible for Conservation*

The unique history of White Sands National Monument (WSNM) is reflected in the superintendents' administrative difficulties as they dealt with operating the monument in spite of the military's countless unauthorized encroachments; overseeing the concession operations; and managing an extremely popular site for hundreds of thousands of visitors, including numerous scientists.

Just months before resigning as WSNM's first custodian, Tom Charles wrote to National Park Service Director Arno B. Cammerer inquiring if he could open a concession at the monument and whether the National Park Service might provide a suitable building for his undertaking. When Charles received authorization to establish his concession, he formed the White Sands Service Company, providing visitors refreshments, sandwiches, and bus tours into the Heart of the Dunes. He charged $1.50 for the round-trip bus ride. Inside the monument Charles collected 25 cents per person for rides over the dunes, and on various occasions passengers would hitch their surf (sand) boards to his car, allowing the former custodian to tow them over and down the dunes![1] These activities occurred without the National Park Service's knowledge, and certainly his actions were inconsistent and inappropriate for the preservation-minded service.

117

As was the usual case, Charles borrowed from earlier ideas for his commercial venture. In fact in 1908, J. F. Milner, the president and manager of the mining operation known as the White Sands Company, operated a Marmon touring automobile for profit. Milner operated his "White Sands car," at $2.50 per adult for a round trip from Alamogordo to White Sands.[2] Charles's dune tours merely continued a longstanding local practice of driving over the dunes. In 1929, the U.S. Forest Service had sponsored auto caravans into the dunes that had provided "plenty of thrills" for tourists.[3] Occasional dune drives continued, even though Charles's successor, Johnwill Faris attempted to curb the practice. Even though Faris tried to stem dune driving, he was just as guilty as his predecessor. Locally, Faris was noted for his "damfool driving" over the dunes.[4] By 1962, Superintendent Forrest Benson initiated ranger patrols to halt unauthorized dune drives because the practice remained inconsistent with the National Park Service's mission of preserving the region's natural features.[5]

Charles's idea of opening a concession at WSNM had originated with Frank L. Ridinger. Ridinger's White Sands Motel and gas station operated until the owner's death on 25 March 1941. In addition to Ridinger, Mrs. Albert B. (Emma Morgan) Fall had expressed an interest to Horace Albright in establishing a cafe at "White Sands National Park" because it would be "right on my road to Three Rivers [Ranch]."[6] Albright responded politely but advised her that a cafe at WSNM "would not be profitable."[7] The issue of concessions did not resurface until 1939, when Tom Charles was preparing to resign from the National Park Service. The state permitted Charles to transport Southern Pacific Railroad, Rock Island Railroad, Greyhound, and New Mexico Transportation Company passengers from Alamogordo to WSNM and return them to Alamogordo. He provided a scenic drive into the Heart of the Dunes, highlighted by an "enjoyable ride" over the dunes. Charles advertised his company's services throughout the local area. Regional National Park Service Director Hillory A. Tolson, alarmed by Charles's publicity campaign, complained that Charles's promotion "sounds too much like [a] Ringling Brothers Circus poster."[8]

Even though his health was failing while operating the White Sands Service Company, Charles placed a concession trailer, in addition to the concession stand in the administration building, in the Heart of the Dunes for the convenience of the tourists. Charles worked unceasingly as concessioner over the next four years until he became critically ill in February 1943.[9] Tom Charles died at age sixty-seven, at 4:15 P.M. on 26 March 1943 in Rousseau Hospital. On 1 April 1943, the *Alamogordo News* announced Charles's death by remarking that "White Sands' Father" had passed away.[10] On 21 November 1943, the Alamogordo Rotary Club held a memorial service at WSNM for Tom Charles. Among the guests who praised Charles's accomplishments were Charles A. Richey, associate regional director of the Park Service, George Frenger, and Edwin Mechem.[11]

Succeeding Charles as WSNM concessioner were his wife, Bula, and son, Ward Charles, who remained with the White Sands Service Company until December 1954.[12] The Charles family's immediate successors Robert Koonce (January 1955–April 1960) and G. Clyde Hammett (April 1960–December 1963) maintained the trailer concession until October 1960 when it was finally discontinued. In January 1964, T. C. Womack took over the reigns as concessioner.[13] As of 1991, the concessioner was former WSNM Superintendent John Turney. Even though the name of the White Sands Service Company had changed to White Sands Concession Company, the services provided had virtually remained the same, except that dune rides were no longer offered. Until 1989, concessioners rented small "surf-boards" to tourists for their enjoyment of the dunes. For many visitors, the attraction of White Sands is, as it has been for decades, as a playground. The concession operations have played an important role by providing comforts, refreshments, and souvenirs to the millions of tourists.

Over the last sixty years, WSNM has witnessed numerous superintendents, rangers, and maintenance personnel. During Tom Charles's tenure as WSNM's custodian, he repeatedly wrote to Frank Pinkley requesting assistance to provide at least adequate services at the monument. Because of the large number of visitors, the requirement for permanent rangers was a priority. At last by 1936, Pinkley finally responded by increasing the WSNM staff. The first documented WSNM ranger/utility men were Barry Mohoun (1935–36), followed by James B. Felton (1937–38), George Sholly (1937–39), and the first full-time ranger, Johnwill Faris, came aboard in 1938. White Sands National Monument's first supervisory or chief ranger William Featherstone arrived on 29 February 1953. The first maintenance worker providing support for Charles and the rangers during those early years was Joe Shepherd, hired in 1937.[14] Supported by numerous seasonal rangers and maintenance personnel, these individuals helped maintain and protect the monument's natural resources.

Ranger Johnwill Faris succeeded Tom Charles as WSNM custodian on 1 November 1939. In contrast to his predecessor, the ranger was a careerist who had entered the National Park Service in April 1929. Faris had transferred from Chaco Canyon National Monument to WSNM in September 1938.[15] He was the first full-time resident custodian at the monument. Faris apparently did not relinquish the title of custodian until November 1948, when National Park Service officials began addressing him in official correspondence as superintendent.[16] This change in title, even though belated, was consistent with general policies of upgrading national monuments that were implemented during the New Deal.[17] While Charles is known as the promoter and father of WSNM, Faris established its administrative and managerial policies and injected professionalism into the superintendent's position.

Faris's administrative duties had expanded unexpectedly in early 1942, when the military entered the Tularosa Basin, initially leasing much of the region for a rocket and bombing range. The military's encirclement of WSNM has resulted in a unique management predicament for the National Park Service. The superintendent repeatedly expressed concerns about the military's encroachment and wrote to the regional directors discussing the difficulties of managing the national monument in such a peculiar situation. During his administration, Faris witnessed numerous V-2 rocket impacts in the Heart of the Dunes, direct hits upon picnic tables, and the arrest and detainment of his rangers by military policemen during the rangers' inspections of the monument's western boundary. Faris reported these incursions to his superiors in Santa Fe and to military commanders. Even though the military sent apologies to the superintendent, the incidents continued while the regional office logged Faris's reports.[18]

Faris supported the recreational nature of WSNM; however, he also encouraged visitors to enjoy the dunes aesthetically. Complying with National Park Service educational and interpretive directives, Faris initiated numerous visitor programs, two of which remain as part of WSNM's programs. Planning for the aesthetic aspects of WSNM, Faris implemented a nature trail, and on 2 September 1954, Faris guided visitors on the first nature trail excursion. Faris and his staff provided interpretive briefings along the trail, turning the occasion into an educational experience.[19] On 14 January 1956, Faris led the first Lake Lucero auto caravan, which consisted of 160 people. Then as now, military policemen escorted the caravan from the highway to Lake Lucero. Lake Lucero's selenite-imbedded banks and grayish appearing ephemeral lake were added attractions that should not be overlooked by the visitor. Currently, and with White Sands Missile Range concurrence, the National Park Service conducts the Lake Lucero caravans monthly.[20]

By 1929 the number of visitors to parks and monuments had increased sufficiently that Horace Albright began to stress the need to educate the public about diverse landscapes in the system.[21] In addition to implementing interpretive programs, Albright and his successors believed that park and monument museums would attract visitors by informing them about what each area had to offer. The directors concluded that museums were the "index to the park itself, which is the real museum of nature."[22]

Following National Park Service guidelines to educate the public and showcase its geologic wonder, naturalist Robert Rose began planning for a WSNM museum in November 1934. Rose proposed that the museum should be constructed at the monument entrance where it would be "an introduction" to the dunes. The unanticipated large number of tourists, approximately 108,000 in 1937, dictated that the museum must be able to accommodate as many people as possible at any time. Rose designed the museum primarily for educating the visitor about WSNM's geology and natural history. Rose also intended that the museum would serve either as a gathering area for visitors to refresh themselves before driving into the dunes or as a rest stop for travelers not entering the Heart of the Dunes.[23]

Rose planned for three subject exhibit rooms in the museum. He believed that the most prominent exhibit should reveal the geology of White Sands and the Tularosa Basin. The exhibit must answer questions about the unique geological features, provoking the visitors to see the dunes firsthand. The exhibit room would also focus on natural history and would contain flora and fauna specimens. Rose subscribed to the idea that tourists must be able to view the region's interesting natural history in order to comprehend the unique adaptations the flora and fauna have undergone to survive in such a harsh and specific environment. The least important exhibit room would be devoted to the historical and archaeological collections. Rose remarked that the two disciplines "should be given some consideration" but "neither subject would require extensive treatment."[24] He suggested that the room be filled with some of Charles's White Sands arrowheads and perhaps some history of the Mescalero Apache.[25] With Recreational Demonstration Projects Administration funds, work on the museum, administration building, ranger residences, and parking area began in early 1937 and was completed in the fall of the same year.[26]

During the first two weeks of June 1940, naturalists Dale King and Natt Dodge assisted and directed the installation of nine exhibits that archaeologist Charlie Steen designed and had prepared by the National Park Service's Western Museum Laboratories in Berkeley, California.[27] Operational in 1941, the museum allowed rangers to brief the visitors on the unique geology, biology, and history of the dunes while simultaneously inducing them to venture into the dune areas. Currently, the museum contains only the monument's geological and natural histories. Regrettably the historical exhibits no longer have any standing in the national monument. The only historical display at the museum is a wagon or *carreta* located in the atrium between the museum and the concession shop.

In 1956, National Park Service Director Conrad L. Wirth ordered a "renaissance" for the National Park Service.[28] The drastic decline in visitor attendance at almost all national parks and monuments prior to and after the Second World War, accompanied by excessive budget cuts during the war, resulted in the deterioration of numerous facilities. Wirth and his staff conceived the idea of Mission 66 "to overcome the inroads of neglect and to restore to the American people a national park system adequate for their needs."[29] Wirth planned to accomplish his goals by 1966. The objective was to refurbish the National Park Service so that it could "provide adequate protection and development" for its current and future visitors.[30] Mission 66 demanded large appropriations in order to upgrade facilities and increase its personnel.[31]

Commenting upon Mission 66 in 1960, Superintendent Faris considered the project a way of procuring the necessary construction materials to "replace or facelift existing artifacts" in the monument.[32] The monument received little if any funds for improving its facilities, even though WSNM recorded high visitation. In June 1965, Forrest Benson's successor, Superintendent Donald Dayton, wrote a poignant memorandum to Regional Director Daniel Beard informing him of the absence of any development at the monument since Mission 66's implementation.[33]

White Sands had evolved from a local attraction into a national tourist stop after the WSNM proclamation. WSNM became an international tourist attraction after the establishment of an allied air defense school center at Fort Bliss, Texas, in 1966. The large contingents of German air force and army personnel and other allied personnel included WSNM as part of their weekend sightseeing trips. A flourishing postwar economy in West Germany contributed to the increasing numbers of Germans spending their vacations in the United States. Fort Bliss, Holloman Air Force Base, and White Sands Missile Range, with their numerous foreign-born dependents, also added to WSNM's international audience. Additionally, many visitors from nearby Mexico included the monument in their travel plans. In response, in 1965, the National Park Service installed two audiovisual machines in the visitor center to make audio tapes available in German, French, Italian, Japanese, Korean, and Spanish.[34]

From its first year as a monument in the Southwestern National Monuments group, WSNM ranked first in tourist travel. In 1934, WSNM recorded 33,900 visitors, easily outdistancing the second-place Montezuma Castle National Monument, located in Yavapai County, Arizona.[35] In 1979, there were 580,000 visitors to White Sands National Monument.[36] The monument rarely experienced a shortage of visitors in its history; only during World War II were significant declines recorded. Superintendent Faris remarked in December 1942 that without the military visitors the monthly count "has dropped to almost nothing."[37] Visitor figures increased sharply following the military's demobilization after the war.

By the mid-1960s, in addition to managing the heavy visitor influx, Superintendent Dayton had to contend with National Park Service officials stationed in Santa Fe and San Francisco who proposed various plans for improving the monument without any on-site inspections. Dayton protested against National Park Service officials who recommended programs or plans that replaced his own staff's investigation reports. Two examples of Dayton's criticisms involved Volney J. Westly, regional chief of master plan coordination, and his team. The superintendent had reported that the Garton Lake area should not be converted into a recreational vehicle camping site as National Park Service planners proposed because the soil quickly turned to gumbo when it rained and into a "fine silty dust" during dry weather.[38] There were sure to be numerous unhappy campers in addition to the funds wasted in attempting to develop the area. Second, Dayton recommended that the monument's principal interpretive program needed replanning, stressing that the area's geology should be the main focus. Dayton argued his case because WSNM's geological and natural histories "have almost been buried under the overriding recreational and historic atmosphere."[39] He convinced his superiors that White Sands geology, followed by the area's natural history, should be the principal themes for National Park Service management and development proposals at the monument.

Dayton urged the Santa Fe regional office to follow his staff's recommendations for improving the visitor center, administration building, and concession facilities. He encouraged his superiors to provide qualitative and effective changes to meet the pressing needs for WSNM's half a million visitors in 1965. Dayton reminded the regional director that if WSNM was expected to follow the National Park Service's directives, then nothing less than the best in monument interpretive services and visitor accommodations should be expected.[40]

Because of its appeal as a major recreational site, White Sands has played host to a variety of special happenings. After the successful opening-day ceremony in April 1934, the first annual scheduled event in WSNM was Play Day, held in April 1935. According to Tom Charles, the event's promoter, the purpose of the special occasion was to permit local children to play in "America's Ideal Playground." White Sands had always been a gathering place for family outings, especially weekend picnics. Noting the successful opening-day ceremonies in 1934, Charles announced that a celebration should be held annually to commemorate that special time. There were numerous Play Day events: old timers' reunions, relay races, band concerts, Mescalero Apache Boy Scout dances, evening and campfire sing-alongs that culminated the festive occasion "in the happy climax of community singing of such songs as The Bear Came Over the Mountain, Merrily We Roll Along, and Good Night Ladies."[41] For the occasion the National Park Service waived the entrance fees.

Attendance at the Play Days averaged more than 3,000 visitors in the 1930s, steadily increasing to 6,171 visitors in 1958, when the event was held for the last time.[42] Although tentatively scheduled for 1959, the Alamogordo Chamber of Commerce and Superintendent Faris could not agree upon the date for Play Day. Faris supported a traditional April date but J. Marion Bell, chamber manager, desired Memorial Day. Faris agreed to reschedule Play Day for 30 May 1959; however, local veterans' organizations opposed the idea of establishing Play Day on Memorial Day, a day set aside for national reflection and remembrance of the nation's war dead. Surrounded by the controversy, Play Day of 1959 never materialized.

By the early 1960s, the National Park Service discontinued its support of such local events. White Sands National Monument as "the nation's sand pile"[43] or "giant sandbox for kiddies" was the only image most visitors held of the monument. Changing the public's perception of WSNM was in large measure due to the publication of books such as Aldo Leopold's *A Sand County Almanac* (1949), Joseph Wood Krutch's *The Desert Year* (1952) and *The Voice of the Desert* (1954), and Conrad Richter's *The Mountain on the Desert* (1955), which contributed to an emerging desert aesthetic.[44]

Johnwill Faris oversaw the passing of Play Day while developing and encouraging new special WSNM events. Regional Director Hugh Miller directed on 3 January 1956 that all superintendents in Region III initiate an Establishment Day for their park or monument.[45] Unlike other official special days, Establishment Day developed as an educational day. At WSNM Faris introduced Establishment Day on 18 January 1956, to coincide with the monument's twenty-third anniversary. The speakers presented historical papers while local photographers and artists displayed their works. The day was designed to acknowledge the person or group responsible for endorsing the establishment of the national monument. On 22 January 1960, acclaimed New Mexico artist Peter Hurd judged the art competition consisting of thirty-one entries.[46] Local artist Regal Leftwich's entry "Tom Charles and White Sands" earned third honorable mention and was the only rendering of Tom Charles presented at the exhibit. Following the show, the artist donated Charles's portrait with its White Sands background to WSNM.[47] Faris accepted Leftwich's gift, and the painting was displayed in the visitor center's lobby until the summer of 1989.

A short-lived event was Founder's Day, celebrating Cabeza de Vaca's sojourn through the Tularosa Basin in 1536. The only Founder's Day date that appears as an entry in the WSNM files is 25 August 1956. Apparently local support was lacking for successive commemorations.

Another brief WSNM celebration was the Fourth of July fireworks. The Alamogordo Chamber of Commerce sponsored this event beginning in 1948. The Fireworks Day drew thousands of spectators and in 1952, 16,723 people celebrated Independence Day in the Heart of the Dunes. The large crowds accompanied by countless beer parties, both of which were inconsistent with preserving a national park or national monument, and the solicitation of money at WSNM by Alamogordo Chamber of Commerce and Lions Club members forced the National Park Service to cancel the popular event after the 1955 celebration.[48] Hugh Miller directed Faris to avoid attracting large local crowds that would interfere with visitors' appreciation of WSNM's "national significance."[49] Miller reinforced the concept of national parks and monuments, that is, parklands belonged to everyone.

128

They were not exclusive sites set aside as local playgrounds.

In addition to its recreational attraction, White Sands also functioned as a spiritual center for many local residents. On Easter Sunday in April 1936, Alamogordo clergymen accompanied by their congregations, numbering more than 1,000 people, assembled in WSNM's Crystal Bowl for sunrise services.[50] The event was so successful that Easter sunrise services continue to attract large crowds every year. On many occasions the Easter sunrise service has drawn some of the largest single-day crowds in WSNM's history. On Easter 1965, 21,809 people congregated in the Heart of the Dunes, marking the day as the greatest visitor count up to that time.[51]

This account of WSNM's formative early years, under its superintendents Johnwill Faris, Forrest Benson, Jr., and Donald Dayton, witnessed a host of changing situations that reflected both national and regional evolution: supervising a national monument while negotiating with the army and air force; coping with a visitation count that rose from 34,000 in 1934 to approximately 380,000 in 1961, to a total of 524,000 in 1965; laying the foundations for the residential and administration buildings; creating a museum and the first educational nature tours of the monument; and managing a monument with a rotating or undermanned staff. The accomplishments of the early superintendents make their shortcomings pale by comparison. Each superintendent and staff member contributed to creating one of the most successful national monuments in the Park Service system.

THE BEST OF A BAD SITUATION IN THE WORLD'S LARGEST SHOOTING GALLERY

Our existence with our Armed Forces neighbors could and probably will be much work.—Johnwill Faris, 1948

W hite Sands National Monument (WSNM), unlike most national parks and national monuments, is surrounded entirely by Department of Defense reservations. Bordered by restricted lands such as White Sands Missile Range and Holloman Air Force Base, the national monument endures an existence that the National Park Service has found undesirable. In contrast to its northern dune field counterpart, Great Sand Dunes National Monument in Colorado, WSNM continues a multiple-use management policy that is inconsistent with National Park Service preservation guidelines. The Interior Department had permitted the War Department to utilize portions of both national monuments for military training during World War II. While Great Sand Dunes National Monument has lost its military importance, WSNM remains an extreme example of a National Park Service reserve forced to accept uses not often associated with a park or monument. National Park Service areas such as Yosemite National Park, Great Sand Dunes National Monument, Death Valley National Monument, and WSNM are threatened continuously by agencies wishing to infringe on the National Park Service's jurisdiction of the lands. At each park or monument, the staff valiantly strives to protect and preserve its landscape.

The first WSNM personnel did not foresee any problems with any potential neighbors. Historian C. L. Sonnichsen wrote that the White Sands region is arguably the most desolate area in the Southwest, which is the reason local residents believed there would be no outside interest in the region.[1] But it was precisely that quality that attracted the War Department's interest. After the National Park Service took over administration of the area, its staff was initially concerned with establishing administrative procedures, constructing appropriate buildings and roads, advertising the unique geological features of the monument, and developing and encouraging a harmonious relationship with local communities. Two significant World War II technological advances made the relatively unpopulated Tularosa Basin an attractive rocket and bombing range. First there was the combination of Germany's development of its V-1 and V-2 self-propelled rockets and the subsequent capture and interrogation by the Americans of Werner von Braun and 500 principal German rocket experts and rockets during late April and the first week in May 1945;[2] second was the introduction of high altitude bombers, such as the B-29. In 1949, National Park Service Director Newton B. Drury poignantly described this relationship between the Interior and War departments as "the best of a bad situation."[3]

Southern New Mexico was not the first location selected by federal officials for a rocket or missile range. The first candidates were Muroc Bombing Range in California, Tonopah Bombing Range in Nevada, Wendover Bombing Range in Utah, and an undesignated area in western Florida. The military discounted these ranges for a variety of reasons.[4] Additionally, the local public vehemently denounced the military's land acquisition efforts. The military desired the White Sands region because the area met its requirements for missile and bombing ranges.

The first indication of military interest in the Tularosa Basin occurred in May 1937 when the interior department became aware of the War Department's interest in possible land acquisition in the Tularosa Basin.[5] The War Department desired to acquire a target range for the New Mexico National Guard.[6] This interest faded quickly and the subject did not resurface until military expediency demanded its attention in 1941.

Surprisingly, the War Department's renewed interest in the White Sands region did not occur immediately following the American naval disaster at Pearl Harbor. Instead the department appears to have anticipated military action somewhat earlier. The War Department's 1940–41 plans included a "premobilization program," that is, the military increased its personnel strength and materiel significantly but short of a total mobilization.[7] Coinciding with an expanding military was the requirement for adequate training for new personnel, especially in remote regions. One such isolated and relatively unpopulated area was the Tularosa Basin.

The War Department requested a withdrawal of 1,249,904.36 acres of land. Secretary of War Henry L. Stimson originally asked for the lands on 2 June 1941, but he withdrew the request until the necessary appropriations for the private lands could be acquired. On 17 December 1941, Stimson renewed his New Mexico land request and demanded the immediate cancellation of all leases.[8]

On 25 October 1941, the first public notice of the War Department's decision to evict ranchers from the Tularosa Basin reached the regional newspapers. The War Department intended to use an area thirty miles wide and sixty miles long as a bombing range. The ranchers received orders to evacuate the area by 15 February 1942 because the army was anxious to survey the territory for a suitable airstrip.[9] According to military spokesmen, the land was an ideal site because of the numerous "natural targets."[10] The military alerted the ranchers to remove their families and their livestock from the grazing lands in the basin. Initially the ranchers protested against the high-handed military demands, but after the United States declared war against Japan on 8 December 1941, the ranchers cooperated with the War Department in the cause for national defense. Approximately 100 ranchers finally acquiesced to the War Department's demands to lease their ranch lands. After the Second World War the displaced ranchers of the Tularosa Basin reclaimed their properties, believing that the necessity for sacrificing their private lands for national defense had passed.

Three years after the war, the military demanded the evacuation of the ranchers again because of the scheduled rocket firings. In 1950, following lengthy negotiations between the ranchers and the military, the lands were leased to the military for twenty years and the ranchers were compensated. The ranchers received approximately $27 million for land purchases and leases by the military over thirty years beginning in 1942. Because of the establishment of a permanent missile range, the ranchers had unknowingly forfeited their rights to reclaim their lands. Demanding appropriate compensation, Dave McDonald, one of twenty-eight surviving ranchers, confronted the military directly on 13 October 1982 by occupying his former ranch house located nine miles south of Trinity Site (location of the first atomic bomb explosion). Accompanied by his niece, Mary McDonald, Dave McDonald surrendered his position when Congressman Joe Skeen and U.S. Sen. Harrison Schmitt promised to have his case reviewed by the U.S. Court of Claims. As recently as March

1989, McDonald announced that he would reoccupy his former ranch if adequate compensation were not forthcoming.[11] Recently, U.S. Senators Pete Domenici and Jeff Bingaman and U.S. Congressman Joe Skeen have introduced the White Sands Fair Compensation Act of 1991 in Congress. The ranchers and their families continue to wait for a decision on their claims.[12]

While the stockmen patriotically surrendered their grazing lands to the federal government, Alamogordo Chamber of Commerce boosters loudly protested the naming of the bombing range as the Las Cruces–Albuquerque Bombing Range.[13] The military responded by trying several other names, including the White Sands Bombing and Gunnery Range, the Alamogordo Bombing and Gunnery Range, and by June 1942, the Alamogordo Army Air Field,[14] finally settling on Holloman Air Force Base in 1948.[15]

To make the ranchers' eviction official, President Franklin D. Roosevelt signed Executive Order 9029 on 20 January 1942, directing local military commanders to consult with National Park Service officials "as to the location of bombing target sites, for the purpose of minimizing the effect of demolition bombing in areas valuable for scientific purposes."[16] It is important to note that there was a stipulation that the lands must be returned to the Interior Department once they had served their purpose.[17] Throughout the period of the military's land acquisitions, the War Department repeatedly included WSNM as an operational area within the confines of the proposed range, thus explaining the military's confusion and ignorance of landholdings in the Tularosa Basin. As late as 1948, Superintendent Johnwill Faris expressed his displeasure with the military's policies concerning land acquisitions because "our area [WSNM] is completely within the rocket research lands," and the maps identified the territory as part of the bombing range.[18] For the duration of the Second

World War the Tularosa Basin remained the air force's focus as a principal high altitude bombing range and the army's major antiaircraft artillery range.

Aware of the military's plans George Fitzpatrick, editor of *New Mexico*, correctly predicted in 1942 that the Tularosa Basin would evolve as "the world's greatest shooting gallery."[19] Three years later, the basin's remoteness, which had once attracted displaced Texas cowmen, was now serving as a magnet for "the scientist laboring to perfect new weapons" for the national defense.[20] In March 1947, the Army Air Force's Air Materiel Command relocated approximately twelve hundred scientists and security personnel from Wendover Air Field, Utah, to Alamogordo Army Air Field (Holloman Air Force Base) in order to conduct secret military research projects.[21]

To the south of Holloman Air Force Base, other military activity was increasing on the proposed White Sands Proving Ground. Superintendent Faris was well aware of WSNM's military encirclement, writing that while there existed some rumors that Holloman Air Force Base might close, "the other side [White Sands Proving Ground] of us seems to be going stronger so we [WSNM] are yet in the middle of excitement."[22] The Army Air Service (Force) began using an airstrip near the eastern foothills of the Organ Mountains, which was suspected of being used by smugglers of contraband. In 1942, the army transformed the airstrip into an emergency landing strip for pilots engaged in training missions from Biggs Field adjacent to Fort Bliss, Texas.[23] By 25 June 1945, the region surrounding Condron Field witnessed the initial construction facilities at White Sands Proving Ground for the United States' rocket program.[24]

Continuing military expansion in the Tularosa Basin forced the Interior and War departments to confront each other and negotiate on the pending problem of rocket firings and their effect upon the public's use of WSNM. Johnwill Faris expressed grave misgivings concerning the army's presence, especially after reviewing a military map that included WSNM within the range's boundaries![25] Initially the solution to the Interior Department's strained relationship with the military was a memorandum of understanding; however, after considerable deliberation, Acting Interior Secretary Oscar L. Chapman decided that a special use permit for allowing the military access to WSNM was more appropriate than a memorandum.[26] Chapman signed the permit on 6 March 1946, forwarding it to Secretary of War Robert P. Patterson, who signed the document on 3 April 1946. The permit would take effect on 1 March 1946.[27]

The special use permit allowed the military access to WSNM under specified conditions. The military agreed to the following provisions: (1) the secretary of the interior could revoke the permit at its discretion, (2) during missile firings all roads to WSNM would be closed, (3) the military would police the impact area and restore its appearance, (4) the military would notify the WSNM superintendent ten days prior to firing periods, and (5) the Defense Department would compensate the National Park Service for damage caused by missile impacts. Of major significance was the inclusion that the National Park Service would judge the quality and thoroughness of the military's restoration projects, implying that the National Park Service would supervise or oversee the impact cleanups.[28] WSNM Chief ranger Robert Schumerth (retired August 1989) and ranger Dave Evans—currently assigned to Big Bend National Park—concurred that this provision had been instrumental in encouraging the military to restore the impact area to the rangers' satisfaction.[29] Schumerth and Evans added that on several occasions military cleanup crews grumbled regarding the rangers' attention to detail while restoring the areas to their unblemished natural condition.[30]

Throughout the late 1940s and early 1950s the military pressed the Interior Department for more land acquisitions. In 1948, Acting Interior Secretary Hillory A. Tolson, responding to the army's request for a time extension of the special use permit, stated that such an extension was unnecessary because the permit did not specify an expiration date. Tolson believed that the army's use of the missile range would be for a minimum of twenty years and added that a permanent permit was, however, "out of the question" because such an arrangement would result in the "virtual disestablishment" of WSNM. He concluded that the National Park Service had no objections to the continuation of the special permit "so long as [it is] needed and its terms are mutually acceptable and adhered to."[31] In 1949, National Park Service Director Newton Drury commented that WSNM's special use permit agreement was "far from satisfactory," adding that the National Park Service would comply with the permit's provisions and "administer it [WSNM] under these conditions if no better arrangements can be worked out."[32] It is obvious that Drury did not favor an arrangement whereby a federal agency other than the National Park Service decided the management policies and the daily openings and closings of National Park Service parks or monuments.

On 25 June 1945, the United States' embryonic rocket range evolved rapidly as contractors worked feverishly to construct the first post buildings and scattered launch pads. On 9 July 1945, the War Department officially designated the range as White Sands Proving Ground, until the Department of the Army changed the name to White Sands Missile Range on 1 May 1958.[33] Lt. Col. Harold Turner, the post's first commander, has received historical recognition for establishing the White Sands prefix, thereby associating the range with the most prominent geological feature in the Tularosa Basin.[34] The military established a neutral position by refraining from associating the range by name with one of the surrounding communities.

On 10 August 1945, 163 military personnel from the 9393d Technical Service Unit arrived from Wendover Air Field, Utah, to provide various support to the American and captured German scientists preparing their missile firings.[35] From the first rocket launching on 25 September 1945 through 31 March 1980, 32,019 missile firings have been recorded at White Sands Missile Range.[36] The steadily growing number of launches, accompanied by a corresponding increase of military and civilian personnel, brought economic prosperity for the tri-city area (Alamogordo, Las Cruces, and El Paso). The three chambers of commerce actively supported and endorsed the military's presence.[37]

However, not all of the residents in the White Sands region were pleased with the military's reluctance to abandon its wartime land acquisitions. Ranchers were outraged after the announcement in local newspapers that the Defense Department wanted to increase its landholdings in the Tularosa Basin. The Las Cruces *Sun-News* warned that the "Government Wants More Land Here" for White Sands Missile Range.[38] The time had arrived for another meeting between military representatives and local and state officials.

On 2 and 3 August 1948, the military and federal officials met with local concerned individuals at New Mexico State University's Hadley Hall. The Department of Defense team included representatives from the secretary of defense, the proving ground, Holloman Air Force Base, and military research and development branches.[39]

Opposing the Defense Department were ranchers, miners, and wool growers affected by the range extension proposal. Their spokesman, G. W. Evans, president of the New Mexico Cattle Growers Association, argued forcefully against the federal government's additional land acquisition requests. Evans remarked that it was one thing to surrender lands to the government during the Second World War, but losing more private and state land during peacetime was unfair. He argued that if the Defense Department achieved its aims, New Mexico would have "its heart cut out" in the process.[40] Also supporting the ranchers was New Mexico State Land Commissioner John E. Miles, who believed that New Mexico was surrendering too much land to the federal government. Additionally, Evans expressed a growing concern that would affect everyone in the Tularosa Basin, the military's potential use of atomic weapons at White Sands Proving Ground. The ranchers' fears were well founded because the first atomic explosion had occurred on 16 July 1945 at Trinity Site located northwest of Oscura Peak and a short distance from the Tularosa Basin.[41] Army spokesmen attempted to allay the residents' fears, assuring them that Defense Department's plans for the area did not include the deployment of atomic warheads.[42]

The two sides engaged in heated arguments. Local chambers of commerce championed the Defense Department's proposal, eyeing the benefits of lucrative government contracts for the region. The land extension advocates accused Evans and his allies of being alarmists, arguing that the ranchers incited unwarranted fears by claiming the expansion would divide the state. Unabashedly, the Las Cruces boosters contended that the discussions would expose the ranchers' selfish motives. Unfairly, Evans and his organization were even accused of stalling in order to gain greater government compensation for the ranchers. The boosters' final argument was perhaps the most provocative: it portrayed Evans and his supporters as unpatriotic Americans who failed to comprehend the significance of scientific research during such a "critical time."[43]

After his meeting with the military on 18 January 1949, Roscoe

E. Bell, associate director of the Bureau of Land Management, relayed the military's request to his colleagues in the Interior Department. The military wanted lands that would possibly affect the Interior Department's WSNM and San Andres National Wildlife Refuge, and the Agriculture Department's Jornada Range and Cibola National Forest. Bell's assessment of the military's proposed thirty-three-mile extension revealed a doubtful future for WSNM, stating that if the army's requests were approved, it was conceivable that the public would be prohibited from visiting WSNM.[44]

Military personnel, local ranchers, and state officials met again on 14 and 15 February 1949. Maj. Gen. Daniel Noce of the army and Maj. Gen. G. Gardner of the air force continued to press for the need to utilize the entire Alamogordo Bombing Range and White Sands Proving Ground in addition to the requested extension. The military ruled out any cooperative use agreement with the ranchers for the desired lands. However, Noce and Gardner supported adequate compensation for the victims of the fledgling United States missile program.[45]

The role of the Department of the Interior during the Defense Department's land withdrawal efforts presented several problems for the National Park Service. Both the Interior and Defense departments desired to continue abiding by the provisions contained in the 1 March 1946 special use permit because by its terms, the monument would remain open to the public except during scheduled missile firings. In other words, it would continue to exist as a national monument.[46]

The principal concern for the Department of the Interior was the WSNM's role in the military's plans. The monument's central location within the military land withdrawal area resulted in some confusion as to its status. The military's expansionist plans surprised Faris, prompting him to write that the "Army has seemingly taken a great interest in us [WSNM]."[47]

While attempting to rescue the monument's integrity, Roscoe E. Bell recommended to Interior Secretary Julius A. Krug that public access to WSNM could be maintained except during missile firings. Although he knew that such an arrangement would be agreeable to the National Park Service, Bell boldly stated that the army would "prefer not to be bothered" with such a settlement.[48] Bell wanted the monument completely closed to the public during all range closures and missile tests. Army officials informed Bell that they would consider this option.[49]

The National Park Service was not at all pleased with the proceedings, and its response to the Defense Department's request for land extensions was unfavorable, accusing the army of having submitted an "unrealistic" proposal. National Park Service Director Newton B. Drury stated that he would "interpose no objection" to the army's request, provided there were no modifications to WSNM.[50] The National Park Service viewed with alarm the increasing number of missile impacts and land encroachments inside the monument's boundaries. Frustrated, Faris frequently expressed his displeasure with the military's missile activities. Commenting upon a rocket impact in WSNM, Faris wrote with displeasure:

> One thing about this firing, you can't call your time your own as they [White Sands Proving Ground] are apt to fire at 4 A.M. with no warning except the customary blanket warning for the entire day. Consequently, we [WSNM] have to be alert for the Army practically all the time.[51]

Characteristically, National Park Service interaction with the army during most of the monument's history can be seen as stressful, especially for the WSNM superintendents. For example, during May 1946, a V-2 rocket landed in WSNM sixteen miles west of the headquarters building. Faris noted that in this incident the army violated two provisions of the 1946 special use permit: physical use of WSNM was not desired because rocket impacts would occur outside the monument, and the army would repair any damage it caused within WSNM. The superintendent discovered military tracks and roads leading into WSNM when no entry permission had been granted. The army initially denied Faris's report, stating that their rocket landed at its designated target. Tongue in cheek, Faris concluded that if the army was correct then WSNM appeared to be the target! In July 1946, the army finally acknowledged that the rocket impacted in WSNM unintentionally.[52] While Faris repeatedly informed his superiors and army officials about encroachments and missile impacts, he resigned himself to the fact that the army's counterargument was always that their work was for the national defense, which they always assumed to take first priority. After another rocket impact within WSNM on 2 June 1949, Faris despondently admitted that the army "generally ignores our existence."[53]

Following the August 1949 Las Cruces meetings the army temporarily abandoned its request for the thirty-three-mile extension, partly because of general opposition in the region. While the ranchers and military argued over possible cooperative use of the range, the army secretly desired exclusive use. By 1 December 1950, Secretary of the Army Frank Pace, Jr., announced that the army had secured exclusive use agreements with the ranchers on 95 percent of the desired lands. The army resubmitted its land withdrawal request, reassuring the Interior Department that WSNM was not included in the proposal.[54]

In 1950, one hundred displaced ranchers, including Dave McDonald, finally signed twenty-year leases with the army contingent upon the promise that the military would return their lands in 1970. However, by 1973 Congress permitted the army to acquire or condemn the Tularosa Basin ranch lands, thereby retaining complete control. Dave McDonald, accompanied by his niece Mary McDonald, continues at the present time his fight to receive adequate compensation for himself and twenty-seven surviving ranchers.[55]

Throughout the 1950s the Defense Department requested revisions to the 1950 special use permit allowing for physical use and an impact area encompassing twenty to thirty miles. On 11 March 1958, Interior Secretary Fred A. Seaton, writing to Defense Secretary Neil H. McElroy, revealed the Interior Department's inability to control unauthorized military activities in WSNM. Seaton stated that his department had "no freedom of choice" in imposing any restraints upon the military. [56]

At long last, Johnwill Faris left WSNM on 1 February 1961, departing for soon-to-be-discontinued Platt National Park. Forrest M. Benson, Jr., Faris's replacement, arrived five days later (see Table 2). One month after his arrival, Benson expressed his amazement at the number of constructed military facilities with-

Table 2. White Sands National Monument Custodians/Superintendents

Thomas (Tom) Charles	10 July 1933—30 September 1939 (appointed 10 July but effective 1 August 1933)
Johnwill Faris	1 November 1939—31 January 1961
Forrest M. Benson, Jr.	6 February 1961—1 July 1964
Donald A. Dayton	25 October 1964—12 August 1967
John F. Turney	8 October 1967—8 December 1973
James M. Thomson	9 December 1973—12 August 1978
Donald R. Harper	13 August 1978—30 December 1988
Dennis Ditmanson	26 March 1989—Present

Compiled by author from White Sands National Monument Library.

in WSNM. Benson and Maj. Gen. John G. Shinkle, White Sands Missile Range commanding general, discussed the army's encroachment into WSNM. Shinkle reassured Benson that when he learned of the unauthorized entries, he had ordered all "further activity of this type to cease."[57] In spite of Shinkle's support, the illegal military entries continued.

In October 1961, Superintendent Benson met with air force representatives to discuss the air force's interest in securing three runways that would extend into WSNM for the purpose of constructing a space port known as Project Dinosaur.[58] The air force wanted to acquire approximately forty square miles of the Alkali Flats region for several reasons: "the area exists!"; the flats would be an appropriate location for space vehicle skids; the Defense Department had existing tracking and instrumentation sites nearby; the White Sands region was identifiable from a manned space craft.[59] The military suggested to National Park Service officials that the Interior Department relinquish the Alkali Flats area; however, Benson recommended to Regional Director Daniel Beard that the National Park Service retain the Alkali Flats and not initiate any administrative action that could result in a congressional withdrawal of the area.[60] Benson indicated that the issue could be resolved by issuing a special use permit for the military's needs.[61] Benson and the National Park Service were coming to believe that the special use permit demanded another revision before the military engulfed WSNM.

On 20 February 1963, Secretary of the Army Cyrus R. Vance wrote Interior Secretary Stewart L. Udall asking for a revised special use permit. Vance stated that the army planned construction of a short-range launch complex that would cost the taxpayers $6 million unless the Department of the Interior would permit the military to utilize the western portion of WSNM as an "impact and instrumentation area."[62] If the army received permission, then the launchings would occur at an existing launch pad nineteen miles south of WSNM, precluding the necessity for a new launch complex.[63] The Defense Department originally submitted a request to the Interior Department for authorization to use two-thirds of WSNM for defense purposes. In answering the request, Assistant Interior Secretary John A. Carver, Jr., instructed Defense Department officials to resubmit their request because the language of the permit implied "unrestricted use of monument lands." The request should also specify the military's plans for the desired area.[64] Carver, answering Vance's letter, believed that by agreeing to the request the National Park Service and the Interior Department would be "abdicating" their responsibilities. Carver stated the army's request included "complex and serious considerations" that could only be settled during formal discussions.[65] Eugene H. Merrill, deputy assistant secretary of the army, notified Carver that a meeting scheduled for 3 July 1963 would be held at the offices of the Department of the Interior in Washington.[66]

At the Washington meeting the army enumerated its desires for the western area of WSNM: there would be no more than thirty-six impacts a year; no live warheads would be used; helicopters would be used for missile recoveries; and mobile test units would be used as temporary instrumentation sites. Included were provisions to permit the necessary installation of telephone lines and road construction. Additionally, the army would establish procedures to protect Lake Lucero from missile impacts and selenite vandalism by civilian and military personnel. The army wanted the permit to be renegotiable pending changing military requirements.[67]

Interestingly, the agreements between the Interior and Defense departments were officially called special use permits; however, the army desired to identify the arrangements as cooperative or co-use. Co-use implied that the two departments shared equally in the administration of the area. Actually, the army acknowledged during the meeting that the agreement would be "intermittent exclusive use."[68] While Hetch Hetchy Valley in Yosemite National Park has been sacrificed to urban expansion, WSNM was clearly becoming a potential National Park Service casualty of the Cold War.

Superintendent Benson wrote to J. M. Carpenter, acting regional director, informing him that the army's draft permit was unacceptable and recommending that he insist upon an amended version. Benson protested vociferously against the army's demands, stating that "regardless of Army use we [WSNM] intend to use all the area," and their requests appear "to give carte blanche to the military, to the exclusion of anything we [WSNM] may want to do."[69] Concerned about the army's draft proposal, Benson strongly urged his superiors in Santa Fe and Washington to "question the ramming through" of a proposal that could jeopardize the National Park Service operation and administration of WSNM. The superintendent continued his warning, stating that if the provisions of any accepted special use permit were not actively enforced, the National Park Service would unknowingly surrender the western half of WSNM by "default." Benson added that "the integrity of the Monument and its purpose" were at risk in concurring with the existing draft. He warned that any draft terms or provisions unacceptable to the National Park Service should be discarded. An unwelcomed voice of protest in the middle of the nation's largest "shooting gallery," Benson admonished the army for its behavior, reminding them that WSNM remained a national monument despite the army's presence.[70]

On 9 October 1963, WSNM and White Sands Missile Range representatives met to review and discuss Benson's arguments. Substituting for Benson, Hugh P. Beattie, acting WSNM superintendent, left the meeting convinced that all major differences had been resolved, and with the exception of a few "semantical" misunderstandings, each side agreed that they now had a "workable agreement." Impressed by the military's "cooperative and reasonable" behavior, Beattie forwarded his findings to Carpenter, who agreed that only a few minor disagreements remained and these could be resolved easily.[71] Advising National Park Service Director Conrad L. Wirth, Carpenter informed him that if the National Park Service and Defense Department documented all existing facilities, whether "authorized or unauthorized," and agreed that no additional buildings or sites would be constructed within WSNM boundaries, then he would recommend approval for the new special use permit.[72] Wirth, supported by Carpenter's endorsement, sent his approval recommendation to Interior Secretary Udall, who approved it on 12 November 1963, followed by Secretary of the Army Vance's signature on 23 December 1963. It became effective on 23 December 1963 and would remain in force for ten years. All previous special use permits were rescinded. The special use permit could be amended or extended only by mutual secretarial consent. The new special use permit allowed White Sands Missile Range to continue to use the western section of WSNM, an area totaling 74,849 acres.[73]

The issuance of a revised special use permit did not eliminate misunderstanding between the National Park Service and the military. Unauthorized road construction by an army recovery crew prompted WSNM rangers to notify White Sands Missile Range officials of the transgression. Maj. Gen. J. F. Thorlin, White Sands Missile Range commanding general, responded swiftly to the news by imposing disciplinary action against the recovery crew. Thorlin desired improved relations with WSNM officials and actively attempted to enforce the provisions of the special use permit.[74] Superintendent Benson added that in order to avoid future disciplinary action, recovery crews would only enter WSNM accompanied by a ranger.[75]

In 1973, the permit was extended until 31 December 1976. A new permit, called the Master Special Use Agreement, was agreed to on 15 March 1977 by Interior Secretary Cecil Andrus and by Secretary of the Army Clifford Alexander, Jr., on 29 April 1977. The new agreement became effective 1 January 1977. In contrast to previous special use permits, the Master Special Use Agreement included a "Memorandum of Understanding By and Between White Sands Missile Range and White Sands National Monument" signed by Maj. Gen. Niles Fulwyler on 20 January 1986 and Superintendent Don Harper on 22 January 1986. Army and WSNM representatives agreed that the memorandum would be reviewed at the end of each calendar year. With this new era of good feelings, the western half of WSNM became known as the Zone of Cooperative Use.[76]

Aside from the army's encroachments, another persistent problem was that of military overflights, or sonic booms, damaging structures in the headquarters area and distracting visitors. Military aircraft had been associated with WSNM since the early 1940s. Numerous planes crashed in the monument; for example, a B-24 crashed on 24 January 1943, killing eleven personnel.[77] Nor was it always the military that desired WSNM's air space. In 1958, Bob Hoffman, president of the Alamogordo Chamber of Commerce, requested Superintendent Faris's permission to allow the air force's flying team, the Thunderbirds, to fly over WSNM during the chamber's sixtieth-anniversary celebration. Faris denied Hoffman's request, citing National Park Service policy of discouraging inappropriate use of parks and monuments.

Displeased with Faris's disapproval, Hoffman telephoned the regional director, Hugh Miller. Miller, after conferring with Faris, agreed to make an exception to National Park Service policy and permit the Thunderbirds's air demonstration because of the special relationship existing between WSNM and the Alamogordo Chamber of Commerce.[78] Miller informed Hoffman that granting permission for the air show did not "constitute a precedent for similar uses" of WSNM.[79]

For the next three decades the WSNM superintendents lodged complaints against the principal air space violators, pilots from the adjacent Holloman Air Force Base. The base commanders received the notifications but responded by stating that the air crews had been alerted to the WSNM overflights and had been advised to be more aware of WSNM air space. The reason for the National Park Service's concern with overflights of any type rests upon the nature of the National Park Service's mission of preserving the integrity of the park or monument. Aircraft noise pollution at any National Park Service region detracts from the natural sounds of the area. For example, as with the overflight problems at Grand Canyon National Park and Fort Jefferson National Monument, Florida, the National Park Service possesses no control authority over the military flights at WSNM. The National Park Service can only notify the Federal Aviation Administration concerning Grand Canyon National Park; however, at Fort Jefferson National Monument the National Park Service tries "to put pressure on the Navy" to discontinue the objectionable overflights. Just as at other parks and monuments, WSNM rangers lodge complaints with local military commanders and occasionally their efforts produce results.[80]

On numerous occasions WSNM Superintendent Donald R. Harper voiced his concern about air force overflights. On 25 May 1984, Lt. Col. Richard Benzingier, the Holloman Air Force Base civil engineer, wrote a letter to the White Sands Missile Range environmental officer informing him that the air force was preparing the third revision of its Environmental Assessment for Supersonic Flight in White Sands Missile Range Air Space (first prepared in 1975 and revised in 1981 and 1982). Previously, the air force was authorized to occupy air space only in the extreme northwest corner of WSNM. The 1984 revision proposed extending the air space farther south to include two-thirds of the co-use area.[81] Joe A. Whiteley, acting director of White Sands Missile Range Engineering and Housing, replied that the air force's proposal to extend their authorized air space into WSNM and the San Andres National Wildlife Refuge was "environmentally unacceptable." He advised against expanding into the proposed areas because of the adverse effect on the endangered desert bighorn sheep and the potential disturbance from supersonic booms to the selenite lake beds next to Lake Lucero. Whiteley, in his concluding response, suggested that the air force should also consult with the U.S. Fish and Wildlife Service and Superintendent Harper and surprisingly remarked that perhaps these two services would "possibly arrive at a finding of no significant impact."[82]

Even though National Park Service officials sent repeated correspondence to Holloman Air Force Base commanders, loud and disruptive WSNM overflights continued. In fairness to the air force, some base commanders were more sensitive to WSNM grievances than others. On 17 September 1985, Col. Walter T. Worthington acknowledged that his planes flying over the WSNM headquarters area could be causing structural damage. He informed Harper that the air force had ordered different departure corridors to prevent WSNM overflights. Worthington reassured Harper that all new pilots were briefed to avoid WSNM and that because Harper had alerted him to the ongoing problem "we [Air Force] have rebriefed all our pilots" in an effort to preclude WSNM overflights.[83] In May 1986, Superintendent Harper received notice that Congress (with House Bill 4430) was initiating an overflight study of National Park Service areas. The bill would permit a minimum altitude of 2,000 feet for overflights over National Park Service areas. Harper quickly asked the regional director to designate WSNM as an appropriate research site. The superintendent justified his request by citing the "numerous and daily" unauthorized overflights occurring over WSNM and by pointing out that his efforts to curb the flights had "met with limited success."[84] Brig. Gen. James F. Record, Holloman Air Force Base commander, in response to Harper's letter concerning House Bill 4430, stated that he would cooperate if required to do so but added that the "potential impact" of the bill disappointed the air force. Record believed that efforts at restricting aviation noise appeared to have succeeded because of the "drastically reduced number of complaints" from WSNM officials.[85] Interestingly, the general interpreted reduced complaints of unauthorized overflights by WSNM as a barometer of change for the better.

Superintendent Harper notified General Record that, in spite of assurances from his office, the flyovers persisted. On 29 April 1987, Harper wrote Record a two-page letter enumerating his complaints and suggesting recommendations to alleviate unauthorized use of WSNM. The most significant entry was Harper's count of 300 to 400 overflights on 14 April 1987. The superintendent stated that during one air force exercise his staff counted as many as sixty planes. Harper also attached a tally sheet to his letter registering thirty-four overflights on the same day from 7:45 to 8:45 A.M. Donald Harper reminded General Record that "quietude" remains an important attraction in any national park or national monument.[86] I can attest to the WSNM's complaints because I have viewed air force jets departing and preparing to land at Holloman Air Force Base after flying over WSNM. On 21 September 1989, I counted seven jets departing the air force base in a westerly direction and banking over the eastern portion of WSNM. I endured the noise and scenic distraction caused by overflights while sitting on top of a gypsum dune in the Big Pedestal area. Frequent visits also reveal low flying military helicopters just above the headquarters and visitors center. Thus, while many auto bumper decals proclaim "jet noise as the sound of freedom," it does not follow that those individuals who desire technological "silence" in the parks and monuments are unpatriotic Americans. The overflights persist to this day.

The history of WSNM's cooperative and sometimes strained relationship with two military installations, White Sands Missile Range and Holloman Air Force Base, emphasizes that each service has its own mandated mission: White Sands Missile Range and Holloman Air Force Base provide for the national defense and WSNM preserves the unique and expansive White Sands. As early as 1942, WSNM endured two threatening problems: numerous military encroachments and repeated military overflights. During the Second World War a host of commercial companies besieged the National Park Service for access to its mineral and natural resources for the war effort. The Interior Department issued 2,396 war use permits during the war.[87] While such diverse National Park Service lands as Grand Canyon, Shenandoah, and Yosemite national parks, and Great Sand Dunes and White Sands national monuments sacrificed their resources during the war, only WSNM continued its sacrifice after the war.[88] Some army and air force commanders have halfheartedly abided by the special use permits, while others, such as Colonel Worthington and General Fulwyler, reflected the phenomenon of environmentally sensitive commanders emerging throughout the military. In an open letter to all White Sands Missile Range personnel, Fulwyler succinctly stated that it was one of the military's responsibilities to "foster and preserve the good will of our many neighbors," emphasizing that the "burden of coexistence" also rests with the military and not solely with "other Government agencies [National Park Service and United States Fish and Wildlife Service] preceding us" in the Tularosa Basin.[89] Ironically, while the military lands surrounding WSNM have been the object of criticism and fears by National Park Service officials with respect to their management policies and procedures, the national monument has been saved from encroaching land developers and real estate agents by the military's presence. After approximately fifty years of coexistence with the Defense Department, the National Park Service and WSNM have attempted and fairly effectively achieved administrative cooperation while enduring "the best of a bad situation."

A BOLD VISION
Struggling for a White Sands Wilderness

I see the preservation of wilderness as one sector of the front in the war against the encroaching industrial state. Every square mile of range and desert saved . . . means another square mile saved for the play of human freedom.—Edward Abbey, *The Journey Home*

In 1985, environmental philosophers Bill Devall and George Sessions, summarized the 1964 Wilderness Act's definition of wilderness as "a landscape or ecosystem that has been minimally disrupted by the intervention of humans, especially the destructive technology of modern societies."[1] Certainly nowhere in the United States can evidence of "destructive technology" be found more readily than within the confines of White Sands Missile Range, New Mexico. The nature of the Defense Department's activities prevented the successful application of wilderness designation to the National Park Service's White Sands National Monument (WSNM), located in the southern portion of the missile range.

The idea of wilderness in the United States evolved from its European origins to contemporary American culture. Arriving in their New World during the fifteenth and sixteenth centuries, the Europeans, who viewed themselves culturally superior to other societies, believed that the American wilderness was not only a haven for noncivilized peoples but that it was also an "unmastered continent" waiting to be subjugated and civilized.[2] Historian Francis Jennings has argued against the popular belief that the Europeans entered a "virgin land, or wilderness"; instead he proposes that they conquered indigenous populations, thereby acquiring "widowed land."[3] Continuous westward progression by non-Hispanic Europeans resulted in the conquest of successive wildernesses, with the next unknown land hidden beyond the next mountain or just over the horizon.

Before the Civil War, the United States pursued its expansionist policies while simultaneously exploiting its natural resources. The nation had subscribed to the myth of superabundance, that is, most Americans believed that there was no foreseeable threat to the nation's apparently inexhaustible natural resources. The nation's rapid expansion from the East Coast to the West Coast, as well as its swift industrialization, alarmed relatively few individuals of the perils that a country would confront when wilderness areas no longer existed within its boundaries. Observing America's shrinking wild lands, artist George Catlin and transcendentalists Ralph Waldo Emerson and Henry David Thoreau were among the few who informed the people of the nation that they must preserve wilderness in order to maintain its spiritual and cultural welfare.

Near the close of the nineteenth century, environmentally destructive industrialization prompted an emerging minority of conservation-minded Americans to take political as well as social steps to preserve endangered landscapes. From the first congressional preservation act in 1864 (enacted to preserve Yosemite Valley and the Mariposa Big Tree Grove by presenting the areas to California) and the subsequent establishment of Yellowstone National Park in 1872, a new American consciousness evolved ushering in a new era for preserving pristine regions.[4] The Sierra Club, formed in 1892 and guided by its energetic founder John Muir, actively promoted wilderness preservation throughout the West, specifically in California. Concentrating principally on Yosemite National Park and the immediate urban threat posed by San Francisco to its Hetch Hetchy Valley, Muir marshalled his forces for the classic fight to prevent the valley's scenic landscape from becoming a reservoir. Historian Roderick Nash has called the Hetch Hetchy affair the beginning of national coverage of "competing claims of wilderness and civilization," for the same region.[5] Even though Muir and his preservation-minded allies waged a bitter and hard-fought campaign for approximately six years, the tragedy of the case was not only the loss of Hetch Hetchy in 1913 but also the polarization within the ranks of the conservation movement. In spite of the setback, Muir and his colleagues instilled the wilderness idea into the American people as a consequence of the public political and legal debates, thereby paving the way for the next generation of preservationists to battle for America's remaining wilderness lands.[6]

Succeeding Muir as the nation's leading wilderness crusader were two members of the U.S. Forest Service: Aldo Leopold, who as a young man in New Mexico learned the meaning of the "howl of the wolf"[7] and who helped establish in 1924 the nation's first designated wilderness, the Gila Wilderness encompassing 438,626 acres near Silver City, New Mexico; and Robert Marshall, the untiring wilderness defender and a founding member, in 1935, of the Wilderness Society. In addition to Leopold and Marshall, other important preservationists such as Howard Zahniser, David Brower, Sigurd Olson, Benton MacKaye, Robert Sterling Yard, Bernard Frank, Harvey Broome, and Harold Anderson contributed to the struggle to establish and preserve wilderness areas.[8]

Preservation of wilderness areas was severely challenged during the 1950s. The site for the conservation conflict was Echo Park in Dinosaur National Monument along the Colorado–Utah border. Fighting to thwart efforts by the Bureau of Reclamation to build a dam at Echo Park, a host of conservation agencies knew that if multiple uses were permitted in the national park then landscapes in all of the nation's parks and monuments would be in jeopardy. Not since Hetch Hetchy had the National Park Service and the preservation idea been threatened so voraciously. Supporting the dam project, Secretary of the Interior Oscar L. Chapman argued that the dam would be more beneficial to society than unspoiled landscapes. Mounting a major publicity campaign, Zahniser, Brower, and the countless wilderness supporters successfully convinced Congress in 1956 that preservation held equal weight with multiple-use arguments; unlike Hetch Hetchy, the argument for preserving unmarred scenery prevailed.[9] This legislative victory was the preservationists' "finest hour to that date."[10] Preservation as an ideal had emerged as a concept that many Americans finally supported in order to salvage those remaining wild landscapes. Environmental lobbyists also flexed their political muscles, revealing that actual or potential encroachments upon legislatively preserved lands and attacks against preservation agendas would be vigorously opposed in the future.

While Echo Park represented the wilderness movement's finest hour, the passage of the Wilderness Act on 3 September 1964 was its greatest triumph because the wilderness idea and its implementation, represented by the Wilderness System, finally became a national responsibility. On 3 September 1989, environmentalists celebrated the Wilderness Act's twenty-fifth anniversary. George T. Frampton, Jr., president of the Wilderness Society, insightfully calls the Wilderness Act "one of the best ideas this country ever had."[11] As a major watershed in America's conservation movement, the act preserved certain regions within public lands in their pristine state, while such areas still existed. Frampton adds that "only with a bold vision"[12] to increase designated wilderness areas beyond the 9 million acres originally set aside could the

United States expect to confront the aesthetic requirements demanded by future generations.

Following the passage of the Wilderness Act, the Interior Department directed the National Park Service to review its system for possible wilderness candidates. The idea of wilderness went against the National Park Service's approach of mass merchandising scenic areas, so it reacted slowly to the mandate. Because of intensive lobbying by preservationists in 1970, Interior Secretary Walter J. Hickel directed the National Park Service to assume a more responsive and responsible role in wilderness designation and recommendation by directing it to draft a proposal detailing how the National Park Service would accomplish the directive. National Park Service Director George B. Hartzog and his staff complied by developing a land management formula consisting of six classes for identifying the National Park

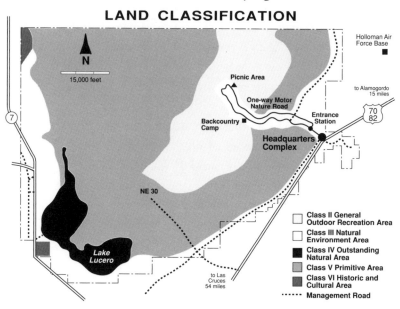

LAND CLASSIFICATION

Map 6. Land Classification, White Sands National Monument ("White Sands New Monument Master Plan, March 1976," Courtesy NPS)

Service's landholdings: "class I—high-density recreational areas; class II—general outdoor recreation areas; class III—natural-environment areas; class IV—outstanding natural areas; class V—primitive areas; and class VI—historical and cultural areas" (see Map 6).[13]

Preservationists such as Anthony Wayne Smith, president of the National Parks and Conservation Association, argued that the National Park Service's classes, especially class III, restricted the size of possible wilderness areas. Essentially the preservationists and the National Park Service could not agree on the question of what entailed wilderness areas and how they should be managed. The National Park Service's early reluctance to endorse fully the act and its mandates is evident in the Park Service's policy of allowing private landholdings in potential wilderness areas within Yellowstone National Park. Park Service management priorities were still intended for the millions of motoring tourists and not for the isolated groups backpacking into the wilderness.[14]

To underscore the preservationist movement, environmental historian Roderick Nash has called the Wilderness Act a "Marshall Plan" for the environment.[15] Reflecting the nation's environmental shift, conservationist and preservationist associations enjoyed flourishing memberships during the late 1960s and early 1970s; however, the number of wilderness areas did not substantially increase between 1971 and 1973. Nash contends that the National Park Service was unenthusiastic in the wilderness review process because of the exhaustive legislative procedures it entailed.[16] The initial wilderness areas were confined within the national forests, thereby revealing the National Park Service's reluctance to pursue wilderness designations for its parks and monuments. In 1971, the Forest Service initiated the Roadless Area Review and Evaluation (RARE) studies for recommending wilderness areas to Congress. The first study, known as RARE I, designated only 11 million acres for wilderness classification of the 56 million examined; this statistical revelation greatly disappointed preservationists. Urged on by the Sierra Club and other environmental groups, the Forest Service prepared RARE II to examine all Forest Service roadless lands.[17] Discounting preservationists' protests, only 15.4 million acres received wilderness status. The National Park Service's first wilderness effort involved the Everglades National Park, which resulted in the establishment of the Big Cyprus Preserve in September 1974. Wilderness designations for Yellowstone and Glacier national parks failed in 1978.[18]

The concept of wilderness has been defined by numerous scholars, as well as by the public. Early wilderness advocates endorsed the preservation of diverse, scenic, and magnificent landscapes because of anthropocentric ideas of nature. Most individuals regarded nature scenes worth saving because of their effect on humans, not because landscapes were inherently valuable. Wilderness debates centered principally on whether nature should be controlled by civilization or whether nature should remain wild for civilization's benefit. By the 1960s, America's increasing population, urban sprawl, industrial pollution, deforestation, and rapid societal upheavals encouraged wilderness supporters to demand that state and federal governments set aside the remaining wildlands from exploitation. Environmentalists viewed wilderness as a significant representation of a new way of seeing nature and how humans should fit into the scheme.

This concept in environmental thinking was not new in intellectual thought. For example, Roman emperor and Stoic philosopher Marcus Aurelius had expressed this idea in his *Meditations*. He wrote that individuals must, "Frequently consider the connexion of all things in the universe and their relation to one another. For in a manner all things are implicated with one another."[19] And according to Roderick Nash, preserving wilderness forced individuals to reconsider "man's relationship to the earth."[20] The need for human restraint was crucial for all life forms' continued existence because of Earth's diminishing natural resources and limited recovery capabilities. During the late 1960s, the counterculture's environmental awareness of ecological destruction culminated in Earth Day on 22 April 1970. The event was held to alert Americans to the need to "reverse our rush toward extinction."[21] Humans had to learn to view themselves and nature in terms of interdependent ecosystems. While the idea of preservation of wilderness had attracted supporters, the fate of wilderness had remained dependent on a "self-restraining civilization."[22]

The relatively unvisited and unknown portion of White Sands National Monument offered a unique opportunity to establish a wilderness area. WSNM's wilderness study and possible approval were hampered at the very beginning of the project. The White Sands Wilderness plan rekindled friction between the Interior and Defense departments. Unlike other prospective National Park Service wilderness candidates, such as Bandelier National Monument (which was reviewed on 18 December 1971 and received wilderness status for 23,267 acres on 20 October 1976),[23] Great Sand Dunes National Monument (which was reviewed in September 1972 and received wilderness status for 33,450 acres on 20 October 1976),[24] and Carlsbad Caverns National Park (reviewed on 7 December 1971 and received wilderness status for 33,125 acres in October 1978),[25] WSNM was a special review case. The monument's disqualification as a wilderness region would not be determined by lack of intrinsic qualifications, legislative burdens, or administrative neglect. The fate of the wilderness status of White Sands hinged on external reasons—the military's presence and its missile tests and aircraft overflights.

A Bold Vision

National Park Service visitor statistics reveal the importance of wilderness areas to millions of American tourists who have fled to the national parks and monuments.[26] Living in stressful surroundings or, as Edward Abbey referred to them, the "smoky jungles and swamps," many individuals accepted the wilderness idea as a necessity for maintaining a healthy life.[27] This theme contributed to an underlying concept that wilderness produces positive feelings. Another important feature of wilderness is the abundance of natural sounds and an absence of civilization's noises. As with all national parks and monuments, enjoying nature's aura is one of WSNM's most important and alluring attractions. The dunes' lure continually invites the sojourner to rest, contemplate, and sense freedom in the relatively untraveled areas within the monument.

As the National Park Service prepared its wilderness investigation of WSNM in 1971, two areas exceeded the wilderness roadless requirements of 5,000 acres. The largest one encompassed 113,500 acres, including most of the principal dunes and Alkali Flats. The second area totaled 5,200 acres covering the southwestern section of WSNM.[28]

In the National Park Service's land classification system, WSNM is designated class IV, an "outstanding natural" site. White Sands National Monument's unique geological and natural features were protected by the National Park Service because of their fragile and inherent values.[29] As a class IV site, WSNM was eligible for wilderness consideration if it met the following criteria specified by the Wilderness Act, 1964:

(1) generally appears to have been affected primarily by the forces of nature, with the imprint of man's work substantially unnoticeable; (2) has outstanding opportunities for solitude or a primitive and unconfined type of recreation; (3) has at least five thousand acres of land or is of sufficient size as to make practicable its preservation and use in an unimpaired condition; and (4) may also contain ecological, geological, or other

features of scientific, educational, scenic, or historical value.[30]

White Sands National Monument met those four conditions. The Wilderness Act did not preclude visitation or recreation. However, motor vehicles such as off-the-road vehicles (ORVs) and all-terrain-vehicles (ATVs) were banned. Wilderness required individuals to hike into the desired area.

Following a preliminary 1971 Wilderness Study, WSNM Superintendent John F. Turney admitted in 1972 that the time was ripe for a detailed wilderness investigation.[31] The superintendent believed that WSNM should qualify because of its pristine ecology.[32] As required by the Wilderness Act, Turney announced in the regional newspapers and the *Federal Register* that a public hearing would be held at the Alamogordo County commissioners' conference room on 1 April 1972. Frank F. Kowski, National Park Service director of the Southwest Region, presided over the morning discussion, while John Preston, former superintendent of Yosemite National Park, chaired the afternoon session. Turney presented a brief about the monument's history, especially its coexistence with the Department of the Army. According to Turney the hearing maintained a "friendly atmosphere" in spite of the provocative nature of the topic.[33]

Written responses concerning the Wilderness Study revealed that wilderness advocates for WSNM outnumbered the wilderness opponents, 338 to 194. Most of those wilderness supporters were not local residents, a fact that caused some resentment on the part of local citizens. Generally, wilderness supporters were from regional offices representing the Sierra Club, the Wilderness Society, and the Audubon Society. These advocates unanimously endorsed a Wilderness Study, stressing the need for wilderness at the monument. As the meeting progressed, the Sierra Club and Wilderness Society representatives insisted on a White Sands wilderness and requested that the Interior

Department and National Park Service terminate the special use permit with the army. Elmer Schooley, representing the Rio Grande Division of the Sierra Club, and Al Conrad of the Albuquerque Wilderness Society, denounced the special use permit and the military's access to the area. Don Campbell of the Santa Fe Wilderness Study Committee agreed, adding that there were too many military roads in the monument.[34] Brent Calkins, representing the Santa Fe Sierra Club, and John McComb of the Tucson Sierra Club, also presented "radical" statements during the hearing. McComb advocated relocating the monument headquarters to Alamogordo, and Calkins recommended replacing private vehicles in the monument with public transportation.[35] Unknowingly, the wilderness advocates undermined their position by viewing the military's co-use agreement with the Interior Department as a temporary relationship until the special use permit's termination.

Local businessmen and concerned citizens countered the wilderness defenders because they were incensed over the perceived intrusion into their recreational area. Echoing community sentiments, the Alamogordo Chamber of Commerce voted unanimously against a wilderness-only designation on 21 April 1972.[36] Also opposing the plan were unexpected allies Claude Warner, representing the National Wildlife Association, and Stan Green, president of the Otero County Wildlife and Conservation Association.[37] It is unclear why these conservation organizations opposed wilderness designation unless they foresaw the inevitable conclusion of trying to negotiate hopelessly with the military for their relocation or complete removal from WSNM or even from the entire Tularosa Basin. C. J. Dugan, president of Otero Mills, Inc., a staunch wilderness opponent, repeatedly wrote letters to the *Alamogordo Daily News* criticizing any project designed to "lock up the White Sands Park."[38]

Dugan's comments revealed his basic lack of familiarity with White Sands and with the wilderness proposal by commenting that "to stagnate our natural resources in the wilderness system is one thing, but to take an already developed area and attempt to revert it to a wilderness is ridiculous."[39] The roadless areas under review in WSNM dunes certainly could not be characterized as developed regions.

Acting in concert with the Chamber of Commerce, the Otero County Planning Commission (only four of the seven commissioners were present) met on 25 April 1972; the last item on their agenda was the WSNM Wilderness proposal. Commissioner George Reed recommended sending a letter to Superintendent Turney denouncing the attempt to attain wilderness status. Reed's motion passed unanimously within his commission.[40] Clearly, local organizations strongly opposed any wilderness designation in WSNM because of the possible losses to the local economy.

The Otero County Commissioners also voiced strong opposition to the wilderness plan. On 1 May 1972, Chairman Clifton G. McDonald submitted County Resolution No. 1972–1977, "Resolution Opposing the Designation of White Sands National Monument as a Wilderness Area," to Turney. It revealed that the principal reasons for opposition were the possibility of personnel reductions or program cutbacks on the part of the Defense Department and a potential decline in tourism. The commissioners concluded that supporting the wilderness plan would only result in "serious adverse" consequences for Alamogordo; therefore, the idea would not be in the best interests of the city.[41]

Bart R. Haigh and George L. Moore, representing the West Texas Geological Society, voiced their own opposition. They were convinced that the missile impacts in the Lake Lucero region made the wilderness plans untenable. They were concerned that if the region received wilderness status, the public's (i.e., geologists') access to the selenite beds would be curtailed. They did, however, suggest that the area required protection from "indiscriminate visitations."[42] Geologists, it seemed, comprised a special-interest group of their own.

Much of the local opposition against any wilderness designation for WSNM reflected several misconceptions concerning the proposal. Many individuals believed that the entire monument would be designated a wilderness area, even though the proposed wilderness areas consisted of 130,900 acres of the central and western sections of WSNM. The remaining 15,635 acres, including the Heart of the Dunes Loop Drive and the headquarters area, would not change status.[43] In an editorial Don Campbell emphasized that "picnicking and frolicking on the sands are in no way threatened."[44] Despite Campbell's reassurances, he could not convince local residents to support the wilderness proposal. Vehemently, the public denounced the preservationists as outsiders attempting to exclude them from their playground. Such a wilderness area would impede military activities; therefore, if the missile programs were halted and relocated to other testing facilities, Alamogordo's economy would suffer immeasurably. Another persistent misconception was the notion that the National Park Service would no longer administer the monument. It was true, and damming to their case, that the principal wilderness supporters demanded not only that the military cease its missile firings into the monument but also that there be a complete military evacuation of the Tularosa Basin.

Commenting on the White Sands proposal, Southwest Regional Director Frank F. Kowski wrote to National Park Service Director George Hartzog that, based upon recommendations submitted to him by reviewing officials, his position was "for non-wilderness."[45] Kowski based his decision on the army's missile impacts, both intentional and unintentional, into WSNM, and not because the region did not qualify for wilderness designation. Kowski added that the army's indefinite presence in the area canceled any favorable wilderness recommendation. Interestingly Kowski concluded his memorandum with a philosophical argument against the special use permit. The regional director strongly opposed the military's using any portion of WSNM as an impact area because the "unique resources of the monument were never intended to be subjected to such adverse use." Kowski confided to Hartzog that the army would never voluntarily relocate its launch complexes unless "pressure, public or otherwise, is applied. Possibly that time has come!"[46] Perhaps Kowski was hoping that the wilderness hearings would snowball into a national issue, causing the public to notice the misuse of a national monument. Clearly, Kowski sympathized and identified with the environmentalists' position on WSNM.

Adhering to its guidelines, the National Park Service notified eight major government agencies of the Wilderness Study plan, and each responded in favor for nonwilderness. Maj. Gen. E. H. deSaussure, White Sands Missile Range commanding general, endorsed the nonwilderness recommendation because the co-use of the western half of WSNM would remain instrumental in the "continued successful accomplishment of the research and development mission [of the missile range]."[47] The military acknowledged that impacts did occur within WSNM, but they stressed that the army avoided missile impacts whenever possible in any portion of the monument. DeSaussure added that while the military might appear to have an adverse impact on monument lands, the co-use zone eliminated any "wanton destruction of ecological assets being trampled by a mass of humanity."[48] The general's remarks reveal the military's rationale for justifying their incursions and implied a curious logic: that human hikers were a greater threat to White Sands ecology than bombs, missiles, and recovery crews!

In 1972, 81 percent (118,700 acres) of WSNM's roadless area had been examined for the purpose of wilderness designation. The principal obstacle blocking the designation was that the majority of the proposed wilderness area was in the western portion of the co-use area of WSNM.[49]

By August 1972, Director Hartzog announced that he supported Kowski's nonwilderness recommendation and cited his reasons. Hartzog concluded that favoring a White Sands Wilderness would be inconsistent and untenable in the face of ongoing missile programs for the nation's defense. The National Park Service could not properly administer the area while military activities continued indefinitely. Director Hartzog concluded:

> The missile impact and recovery program under the cooperative-use agreement with the Army is incompatible with the mandates of the Wilderness Act. The future plans of the White Sands Missile Range include a portion of the zone of cooperative use for testing and evaluating missiles. Since it is a permanent base, the use of the missile range will continue into the indefinite future.[50]

The wilderness fight in WSNM was not over, however. In early 1973, environmental organizations and the National Park Service renewed their interest in the White Sands Wilderness Study because the military's special use permit expired on 23 December 1973. Superintendent Turney and a new Wilderness Study team, composed of Don Campbell, Bonnie Campbell, Bob Rose, and Bill Ingersoll, from the National Park Service Western Office, toured the monument boundaries by jeep and army helicopter, allowing the team to examine the entire monument. The survey team recommended a wilderness area covering 30,000 acres located in the eastern portion of the monument. Following the inspection, Turney submitted the team's findings to Kowski. During an interview, when asked what happened to the second wilderness proposal, Turney replied that it just faded away or was just "pigeonholed somewhere."[51]

John A. McComb, a representative of the Southwest Sierra Club; Harry B. Crandell, director of Wilderness Review of the Wilderness Society; and Conservation Coordinator Phillenore D. Howard of the Rio Grande Chapter of the Sierra Club closely monitored the special use permit expiration by writing inquiries to Deputy Assistant Interior Secretary Curtis Bohlen asking if the permit would be renewed or allowed to expire.[52]

Bohlen, responding to a letter from Harry B. Crandell, said that he believed that the issue of national defense for maintaining the cooperative use agreement with the military was no longer valid because of the available technology for directing missiles away from the monument. Bohlen stressed that WSNM could not endure continued missile impacts and military encroachments for two more decades.[53] He emphasized the argument that "we [Interior Department] adjusted our priorities during a time of national necessity. That period is now over."[54] Bohlen's remarks leave few doubts about the frustrations resulting from the undesirable association WSNM has with the military. Optimistically, Bohlen hoped that the military would evacuate its facilities from WSNM, commenting that he looked "forward to the day when monument resources are free" from Defense Department influences.[55] Only with the termination of the Cooperative Use Agreement and the military's evacuation of the Tularosa Basin could wilderness designation and modern ecological protection become a reality in White Sands. In a memorandum to McComb on 18 October 1973, Bohlen perhaps naively expressed the hope that the Interior Department would be able to negotiate with the Defense Department and the army, allowing for a five-year period to permit the military's evacuation resulting in the closing or drastic reduction of White Sands Missile Range.[56] If the army agreed to terminate its WSNM missile operations, then a wilderness study and environmental assessment statement could be proposed again. As recently as 1975, the National Park Service still listed WSNM as an area "awaiting [wilderness] enactment" or one where "reevaluation would be made at a later date."[57] Essentially, the White Sands Wilderness proposal remains in an indefinite hold status.

From its inception in 1971, the WSNM wilderness proposal was an exercise in futility. While White Sands meets the prerequisites for a potential wilderness, the Defense Department's expanding activities precluded any favorable recommendation. This defeat was a startling revelation for the National Park Service because the outcome revealed its limited control over WSNM. The Defense Department emerged victorious because it still possessed the secret weapon that had allowed it to acquire most of the Tularosa Basin during the Second World War. The time-worn justification of its actions in the name of national defense, or "legal thievery" as Edward Abbey's fictional character John Vogelin in *Fire on the Mountain* called it, had won out again.[58] Additionally, the taxpayers' billions of dollars already invested in the region would not justify facility relocations just for the sake of wilderness. While the Interior and Defense departments continue to cooperate to fulfill their respective missions within WSNM, the Interior Department and the National Park Service discovered to their regret that national defense programs continue to maintain priority over any national wilderness programs for White Sands.

RETROSPECT
Beyond the Desert

Put aside for a while the plastic alligators of the amusement park, and I will show you that nature, taken on its own terms, has something to say that you will be glad to hear. This is the essence of the preservationist message.—Joseph L. Sax, *Mountains Without Handrails*

The need to preserve White Sands did not originate as a result of the public's environmental outcries. As has been the case with other areas within the National Park system, the impetus for preserving the dunes resided with a small, vocal special interest group, namely the Alamogordo Chamber of Commerce. Motivated principally by the lure of tourist dollars—with the importance of aesthetic/preservationist philosophy lagging far behind—the chamber and its leading spokesman, Tom Charles, promoted White Sands as a potential playground to state and federal officials. While mining ventures seemed to promise jobs and riches for the region, these expectations were never fulfilled. In short order the value of White Sands shifted from purely commercial exploitation to the possibility of developing a lucrative tourist industry. Motivation behind the preservation of the dune field remained economic; an alternative method for securing benefits from it had evolved. Thanks to the National Park Service's intervention, values other than economic ones finally triumphed.

The shift in emphasis from mining to tourism suggests that local developers and residents continued to view White Sands as an economic asset. Locals endorsed the federal government's willingness to administer the dune field as long as a profitable arrangement could be made for the community. In order to preserve the potential for commercial ventures, the promoters supported a park area that was as restricted in size as possible. Had it been left to the chamber, a portion of White Sands might have been developed as a gypsum theme park, complete with its own man-made lake and graded scenic route barely disguising the view of large trucks and trains hauling gypsum in the distance. This close brush with an environmentally tragic fate is symbolic of the history of WSNM and the threats to its integrity over the years.

It was the preservation-oriented National Park Service that insisted on the maintenance of White Sands as a natural area. Roger Toll's understanding of the significance of such natural landscapes as White Sands National Monument ensured its survival as a unique member in the National Park system and its preservation for its national significance, not merely as a money-making enterprise for the local community. The geologic composition of White Sands, as well as its aesthetic qualities, made it appropriate for designation as national monument status.

As was the case with many earlier national parklands, the entire White Sands ecosystem failed to receive monument designation because of opposition by public and special interests and by the National Park Service's practice of limiting areas to specific attractions. The area set aside as a national monument included the most remarkable or well-formed dunes, alkali flats, marginal dune areas, Lake Lucero, and two detached areas, Dog Canyon and Garton Lake. Overcoming initial protests, Roger Toll insisted that if admitted into the National Park system White Sands must encompass a large enough area to showcase its most attractive natural features. Also the very spaciousness or expansiveness of a large monument would only enhance its magnificence. To have created a relatively tiny geologic national monument of only 27,000 acres in the vast expanse of the Tularosa Basin would have undermined the National Park Service's plans for the dunes. While the National Park Service did not go after the entire dune field when it had the opportunity in 1930–31, officials managed to acquire a sufficient area despite local opposition.

For its first custodian, Tom Charles, WSNM was a place to have fun, in effect a gigantic natural sandbox. Charles encouraged his visitors to leave their cars, kick their shoes off, and frolic in the dunes; he also actively urged visitors to collect gypsum samples for mementos of their White Sands stay.[1] The appointment of Johnwill Faris initiated an era of professionally trained superintendents, groomed from within the National Park Service ranks. During the next forty years they were confronted with a host of complex situations that threatened the integrity of the national monument, the most severe brought on by the creation of Alamogordo Bombing and Gunnery Range in 1942 (later designated Holloman Air Force Base), and White Sands Proving Ground in 1945 (later renamed White Sands Missile Range). The military's encirclement of White Sands ushered in problems never encountered by other parks and monuments. These problems include military encroachments, missile impacts, road closures, overflights by aircraft, and trespass by military and civilian personnel.

The relationship between the Interior and the Defense departments has proved a mixed blessing. On the one hand the military prevented the private and commercial exploitation and despoliation of the land surrounding the monument and its resources. On the other, the nature of Defense Department activities has continuously undermined the National Park Service's mandate for preserving the dune field and its flora and fauna.

The Defense Department has not been the only agency causing administrative headaches for the National Park Service at

WSNM. The importation of the exotic African oryx during 1969–73 by New Mexico's Department of Game and Fish and the U.S. Department of Agriculture's introduction of colonies of saltcedars into the Southwest between 1899 and 1915 have threatened the endemic flora in the area. The National Park Service has experienced only limited success in its attempts to control the exotic flora and fauna.

Undaunted by administrative hurdles, the National Park Service has confronted each of these challenges. The WSNM superintendents have struggled to develop harmonious relationships with the military in order to minimize intrusions by the army and air force into the monument. Whether dealing with the military or exotic flora and fauna, the WSNM staff's efforts have not always produced desired results. As ecological concerns have increasingly gained sway in the National Park Service, however, local monument administrators have hoped for, and sometimes pushed for, a monument with a more pristine and protected desert ecology.

Immediately after the passage of the Antiquities Act, supporters perceived national monument status as secondary to that of national park. In spite of disappointment at the designation, White Sands National Monument never suffered the second-class stigma associated with earlier national monuments. The proclamation of its status occurred at the very end of Herbert Hoover's presidency, so it benefitted almost immediately from Franklin Roosevelt's New Deal programs, Interior Secretary Harold Ickes's directives, and the National Park Service directors' guidance policies and the superintendents' implementations of those directives.[2]

Pressured by environmental organizations such as the Sierra Club and the Wilderness Society, the National Park Service undertook plans to survey WSNM as a possible wilderness candidate in 1971. White Sands National Monument's wilderness reviews during 1972 and 1973 were conducted by the National Park Service to designate a sizeable portion of the monument as a wilderness area. While the National Park Service examination of the region concluded that it qualified as a potential wilderness, the military's missile firings prevented a favorable verdict. The National Park Service's recommendation was something of a foregone conclusion. It also revealed to the National Park Service and to the Interior Department the limitations on their management control over White Sands in contrast to other National Park Service lands. The prospect of a White Sands wilderness area depended on an unlikely Defense Department decision to curtail its missile tests or completely evacuate the Tularosa Basin. In spite of the Interior Department's unholy alliance with the military in the Tularosa Basin, environmental groups remain interested in the White Sands wilderness idea and continue to monitor military activities. The uniqueness of White Sands within the National Park system thus makes it a potential battleground for environmental activists and a regional economy tied closely to the defense industry.

In one respect WSNM actually represented the National Park Service's early emphasis on monumentalism. During its early years White Sands was frequently advertised as the world's largest gypsum concentration (which it is) and as the "Great White Sands." Interestingly, all of Albert Fall's 1922 proposed "spots" for the All-Year National Park except the Mescalero Apache Indian Reservation are currently preserved by state or federal conservation agencies. The former spots are Elephant Butte Lake State Park, Valley of Fires Recreation Area and Carrizozo Lava Flow Wilderness Study Area, and WSNM. Only White Sands and Valley of Fires are a part of the federal preservation system, however.

White Sands National Monument has never, excluding the Second World War, experienced a tourist drought. What began as a Tularosa, La Luz, and Alamogordo picnic spot, evolved into a regional attraction, then into a national "drawing card," and finally matured into an international monument. Attendance figures reflect the astronomical increase of visitors, from approximately 34,000 in 1934 to nearly 650,000 in 1988. The WSNM tourist influx has increased the National Park Service's revenues dramatically while contributing to the economic welfare of Alamogordo. Tourists arrive from all parts of the globe to experience the gypsum dune field.

Annually WSNM ranks second only to Carlsbad Caverns National Park in attendance in the National Park Service's Southwest Region. White Sands National Monument's popularity as a recreational area contributes immeasurably to New Mexico's tourism industry and to the economies of the surrounding communities. El Paso metropolitan population projections predict 3.5 million people for the sprawling El Paso–Juarez–Las Cruces area by A.D. 2010.[3] Coupled with the growth of environmental awareness in general in the Southwest, the need for recreational and inspirational regions will be greater than ever. Currently consisting of 145,334 acres (or 234 square miles), White Sands National Monument will continue to play a major role in the region's ties with its desert landscape.

At various times WSNM has been described affectionately as a "freak of nature," as one of the "Saharas of America" (Great Sand Dunes National Monument is the other Sahara), "Uncle Sam's Biggest Sand Pile," "The Nation's Sand Pile," "Uncle Sam's Newest Play Ground," and "The Great White Sands."[4] Each of these descriptions attempted to provide a graspable metaphor for some distinctive quality of White Sands.

Restrospect

An appreciation of these qualities requires time. To dash through the visitors center is to miss entirely the parkland's magic. The museum is but a gateway to a unique experience. White Sands offers a cornucopia of aesthetic pleasures to tantalize the senses: magnificent desert sunrises bursting over the crests of the Sacramento Mountains; striking fiery sunsets silhouetting the distant Organ and San Andres mountains; blinding gypsum windstorms; driving winter snowstorms; searing summer days and refreshingly cool evenings; spectacular thunder and lightning storms; sporadic and intense lifegiving desert rainstorms; and Lake Lucero's mirror-like waters and its shoreline holding the protruding selenite deposits. Equally memorable is a full moon excursion into the Heart of the Dunes—a night sky, crisp and clear, with a million stars, a full moon, and the wide expanse of rolling gypsum dunes. Even a walk among the cattails in Garton Lake offers a unique experience. Lastly, finding a shady spot under the cottonwoods in the Big Pedestal area allows a visitor to listen to the wind as it sweeps across the dune field— rustling leaves, swaying trees, and if one listens carefully, the sound of millions of colliding gypsum particles. All of these natural happenings are available to visitors who take the time to experience them. Even more can be gained if visits to the monument occur over the cycle of seasons. A major change in consciousness can result from the realization that the monument's impression on an individual could last a lifetime, but any impact that an individual makes on the dunes lasts but a second.

The emergence of an evolving desert consciousness in the West has played an important preservation role for the National Park Service and for America's popular culture. White Sands has become much more than just a site for picnics or a recreational playground; the dune field's fragile ecosystem and gypsum scenery have at last become important for their own intrinsic values.

Perhaps the anticipated peace dividends from the end of the Cold War could benefit White Sands. For the environmentalist the ideal White Sands scenario would be a military-free Tularosa Basin incorporating the entire dune field into the monument with the remaining lands designated as part of the federal wilderness system. Imagine almost an entire basin's ecosystem preserved intact! The realization of a vast wilderness of such proportions (perhaps 3,000–6,000 square miles) enclosing an enlarged WSNM (nearly 300 square miles) would more than delight, it would induce environmental ecstasy. But this remains only a dream. If the military should leave, then those persons holding ranch claims would challenge any such plan, in addition to the land developers waiting to pounce on such an easy prey.

As we close in on the twenty-first century the urgency to protect our natural resources as well as expand the National Park System is greater than ever. The principal challenge confronting America's survival is no longer an external threat emanating from the Russian steppes, rather the solutions to our most pressing problems reside within the geopolitical boundaries of the United States. As the world's military and political balance has clearly shifted in the United States' favor what an opportunity for the federal government to provide leadership, funding, and manpower to protect the environment. It is possible to envision a preservation bill, similar to the 1991 Highway and Transit Bill ($151 billion), offering permanent meaningful employment in a national environmental crusade. Though we have won the Cold War it would indeed be a shallow triumph if we neglect to channel the same energies to preserve our portion of spaceship Earth. Imagine a national offensive designed to refurbish, enlarge, and preserve our natural environment. Clean air, clean water, wild and beautiful landscapes, and a healthy economy, all in one package! At long last the Defense

Department's dominance over Interior Department agendas would be swept aside.

Today almost every national park area experiences new administrative and environmental issues. Contemporary problems include law enforcement, managing the monument with an undermanned and underpaid staff, upgrading park facilities within budget restraints, and ensuring quality of life for National Park employees. To make matters worse, the measured decline of air quality in the region, structural damage to the buildings caused by low flying aircraft and sonic booms, simulated A-bomb tests at White Sands Missile Range, and overwhelming numbers of tourists tax the monument's staff and the regional director in Santa Fe.[5] National park areas are special landscapes or unique sites that must be preserved for all generations. Encroachment upon one park must be perceived as a potential assault against the entire system of national parks.

This history of WSNM has examined a national monument that shares qualities similar to other national parks and monuments yet retains its own peculiar characteristics. It has analyzed the historical events that led to the establishment of a national monument in a previously remote area in Southern New Mexico. The monument's geology, natural history, its development from idea to reality, and its administrative history from 1933 through contemporary issues give White Sands National Monument an extraordinary place in environmental and National Park Service histories in particular and in the history of the American West in general. In spite of a difficult beginning and a perilous history, WSNM has lived up to Tom Charles's belief that "there is something more to the White Sands than just gypsum."[6]

NOTES

Preface

1. Eugene Manlove Rhodes, *Once in the Saddle* and *Paso Por Aqui* (Boston: Houghton Mifflin Company, 1927), 153.

Chapter 1

1. See "Southwestern National Monuments Monthly Report," 1933-40, WSNM library. James A. MacMahon, ed., *The Audubon Society Nature Guides: Deserts* (New York: Alfred A. Knopf, 1985), 83; also see John McPhee, *Basin and Range* (New York: Farrar, Straus and Giroux, 1981).

2. Ibid., 83-84.

3. Edward Abbey, *Fire on the Mountain* (Albuquerque: University of New Mexico Press, 1962), 4.

4. William R. Seager, *Geology of Organ Mountains and Southern San Andres Mountains, New Mexico* (Socorro, N.M.: New Mexico Institute of Mining and Technology, 1981), 13.

5. William M. Sandeen, "Geology of the Tularosa Basin, New Mexico," in *New Mexico Geological Society Guidebook of Southeastern New Mexico* (New Mexico Geological Society, 1954), 81.

6. George O. Bachman, "Paleotectonic Investigations of the Pennsylvanian System in the United States Part I, Regional Analyses of the Pennsylvanian System—New Mexico," *Geological Survey Professional Paper 853* (Washington, D.C.: Government Printing Office, 1975), 239.

7. D. S. Wilkins, "Geohydrology of the Southwest Alluvial Basins, Aquifer-Systems Analysis, Parts of Colorado, New Mexico, and Texas." *U.S. Geological Survey Water-Resources Investigations Report 84-4224* (Albuquerque: U.S. Geological Survey, 1986), 48.

8. Henry L. Jicha, Jr., and Christina Lochman-Balk, *Lexicon of New Mexico Geologic Names: Precambrian through Paleozoic* (Socorro, N.M.: New Mexico School of Mines and Mineral Resources, 1958), 32.

9. C. L. Herrick, "Lake Otero, An Ancient Salt Lake Basin in Southeastern New Mexico," *American Geologist* 34 (1904): 174-89. Approximately 250 million years ago, seas submerged low-lying areas throughout New Mexico. The abundance of limestone reveals that the seas were clear, and the numerous corals and fossils are evidence of abundant marine life. Repeated submersion and evaporation uncovered gypsiferous sediments and silt as well as creating the nearby mountains' Yeso (gypsum) Formation layer.

With widespread and sporadic earth shiftings, additional sediment accumulated throughout the region, resulting in the seas' ultimate recession. The enormous amount of valley fill that followed caused the seas to become isolated from each other. As the seas advanced and retreated repeatedly, only small enclosed basins remained. Downwarping (shifting of the earth's plates), volcanism, aridity, and southern hemispheric glacial activity had contributed collectively to the seas' stagnation and thus the seas finally disappeared from the Tularosa Basin, exposing the gypsiferous sand.

10. Bachman, "Paleotectonic Investigations," 237-78.

11. Seager, *Geology of Organ Mountains and Southern San Andres Mountains,* 35.

12. Ibid.

13. Senate, *Report of the Secretary of War,* 31st Cong., 1st sess., S. Exec. Doc. 64, 198.

14. Ibid., 14.

15. A. S. Packard, Jr. and F. W. Putnam, eds., "Salt Lake Plain in New Mexico," *American Naturalist* 4 (1870): 695-96; also see Fayette Alexander Jones, *New Mexico Mines and Minerals* (Santa Fe: The New Mexican Printing Company, 1904), 235; George I. Adams, "Geology, Technology, and Statistics of Gypsum," *U.S. Geological Survey 223* (Washington, D.C.: Government Printing Office, 1904), 13; and Jones, *New Mexico Mines and Minerals,* 235. By the late 1800s, three diverse groups developed an interest in White Sands: the scientific community, the private commercial companies, and the regional commercial clubs (predecessors of the chambers of commerce). In 1904, geologist Fayette A. Jones, predicted that gypsum would become a principal mineral for New Mexico's economic future. Gypsum could be used for many purposes, such as cement plaster, stucco, dental plaster, cement paint, and plaster of Paris. Geologist George I. Adams also reported in 1904 that when gypsum is "fine grained and suitable for carving and sculpturing" it is identified as alabaster. Gypsum was also an important building material for home construction. Jones remarked that geologists knew that there were many gypsum deposits in New Mexico; however, he added that the "virgin deposits of this useful material" had remained undeveloped.

16. Edwin D. McKee, ed., "A Study of Global Sand Seas," *Geological Survey Professional Paper 1052* (Washington, D.C.: Government Printing Office, 1979), vii.

17. O. E. Meinzer and R. F. Hare, "Geology and Water Resources of Tularosa Basin, New Mexico," *U.S. Geological Survey Water-Supply Paper 343* (Washington, D.C.: Government Printing Office, 1915), 13; G. B. Richardson, "Report of a Reconnaissance in trans-Pecos Texas," *U.S. Geological Survey 166* (Washington, D.C.: Government Printing Office, 1909), 2; C. S. Slichter, "Observations on the Groundwaters of Rio

Grande Valley," *U.S. Geological Survey Water-Supply Paper 141* (Washington, D.C.: Government Printing Office, 1905), 15; C. L. Herrick, "Lake Otero, An Ancient Salt Lake Basin in Southeastern New Mexico"; M. W. Harrington, "Lost Rivers," *Science* 6 (1885): 265-66; R. T. Hill, "The Texas-New Mexican Region," *Geological Society American Bulletin* 3 (1891): 85-100; Thomas H. MacBride, "The Alamogordo Desert," *Science* 21 (1905): 90-97; L. C. Graton, "The Alamogordo Desert," *U.S. Geological Survey Professional Paper 68* (Washington, D.C.: Government Printing Office, 1910), 25 and 184; C. R. Keyes, "Geology and Underground-Water Conditions of the Jornado del Muerto, New Mexico," *U.S. Geological Survey Water-Supply Paper 123* (Washington, D.C.: Government Printing Office, 1905), 15; also see C. L. Herrick, "The Geology of the White Sands of New Mexico," *New Mexico University Bulletins Geological Series* 1 and 2 (1900): 1-14; F. W. Brady, "The White Sands," *Mines and Minerals* 25 (1905): 529-30, and H. N. Herrick, "Gypsum Deposits in New Mexico." *U.S. Geological Survey Bulletin 223* (Washington, D.C.: Government Printing Office, 1904), 89-99; Meinzer and Hare, "Geology and Water Resources of Tularosa Basin, New Mexico," 69; Nelson H. Darton, "Red Beds and Associated Formations in New Mexico," *U.S. Geological Survey Bulletin 794* (Washington, D.C.: Government Printing Office, 1928), 59; Charles W. Botkin, "The White Sands National Monument," *Pan American Geologist* 60 (1933): 304; "White Sands, Nomadic in Nature, May Enter Alamogordo in about 4097 A.D.," *Alamogordo News,* 4 August 1932, p. 3, col. 1 and 4; and Vincent W. Vandiver, "White Sands Geological Report," Southwestern Monuments Special Report 3, National Park Service, May 1936, 391-98.

In 1900, geologist Clarence L. Herrick, published one of the first in-depth monographs on the Tularosa Basin, with specific attention to the gypsum dunes. He never identified the Tularosa Basin by name; Herrick merely referred to the basin as "an extensive valley." He investigated the northern and central portions of the basin reporting that the gypsum deposits were the product of the gypsum layers in the San Andres Mountains. According to Herrick, the gypsum dunes evolved as a result of wind and rain weathering the exposed selenite crystals in the alkali flats. Herrick argued against the idea that springs and floods accounted for the gypsum field's evolution. Despite Herrick's brief and unsatisfactory analysis, the study was the first major effort by the scientific community to account for the gypsum dunes.

In 1915, the U.S. Geological Survey published a lengthy tract co-authored by geologists O. E. Meinzer and R. F. Hare entitled "Geology and Water Resources of Tularosa Basin, New Mexico." Meinzer's and Hare's work was a comprehensive report on the physiography and topography of the Tularosa Basin. The authors contended that the gypsum originated in the gypsum deposits in the rock formations found in the adjacent mountains. Accordingly, the gypsum arrived at its present location as a consequence of surface and subsurface water reducing the selenite formations into gypsum crystals and forcing the gypsum to the surface. The gypsum crystals resettled when the waters evaporated and these gypsum deposits were altered continuously by "repeated resolution and redeposition and by wind work."

Geologist Nelson H. Darton, in 1928 advanced another concept for the White Sands' origin. Darton's idea was that the gypsum reached the surface of the Tularosa Basin as a result of water flowing from the adjacent Yeso formation beds. The natural weathering processes, which occurred over many centuries, reduced the gypsum deposits to gypsum particles and the wind subsequently formed the gypsum crystals into dunes.

The significance of the pre-1933 White Sands geological reports was the important information they contained for study by the National Park Service. Subsequent to the creation of WSNM on 18 January 1933 the quality of the White Sands gypsum reports improved considerably. In 1933, following the establishment of WSNM, chemist Charles W. Botkin, wrote that a large deposit of gypsum crystals (micro crystalline-selenite) existed in the dry lakebed of the Tularosa Basin, and as a consequence of prolonged wind erosion of the crystal deposits the gypsum particles were formed into dunes. Shortly thereafter, geologist L. M. Richard, proposed that gypsum dunes developed because "tiny wavelets" crystallized as the wind blew over the lake area and the intensive eastward winds carried the gypsum crystals to the lakeshore. Richard concluded that the continuous gypsum accumulation along the lakeshore evolved as the White Sands dune field. Most geologists now agreed that the original source of the gypsum was the Yeso layers and that high winds eroded the selenite that had been washed into the basin.

Writing for the National Park Service in 1936, geologist Vincent W. Vandiver agreed that the initial gypsum deposits originated in the Yeso formations found in the adjacent mountains. During the Quaternary Period, streams transported red clay, gypsum, sand, and gravel from the mountains and deposited them on the basin floor. Water erosion created salt deposits that were "redissolved and redeposited," eventually forming the alkali flats.

Vandiver argued that the gypsum (selenite) in the alkali flats disintegrated because of hydraulic forces and were transported by the prevailing southwesterly wind to the eastern region of Lake Lucero. He proposed that because the gypsum dunes lay on the eastern fringe of the ancient lakebed, the principal gypsum source for the White Sands originated from Lake Otero. Vandiver rejected the idea that the majority of the gypsum dune field originated as a result of the subsurface water pressures forcing the selenite—located in the subsurface Yeso formation—to the surface. Vandiver concluded that the initial gypsum and saline (salt) deposits of the Yeso formation originated from the heavy summer rains pouring into the Tularosa Basin accompanied by high rates of evaporation.

18. Roger J. Allmendinger, "Hydrologic Control over the Origin of Gypsum at Lake Lucero, White Sands National Monument, New Mexico" (M.A. thesis, New Mexico Institute of Mining and Technology, 1971), 78; for additional information also see Robert H. Weber and Frank E. Kottlowski, *Gypsum Resources of New Mexico* (Socorro: New Mexico Bureau of Mines and Mineral Resources, 1959), 13-14.

19. J. S. McLean, "Saline Ground-Water Resources of the Tularosa Basin, New Mexico," *U.S. Geological Survey 561* (Washington, D.C.: Government Printing Office 1970), 16; also see R. E. Neher, et al., "Soils and Vegetation Inventory of White Sands Missile Range," *U.S. Department of Agriculture, Soil Conservation Service, West Region* (Washington, D.C.: Government Printing, Office, 1970), 3.

20. McKee, "Global Sand Seas," 87; also see Frank Byrne, *Earth and Man* (Dubuque, Iowa: William C. Brown Company, 1974), 326-28; Charles J. Cazeau, ed., *Physical Geology: Principles, Processes, and Problems* (New York: Harper and Row Publishers, 1976), 318; R. A. Bagnold, *The Physics of Blown Sand and Desert Dunes* (London, 1941. Reprint. Chapman and Hall, 1971), 32, 34, 37, and 189; Vandiver, "White Sands Geological Report," 398-99; "White Sands, Nomadic in Nature, May Enter Alamogordo in about 4097 A.D.," *Alamogordo News,* 4 August 1932, p. 3, col. 4; Vandiver, "White Sands Geological Report," 399; also see R. O. Stone, "Desert Glossary," *Earth-Science Reviews* 3 (1967): 217-18; Edwin D. McKee, "Structures of Dunes at White Sands National Monument, New Mexico," *Sedimentology,* Special Issue 7, no. 1 (1966): 69; Edwin D. McKee and John R. Douglass, "Growth and Movement of Dunes at White Sands National Monument, New Mexico," *U.S. Geological Survey Professional Paper 750-D* (Washington, D.C.: Government Printing Office, 1971), D-108; and Edwin D. McKee and Richard J. Moiola, "Geometry and Growth of the White Sands Dune Field, New Mexico," *U.S. Geological Research* 3, no. 1 (January-February 1975), 59.

Wind erosion alters the landscape through a series of processes: corrosion, the relocation of rock sediments; deflation, the relocation of sand particles; and abrasion, a process similar to sandblasting. Many geologists believe that deflation is the most important of the elements of wind gradation. Winds such as dust devils and tornados become the vehicles for transporting fine dust particles.

Wind turbulence is important in the transportation of dust particles or fine gypsum crystals. Near the land surface, forward wind speed is five times as fast as the rate of upward wind gusts. Dust particles that possess a forward velocity greater than 1/5 of the speed of the wind will not be conveyed through the air. Thus the rate of wind speed is important for a dune's evolution because the duration of a dune's growth and the distance of a dune's migration are dependent upon wind velocity.

In 1936, Vandiver remarked that he knew "of no proper records as to the rate of migration of the sand dunes." Vandiver acknowledged geologist D. T. MacDougal's 1910 migration theory that the dunes advanced one mile every twenty years; however, he believed that MacDougal exaggerated his estimation. Vandiver suggested that there was a possible correlation between the distance a dune traveled and the age of yuccas in the area. In 1932, L. M. Richard predicted that the gypsum dunes would reach Alamogordo by A.D. 4097. Vandiver responded to Richard's commentary by arguing that Richard did not take into account the quantity of gypsum particles in Lake Lucero or that well-established, hardened dunes did not permit the transportation of gypsum particles as easily as more recently formed dunes. Vandiver did not furnish any of his own migration projections; however, he suggested with tongue in cheek that the residents of Alamogordo and Tularosa "have little to fear for some time nor need the (National) Park Service take out protection in lands to the east in order to have White Sands for a monument in later years."

As a consequence of the National Park Service's revitalization program, known as Mission 66, the agency in 1962 recommended that more current and extensive geological research was needed for the White Sands dunes. Edwin D. McKee of the U.S. Geological Survey initiated the first of three research expeditions into the gypsum dune field in late 1962. In the first study McKee's principal research objectives were to analyze the four major types of dunes found at White Sands; to discover common structural characteristics of the dunes; to investigate dune movement; and to record the evolution of "individual structural units within dunes." In 1966, Maj. Gen. John M. Combs, the commanding general at White Sands Missile Range, provided bulldozers and army personnel for McKee's research project. In the spirit of cooperation the U.S. Air Force, at nearby Holloman Air Force Base, furnished aerial photographs of the gypsum dunes and meteorological information to the research team. The second study examined the growth and migration of the dunes. McKee's third research phase, conducted in 1973, analyzed the composition and development of the dune field. Collectively, the three scientific articles produced by the field work provide a "general analysis. . . of the nature and development of the dune field."

21. McKee, "Structures of Dunes," 27. McKee states that "in early stages they (the embryonic dunes) advance by removal of sand through beveling of the low-angle windward face and by avalanching of the slip face on the steep lee side as shown by upward structures."

22. Ibid., 26.

23. Ibid., 27.

24. Ibid., 39.

25. Ibid., 50. Ibid., 10-11; Ibid., 11; also see McKee and Douglass, "Growth and Movement of Dunes at White Sands National Monument, New Mexico," D-110; Ibid., D-113.

26 John C. Van Dyke, *The Desert: Further Studies in Natural Appearances* (New York: Charles Scribner's Sons, 1904), 16-17.

27. McKee and Moiola, "Geometry and Growth of the White Sands Dune Field, New Mexico," 60.

28. Ibid., 61.

29. Ibid. Interdune areas contain structures different from the dunes' internal structures. Interdune areas possess "subparallel layers that are structureless, flat bedded, or irregularly bedded" in comparison to the contiguous dunes that are "cross-stratified." Various colored particles accumulate as the dunes and interdune areas migrate over the dune field.

30. "Southwestern National Monuments Monthly Report," 1933-1940. Early on, national parks were referred to as emeralds while monuments were diamonds.

Chapter 2

1. John Burroughs, *Pepacton* (Boston: Houghton, Mifflin and Company, 1881), 101.

2. Joseph W. Krutch, *The Voice of the Desert: A Naturalist's Interpretation* (New York: William Sloane Associates, 1954), 17.

3. George M. Wright, Joseph S. Dixon, and Ben H. Thompson, *Fauna of the National Park Service of the United States* (Washington, D.C.: Government Printing Office, 1933), 1.

4. David E. Brown, "Chihuahuan Desert Scrub," *Desert Plants,* 4, 1-4, (1982): 170.

5. James A. MacMahon, ed., *The Audubon Society Nature Guides: Deserts* (New York: Alfred A. Knopf, 1985), 22-4.

6. Ibid., 83.

7. Phillip S. Derr, et al., *Soil Survey of Otero Area, New Mexico* (U.S. Department of Agriculture, Soil Conservation Service, 1981), 1.

8. C. L. Sonnichsen, *Tularosa: Last of the Frontier West* (New York: The Devin-Adair Company, 1960), 3.

9. John Wesley Powell, *Report on the Lands of the Arid Region* (Washington, D.C.: Government Printing Office, 1879), 20.

10. Senate, *Reports of the Secretary of War,* 31st Cong. 1st sess., 1850, S. Exec. Doc. 64, 198.

11. William A. Dick-Peddie, "Vegetation of Southern New Mexico," in *Arid Lands in Perspective,* ed. W. O. McGinnies and B. J. Goldman (Tucson: University of Arizona Press, 1969), 165.

12. Charles J. Whitfield and Hugh L. Anderson, "Secondary Succession in the Desert Plains Grassland," *Ecology* 19, no. 2 (April 1938): 171-2.

13. R. A. Wright and J. H. Honea, "Aspects of Desertification in Southern New Mexico, U.S.A.: Soil Properties of a Mesquite Duneland and a Former Grassland," *Journal of Arid Environment* 11 (1986): 140.

14. Ibid., 143-4. Also see *Alamogordo News,* 27 April 1933, p. 1, col. 6; Forrest Shreve, *Vegetation of the Sonoran Desert* (Washington, D.C.: Carnegie Institution of Washington Publications 591, 1951), v; *Alamogordo News,* 30 April 1942, p. 1, col. 5. On 4 May 1933, the American Association for the Advancement of Science met at WSNM. Although WSNM was established principally to preserve the earth's most expansive gypsum deposit, the principal speakers were two eminent Southwestern botanists, professor Clayton W. Botkin of New Mexico College of Agriculture and Mechanic Arts (currently New Mexico State University) and Forrest Shreve, associated with the Desert Laboratory of the Carnegie Institution of Washington in Tucson and the University of Arizona. White Sands National Monument's unique environment encouraged the association's members to meet again at the monument on 27 April 1942, this time listing among its distinguished guests botanists Fred W. Emerson, New Mexico Highlands University; W. B. McDougall, Santa Fe; S. B. Talmage, New Mexico School of Mines (New Mexico Tech); and A. L. Hershey of New Mexico State University who was the meeting's presiding officer. The minutes of the meetings are unknown; however, the significance of the meetings lies in the acknowledgment by the botanists that the White Sands was a unique ecosystem worthy of study.

Note to page 18

For historical overview of flora and fauna studies see *Science* 21, no. 187 (29 July 1898): 119, 121; E. O. Wooton and Paul C. Standley, *Flora of New Mexico* (Washington, D.C.: Government Printing Office, 1915), 9-11; Edward Ray Schaffner, "Flora of the White Sands National Monument of New Mexico," Master's thesis, New Mexico Agriculture and Mechanic College, 1948, 10-6; *Science* 21, no. 525 (1905): 90, 93; Fred W. Emerson, "An Ecological Reconnaissance in the White Sands, New Mexico," *Ecology* 16, no. 2 (April 1935): 226-33. For more interesting information see U. T. Waterfall, "Observations on the Desert Gypsum Flora of Southwestern Texas and Adjacent New Mexico," *The American Midland Naturalist* 36 (1946): 458; Lora Mangum Shields, "Zonation of Vegetation Within the Tularosa Basin, New Mexico," *The Southwestern Naturalist* 1, no. 2 (April 1956): 52, 55, 61.

While the principal White Sands naturalist studies were published following the creation of the WSNM in 1933, there were also earlier scientific studies of the gypsum field's flora and fauna, demonstrating that geological studies were not the only ones of interest. Several of the earliest scientific studies revealed the abundant vegetation along the dune field margins. As early as 1896, Professor A. Guss recorded that there was an abundance of grass growing along the dune margins. Botanists T. D. A. Cockerell and Fabian Garcia conducted experiments to demonstrate that "plants [wheat and peas] will grow in nearly pure gypsum." Their wheat experiments lasted from 17 February until 11 June 1898 and the pea study from 26 February to 1 April 1898. They used five types of soils: gypsum from White Sands; Larrea, that is, soil in which creosote grows, composed mainly of Organ Mountains sedimentation; mesquite soil; Pluchea soil-sandy soil from the river region; and adobe soil. In their summary the botanists concluded that "gypsum will nourish plants as well as ordinary soil, or even better."

In 1897, Elmer O. Wooton, became the first botanist known to have collected floral specimens from the gypsum dunes. Over the next decade Wooton and his assistant, Paul C. Standley, gathered flora specimens from White Sands and throughout New Mexico, producing their principal reference work, *Flora of New Mexico*. Wooton and Standley catalogued eight species from White Sands: sand verbena (*Abronia angustifolia*), giant dropseed (*Sporobolus giganteus*), gyp moonpod (*Selinocarpus lanceolatus*), globemallow (*Sphaeralcea arenaria*), stick-leaf (*Mentzelia pumila*), yellow evening primrose (*Calyrophus hartwegii*), white evening primrose (*Oenothera pallida runeinata*), and gype nama (*Nama carnosum*). Because of Wooton's and Standley's tome, botanists' interest in White Sands continued.

During an address in 1904 to an "ecologically minded" scientific gathering in Philadelphia, Pennsylvania, Thomas H. MacBride discussed the geomorphology and botany of the Tularosa Basin in general and the White Sands dunes in particular. MacBride told his audience that the entire Tularosa Basin should be examined for its peculiar flora because the basin's flora is unlike that of any other region, "not that it has peculiar species, perhaps, but that it has its own particular groups of species." He added that it was important to study the local environment in its totality because the region's peculiarities would emerge more readily.

While traveling throughout the Tularosa Basin, MacBride recorded its flora. As he approached the dunes, he noted that he anticipated new species, but upon closer examination concluded that the dunes "are sands first of all," regardless of the chemical composition. The nature of the environment supported his contention that only a hardy vegetation could endure in such mobile habitat. MacBride noted that the yucca (*Yucca radiosa*), and the mesquite (*Prosopis glandulosa*) were the dune field's dominant vegetation.

Botanist Fred W. Emerson, surveying White Sands during the spring and summer of 1934, noted that plants were migrating into the marginal dune areas from the surrounding desert. He discovered that seedlings established themselves only in the interdune areas because the water table is only two to three feet below the surface and that the open spaces prevented interference in the seedlings' growth. Observing the dunes' continuous advancement, Emerson concluded that of the sixty-two reported plant species in the White Sands region, only seven species were capable of growing upward fast enough to survive gypsum engulfment. The remaining fifty-five species survived only in the flat interdune areas because of their inability to produce elongated root systems. While Wooton and Standley had listed fifty-seven White Sands species in 1915, only twenty years later Emerson added five species not previously mentioned.

Edward R. Schaffner completed his studies of the dune field in 1948, the most comprehensive work up to that time. He examined the plants in six plant habitats: the Alkali Flats area, Lake Lucero, the Heart of the Dunes, the embryonic dune area, marginal dune areas, and Garton Lake. The young botanist identified five "gypsum indicator" plants: frankenia (*Frankenia jamesitti*), gype nama, gyp grama (*Bouteloua breviseta*), narrowleaf greggia (*Nerisyrenia linearifolia*), and gyp moonpod. These plants' survival depends upon the presence of gypsum in the sand.

Eight years later, botanist Lora Mangum Shields compared plant species of the lava beds with those of White Sands. She collected 62 plant species from White Sands and 134 species from the lava beds and reported that there were 23 species common to both areas. Shields's research supported Wooton's and Standley's 1915 listing of only five gypsum indicators: frankenia, gype nama, narrowleaf greggia, goosefoot moonpod (*Ammocodon chenopodoides*), and gyp grama. The conclusion was that dune migration and the high concentration of calcium sulfate prevented the propagation of most of the adjacent plant species in the gypsum dune field.

15. Rogelio Lozano, "The Distribution and Ecology of Two *Echinocereus triglochidiatus* Populations in White Sands National Monument, New Mexico," Master's thesis, University of Texas at El Paso, 1979, 3-4.

16. Kenneth D. Heil and Steven Brack, "The Rare and Sensitive Cacti of White Sands National Monument," Contract Report for the National Park Service by Ecosphere Environmental Services, Farmington, New Mexico, 1985, 1-2.

17. Ibid., 5.

18. Ibid., 8-9.

19. Ibid., 1-12.

20. Ibid., 8.

21. Janice E. Bowers, "Plant Geography of Southwestern Sand Dunes," *Desert Plants* 6, no. 1 (Summer 1984): 37-8.

22. Ibid., 39.

23. Ibid., 51.

24. "White Sands National Monument Master Plan 1965," National Park Service, WSNM library, 3.

25. David V. Petticord, acting superintendent, "White Sands National Monument Information Letter," 8 March 1971, Southwest Regional Office (SWRO), National Park Service (NPS), library, White Sands National Monument (WHSA) file NS-19.

26. "Plants and Animals of the White Sands: A Discussion of Dunes Ecology, 1983," National Park Service, WSNM library, 1.

27. Craig McFarland, "Habitat Partitioning Among the Three Species of Lizards from White Sands National Monument, New Mexico," Master's thesis, University of Wisconsin, 1969, 1-10.

28. William H. Reid, untitled report, examining the salt cedar in White Sands National Monument, undated, WSNM library, natural history file, typescript, 1-9.

29. William H. Reid, *Final Report: White Sands National Monument Natural Resources and Ecosystem Analysis,* CX702900001, 1, Laboratory for Environmental Biology, Research Report, 12, 1980, University of Texas at El Paso, 5, SWRO, NPS, library, WHSA file 1.b NS-30. Also see Michael R. Kunzmann, et al., "Tamarisk Control in Southwestern United States," *Proceedings of Tamarisk Conference,* Special Report No. 9, 1989.

30. Alexander G. Ruthven, "A Collection of Reptiles and Amphibians from Southern New Mexico and Arizona," *American Museum of Natural History Bulletin* 23 (1907): 483-603.

31. Lee R. Dice, "Mammal Distribution in New Mexico," *Special Report,* 1927, SWRO, NPS, library, WHSA file NS-11, 1-3.

32. Ibid., 3.

33. *Albuquerque Journal,* 29 September 1938, p. 2, col. 4.

34. Seth B. Benson, "Concealing Coloration Among Some Rodents of the Southwestern United States," *University of California Publications in Zoology* 40 (1933): 60-70.

35. Adrey E. Borell, "Birds of White Sands National Monument," Special National Park Service Report, 1938, 5, SWRO, NPS, library, WHSA file NS-6.

36. Arno Cammerer to T. A. Walters, 12 June 1935, National Archives (NA), Record Group (RG) 48, Monuments file 12-1, 16 January 1930-3 November 1936.

37. W. B. McDougall, "Wildlife Project at White Sands National Monument," Special Report, 1939, SWRO, NPS, library, WHSA file NS-8.

38. W. B. McDougall, "Some Wildlife Problems at White Sands National Monument," *Special Report,* 1939, SWRO, NPS, library, WHSA file NS-7; *Southwestern National Monument Monthly Report,* January 1941, WSNM library. In 1941, WSNM custodian Johnwill Faris commented that the state had introduced a small pronghorned antelope herd within the monument. It is unclear whether the state had received permission or the Interior Department had failed to inform the custodian of the agreement

because of Faris's bewilderment.

For recent herpetological/reptile studies see Roy E. Bundy, "Color Variation in Two Species of Lizards: *Phrynosoma modestum* and *Holbrookia maculata* Subspecies," Ph.D. diss., University of Wisconsin, 1955, 2-4; Delbert Eugene Meyer, "Studies On Background Color Selection in Two Species of Lizards: *Holbrookia maculata* subspecies and *Phrynosoma modestum,*" Ph.D. diss., University of Wisconsin, 1959, 4-6; McFarland, "Habitat Partitioning Among the Three Species of Lizards from White Sands National Monument, New Mexico," 4.

White Sands has also seen the study of the evolution of unique varieties of its reptiles. Herpetologists have shown interest because they are intrigued by color adaptations among lizards to a habitat of snow-white dunes. In 1955, herpetologist Roy E. Bundy examined the round-tailed horned lizard (*Phrynosoma modestum*) and the lesser-earless lizard (*Holbrookia maculata*). Bundy described the round-tailed horned lizard as a small "somewhat sedentary" lizard while the lesser-earless lizards, the *H.M. ruthveni, H.M. maculata,* and *H.M. approximans,* excepting *ruthveni,* were more agile and quicker. Bundy experimented with varying temperatures and alternating black cinders and gypsum environments to document what effect each would have upon the lizards. After experimenting for several months, he was unable to prove that the lizards could alter colors (black to white or vice versa). However, Bundy did notice a "paling on the white background and a darkening on the black," on the lizards. He concluded his research by asserting that environmental changes by themselves do not force color variation; instead, the lizards' adaptive coloring resulted because of biologic and genetic "divergence of local populations" occupying areas of varying colors.

Four years later, herpetologist Delbert E. Meyer, investigated the round-tailed horned lizard and the lesser-earless lizard to determine their color preference regarding the environment. Assuming that the lizards can detect color, Meyer conducted experiments that revealed that both species of lizards chose red sand for the preferred surroundings. The lesser-earless lizards preferred the coarsest and warmest sand grains. Meyer deduced that if the lizards duplicated their laboratory behavior in the field then "color mutations accompanied by changes in specific habitat selection" do not produce the diverse colors of the lizards. In the end, Meyer failed to prove that lizards select their environments because of "strong innate preferences" that determine the lizards' coloring in the field.

In 1969, another herpetologist, Craig McFarland, researched the relationship of similar diurnal lizard species coexisting in the interdune and marginal dune areas. He examined the probability of one species population affecting the population size of neighboring species. McFarland studied the cowles prairie lizard (*Sceloporus undulatus cowlesi*), the lesser-earless lizard, and the little striped whiptail (*Cnemidophorus inornatus*). McFarland's project did not conclusively reveal that the three species limited each other's population size.

39. J. Stockley Ligon, *Wild Life of New Mexico: Its Conservation and Management* (Santa Fe: Santa Fe New Mexican Publishing Corp., 1927), 50.

40. Vernon Bailey, "Mammals of New Mexico," *United States Department of Agriculture, North American Fauna No. 53* (Washington, D.C.: Government Printing Office, 1931), 303-8.

41. David E. Brown, "Return of the Natives," *Wilderness* 52 (Winter 1988): 49; Jim Burbank, "Fate of Mexican Wolf Has People Howling," *New Mexico* 68 (February 1990): 52-57. Also see James C. Bednarz, "The Mexican Wolf: Biology, History, and Prospects for Reestablishment in New Mexico," *Endangered Species Report 18,* U.S. Fish and Wildlife Service, 1988; as well as his, "An Evaluation of the Ecological Potential of White Sands Missile Range to Support a Reintroduced Population of Mexican Wolves," *Endangered Species Report 19,* U.S. Fish and Wildlife Service, 1989. *Las Cruces Sun-News,* 11 March 1992, p. 5A, col. 2–3.

42. *Albuquerque Journal,* 7 May 1987, section C, p. 3, col. 1-3.

43. *Missile Ranger,* 9 April 1972, section B, p. 1, col. 3.

44. Milford Fletcher, "Through Darkest New Mexico with Tongue in Cheek or the Exotic African Oryx," *Park Service* 6, no. 2 (Winter 1986): 25. See also Donald Harper to Chief, Division of Natural Resources Management, 26 May 1983, WSNM library, file N-14-Animal and Plant Life. In 1983, WSNM superintendent Harper, in cooperation with White Sands Missile Range officials, conducted an aerial survey of oryx crossing the monument. Surveying from an army helicopter, Harper counted sixty-eight oryx in the monument.

45. Field Solicitor memo to Regional Director, 16 March 1979, SWRO, NPS, library, WHSA file W-18.

46. Ibid.

47. "Preliminary Draft Resources Management Plan and Environment Assessment for White Sands National Monument," December 1981, 9, SWRO, NPS, library, WHSA file W-19.

48. William H. Reid and Gail R. Patrick, "Gemsbok (Oryx Gazella) in White Sands National Monument," *The Southwestern Naturalist* 28, no. 1 (18 February 1983): 99.

49. Robert Ferrari memo to Donald Harper, 13 February 1984, WSNM library, file N-14-Animal and Plant Life.

50. "Plants and Animals of the White Sands," 17-8.

Chapter 3

1. Edgar L. Hewett, *Ancient Life in the American Southwest* (Indianapolis: The Bobbs-Merrill Company, 1930), xiii.

2. Ibid., 274-5.

3. Ibid., 275.

4. William D. Lipe, "The Southwest" in *Ancient Native Americans,* ed., Jesse D. Jennings (San Francisco: W. H. Freeman and Company, 1978), 332-5.

5. Peter L. Eidenbach and Mark L. Wimberly, "Archaeological Reconnaissance in White Sands National Monument," 1980, 28, 76, 79-80, 93, and 97. For prehistoric references see J. Jefferson Reid and David E. Doyel, eds., *Emil W. Haury's Prehistory of the American Southwest* (Tucson: University of Arizona Press, 1986), 12, 441, 445, and 452-3; Erik F. Reed to Director National Park Service, 7 May 1937, *Special Report,* SWRO, NPS, library, White Sands National Monument (WHSA) file A3, Santa Fe, NM; Mark L.

Note to page 30

Wimberly and Peter L. Eidenbach, "Preliminary Reconnaissance of Archaeological Potential of White Sands National Monument," 28 August 1973, 4. See also Victor Michael Giammattei and Nanci Greer Reichert, *Art of a Vanished Race: The Mimbres Classic Black on White* (Woodland, Calif.: Dillon-Tyler, 1975), 7; Roberta A. Jewett and Kent G. Lightfoot, "The Shift to Sedentary Life: A Consideration of the Occupation of Early Mogollon Pithouse Villages," in *Mogollon Variability,* ed. Charlotte Benson and Steadman Upham (Las Cruces: New Mexico State University, University Museum, 1986), 43; Trace Stuart and Mary Sullivan, "Archaeological Clearance Survey of Approximately 15 Miles of Fence Line at White Sands National Monument," Report 594, New Mexico State University, August 1984, 13.

Until the 1930s, anthropologists subscribed to the idea that the Anasazi (Basket Makers) were the sole early Southwestern Culture. In 1934, preeminent Southwestern archaeologists Emil W. Haury and Harold S. Gladwin proposed the term *Hohokam* to delineate the differences between the southern Arizona peoples and the Anasazi. Two years later Haury further differentiated the Mogollon Culture as distinct from the Hohokam and the Anasazi. The Jornada Mogollon lived in the Tularosa Basin and the specific group associated with White Sands was the Bajadan Community. The Jornada Mogollon concentrated their villages along alluvial fans and bajadas to capture the water runoff from the mountains.

National Park Service archaeologist Erik Reed conducted one of the earliest archaeological investigations of White Sands National Monument in 1936-37. Reed examined numerous campsites near White Sands and determined that the sites belonged to Puebloan bands and not to Apache as he had previously believed. He had observed Folsom projectiles that had been removed from White Sands in local private collections. Aside from Reed's report, until the 1970s, archaeological examinations were conducted by amateurs who filled their private arrowhead and pottery collections with pilfered artifacts.

In 1972, archaeologists Mark L. Wimberly and Peter Eidenbach led the initial major archaeological research at White Sands. They categorized White Sands into four archaeological occupation zones: the San Andres Mountains alluvial slopes along the western fringe of Lake Lucero; the eastern edge of Lake Lucero; the southern marginal dune areas; and the eastern marginal dune areas. The interdune areas were not considered for study because of the shifting gypsum dunes. Eidenbach and Wimberly speculated that 300-600 sites had existed in the White Sands region. In the eastern and southern dune areas hearths were situated within an interdune area and identified as seasonal occupation camps. The significance of these hearths is that these ancient site impressions are not found outside the gypsum dune field. The numerous hearths and adjacent camp sites indicate that human interaction in White Sands was extensive over a long period of time.

In 1977, Wimberly, Eidenbach, and ceramics consultant Terry Knight surveyed White Sands for archaeological sites at the northwestern and southwestern corners of the region and for the possible existence of other bajadan community activities. The archaeologists' principal areas of interest were the Lucero Lake and Huntington sites. The Lucero Lake Site is an extensive pueblo village ruin situated on the western side of the ephemeral lake; however, Wimberly and Eidenbach did not find any surface structures. They discovered fire-cracked rocks and excavated a human burial site. Numerous bone fragments and an exposed femur were located. The archaeologists concluded that the bones' arrangement and location suggested that the body had been buried in a flexed position, a distinctive feature in distinguishing the Mogollon from the Hohokam and the Anasazi. The Huntington Site was a pueblo village revealing a dense artifact area and, like the Lucero Lake Site, the village's structures were no longer visible because of extensive erosion. These sites demonstrate that early Southwest cultures located near White Sands in order to utilize mountain water runoffs, to hunt the big game animals in the mountains, and to employ adjacent mountain lookout points to alert the residents of potential enemy threats.

Agricultural advancements in Mesoamerica had immeasurable impacts upon the Southwest cultures. Emil Haury credits this agricultural advance as the moving agent for the establishment of Mogollon villages in the Southwest. While some anthropologists believed that the Mogollon were sedentary peoples, others claim that the traditional sedentary concept is an inapplicable explanation for the Mogollon settlements. These scientists contend that the Mogollon's evolution to early pithouse settlements does not necessarily imply a break with their nomadic lifeways, calling the Mogollon lifeway semisedentary.

In July 1984, archaeologists Trace Stuart and Mary Sullivan surveyed a proposed fence line along the southern and western borders of these early cultural sites and counted at least eight scattered artifact areas. Eidenbach and Wimberly had identified the Lucero Lake Site as pueblo remains; however, Stuart and Sullivan theorized that Lucero Lake Site's low mounds resulted principally from washouts.

Why the Mogollon Culture vanished remains a principal anthropological question in the Southwest. Emil Haury discounts the theory that the Mogollon were overwhelmed by the Anasazi. Haury speculates that the Mogollon's acceptance of the Anasazi-Pueblo Culture resulted in the Mogollon's progression from pithouse structures to pueblo dwellings. As a consequence of the Mogollon's cultural receptivity, Haury adds, the appropriate identification of the Mogollon should be Mogollon-Pueblo. Haury selects the Tarahumara of Chihuahua, Mexico, as the most promising candidates as descendants of the Mogollon. He states that continuous archaeological investigations may "cause us to reassess our notions of Mogollon territoriality, and that what we see as Mogollon north of the International line was in truth no more than a robust arm from a heartland centered in the Sierra Madre Occidental of Mexico."

6. Reid and Doyel, *Prehistory,* 303.

7. Peter L. Eidenbach and Mark L. Wimberly, *Future Past: The Research Prospectus* (Tularosa: Human Systems Research, 1977), 34; Carroll L. Reilly, *The Frontier People* (Albuquerque: University of New Mexico Press, 1987), 285. The Tularosa Basin's exodus was completed and during the period following the drought-induced dispersal, the Mogollon-Mimbres, Hohokam, and Anasazi survivors concentrated in areas anthropologist Carroll L. Reilly designated as provinces. Reilly identifies the La Junta Province situated at the junction of the Conchos River and the Rio Grande in Mexico as the

sanctuary for the fleeing Mogollon-Mimbres. The vacated areas such as the Tularosa Basin remained uninhabited until the arrival of diverse Apache bands.

8. Morris Edward Opler, "Mescalero Apache," in *Southwest Handbook of North American Indians,* ed. Alfonso Ortiz (Washington, D.C.: Smithsonian Institution, 1983), 419.

9. Department of Interior, Bureau of Ethnology, *8th Annual Report 1886-7* (Washington, D.C.: Government Printing Office, 1891), 73-4. Also see Eve Ball, *Indeh: An Apache Odyssey* (Provo, Utah: Brigham Young University Press, 1980); and *In the Days of Victorio: Recollections of a Warm Springs Apache* (Tucson: University of Arizona Press, 1970); Morris Edward Opler, *An Apache Life-Way: The Economic, Social, and Religious Institutions of the Chiricahua Indians* (Chicago: University of Chicago Press, 1941), 261.

10. Elizabeth A. H. John, *Storms Brewed in Other Men's Worlds: The Confrontation of Indians, Spanish, and French in the Southwest, 1540-1795* (College Station: Texas A&M University Press, 1975), 13-5.

11. Herbert E. Bolton, "Coronado in Perspective," in *New Mexico, Past and Present,* ed. Richard N. Ellis (Albuquerque: University of New Mexico Press, 1971), 5-7. Also see Cleve Hallenbeck, *Journey and Route of Cabeza de Baca* (Port Washington: Kennifat Press, 1940; reissue, 1971), 195-98.

12. John, *Storms Brewed in Other Men's Worlds,* 39-52.

13. Albert H. Schroeder, *Apache Indians* (New York: Garland Publishing, Inc., 1974), 1-75.

14. David J. Weber, *The Mexican Frontier 1821-1846: The American Southwest Under Mexico* (Albuquerque: University of New Mexico Press, 1982), 92.

15. Josiah Gregg, *Commerce of the Prairies,* ed. Max L. Moorhead (Norman: University of Oklahoma Press, 1954), 272.

16. Weber, *The Mexican Frontier,* 130-4. Dan L. Flores, ed., *Jefferson and Southwestern Exploration: The Freeman and Custis Accounts of the Red River Expedition of 1806* (Norman: University of Oklahoma Press, 1984), 288-91; William H. Goetzmann, *Army Exploration in the American West 1803-1863* (New Haven, Conn.: Yale University Press, Inc., 1959; reprint, Lincoln: University of Nebraska Press, 1979), 40-4.

17. Gregg, *Commerce of the Prairies,* 124.

18. Ralph Emerson Twitchell, *History of the Military Occupation of the Territory of New Mexico from 1846-1851* (Denver: The Smith-Brooks Company, 1909), 72-9.

19. Senate, *Treaty Between United States and Mexico,* 30th Cong., 1st sess., 1848, S. Exec. Doc. 52, 43.

20. Ibid., 50.

21. A. B. Bender, "Government Explorations in the Territory of New Mexico 1846-1859," *New Mexico Historical Review* 9, no. 1 (January 1934): 1.

22. George P. Hammond and Edward H. Howes, eds., *Overland to California on the Southwestern Trail 1849: Diary of Robert Eccleston* (Berkeley: University of California Press, 1950), i.

23. William Goetzmann, *Exploration and Empire: The Explorer and the Scientist in the Winning of the American West* (New York: Alfred A. Knopf, 1966), xiii; and *New Lands, New Men: America and the Second Great Age of Discovery* (New York: Penguin Books, 1986), 399-418. Also see Richard A. Bartlett, *Great Surveys of the American West* (Norman: University of Oklahoma Press, 1962), xiv.

24. Senate, *Notes of a Military Reconnoissance,* 30th Cong., 1st sess., 1848, S. Exec. Doc. 7, 7.

25. Ibid., 56.

26. Senate, *Report and Map of the Examination of New Mexico,* 30th Cong., 1848, 1st sess., S. Exec. Doc. 23, 3.

27. *Notes of a Military Reconnoissance,* 43.

28. *Report and Map of the Examination of New Mexico,* 44.

29. Ibid., 74-6.

30. Ibid., 83.

31. Senate, *Reports of the Secretary of War with Reconnaissances of Routes from San Antonio to El Paso,* 31st Cong., 1st sess., 1850, S. Exec. Doc. 64, 50.

32. Ibid.

33. Ibid., 169.

34. Ibid., 196.

35. Ibid.

36. Ibid., 197.

37. Ibid., 198.

38. Ibid., 202.

39. Ibid., 14.

40. Ibid.

41. C. L. Sonnichsen, *El Paso Salt War* (El Paso: Texas Western Press, 1961), 7.

42. H. H. Bancroft, *History of Arizona and New Mexico: Works of Bancroft,* vol. 17 (San Francisco: The History Company, 1889), 670.

43. C. L. Sonnichsen, *Tularosa: Last of the Frontier West* (New York: The Devin-Adair Company, 1960), 9-12.

44. S. C. Agnew, *Garrisons of the Regular U.S. Army: New Mexico 1846-1899* (Santa Fe: Press of the Territorian, 1971), 1-9.

45. Francis Paul Prucha, *The Sword of the Republic: The United States Army on the Frontier, 1783-1846* (Bloomington: Indiana University Press, 1969), xvii.

46. A. S. Packard, Jr., and F. W. Putnam, eds., "Salt Lake Plain in New Mexico," 4, *American Naturalist* (1870), 695-6.

47. *Rio Grande Republican,* 23 July 1881, p. 3, col. 3.

48. C. L. Sonnichsen, *The Mescalero Apaches* (Norman: University of Oklahoma Press, 1958), 192. Francis B. Heitman, *Historical Register and Dictionary of the United States Army* (Washington, D.C.: Government Printing Office, 1903; reprint, Urbana: University of Illinois Press, 1965), 446. Nana succeeded Victorio as leader of Mimbres Apaches following the Tres Castillos Massacre in 1881.

49. Sonnichsen, *Tularosa,* 15.

50. William A. Keleher, *The Fabulous Frontier: Twelve New Mexico Items* (Santa Fe: The Rydal Press, 1945), 213.

51. Harwood P. Hinton, "John Simpson Chisum, 1877-84," *New Mexico Historical Review* 31, no. 3 (July 1956): 190.

52. Keleher, *The Fabulous Frontier,* 214-5.

53. A. M. Gibson, *The Life and Death of Colonel Albert Jennings Fountain* (Norman: University of Oklahoma Press, 1965), 282-3; Keleher, *The Fabulous Frontier,* 233.

54. Gibson, *Albert Jennings Fountain,* 282; Keleher, *The Fabulous Frontier,* 235-7.

55. Gibson, *Albert Jennings Fountain,* 281.

56. Keleher, *The Fabulous Frontier,* 247.

57. Gustav Leonard Seligmann, Jr., "The El Paso and Northeastern Railroad System and Its Economic Influence in New Mexico," Master's thesis, New Mexico State University, 1958, 42.

58. Eugene Manlove Rhodes, *Once in the Saddle* and *Paso Por Aqui* (Boston: Houghton Mifflin Company, 1927), 178.

59. Robert H. Sholly, "Alamogordo, New Mexico: A Case Study in the Dynamics of Western Town Growth," Master's thesis, University of Texas at El Paso, 1971, 38.

60. Inventory of the County Archives of New Mexico, 18, Otero County (Alamogordo) (Albuquerque: Historical Records Survey Program, 1939).

Chapter 4

1. Eugene Manlove Rhodes, *Bransford of Rainbow Range* (New York: H. K. Fly, 1920), 86, 43.

2. *Alamogordo News,* 29 March 1900, p. 4, col. 3.

3. Ibid., 7 January 1905, p. 4, col. 4.

4. Ibid., 29 March 1900, p. 1, col. 3.

5. William Kamp Charles, "The Davies-Charles Family in the U.S.A.," December 1960, 2. Tom Charles Family Papers, box 3, folder 9, MS 18, Rio Grande Historical Collections/Hobson-Huntsinger University Archives, New Mexico State University, Las Cruces.

6. Louise Charles Rutz, interview with author, 11 September 1990.

7. Charles, "The Davies-Charles Family," 9.

8. Louise Charles Rutz, "Early Days in New Mexico with the Charles Family," in *Otero County Pioneer Family Histories,* vol. 2 (Alamogordo: Tularosa Basin Historical Society, 1981), 103.

9. Charles, "The Davies-Charles Family," 6. Also see Rutz, "Early Days in New Mexico," 103.

10. *Alamogordo News,* 16 November 1907, p. 3, col. 3.

11. Ibid., 4 January 1908, p. 4, col. 3. Also *Tularosa Valley Tribune,* 20 March 1909, p. 1, col. 3.

12. Ibid., 18 April 1908, p. 4, col. 1; and *Alamogordo News,* 5 October 1907, p. 3, col. 3.

13. Ibid., 28 March 1908, p. 2, col. 2.

14. Ibid., 13 June 1908, p. 1, col. 4.

15. Ibid., 15 August 1908, p. 2, col. 1.

16. Otero County Court House, Marriage Records, books 1 and 2, 335.

17. Mrs. Tom (Bula) Charles, *Tales of the Tularosa* (Alamogordo: Pass of the North, 1953), 51.

18. O. E. Meinzer and R. F. Hare, "Geology and Water Resources of Tularosa Basin, New Mexico," *U.S. Geological Survey Water-Supply Paper 343* (Washington, D.C.: Government Printing Office, 1915), 260.

19. Rutz, "Early Days in New Mexico," 103.

20. Alamogordo Chamber of Commerce Museum of History.

21. Murray Morgan, telephone interview with author, 4 June 1987. Notes in possession of the author.

22. Rutz, "Early Days in New Mexico," 104.

23. Ralph Emerson Twitchell, *The Leading Facts of New Mexican History,* vol. 3 (Cedar Rapids, Iowa: The Torch Press, 1917), 434. Inventory of the County Archives of New Mexico, 18 Otero County (Alamogordo) (Albuquerque: Historical Records Survey Program, 1939).

24. *Alamogordo News,* 5 October 1907, p. 3, col. 1.

25. Ibid., 28 September 1907, p. 2, col. 1.

26. Ralph Charles to the author, 9 September 1986. In possession of the author. *Alamogordo News,* 28 April 1921, p. 2, col. 4. He held numerous positions within the lodge, including at least one term as Worshipful Master. In 1921, Charles was one of fifteen Alamogordo masons who earned the Shriners' degree in the Ancient Order of the Mystic Shrine in El Paso, Texas.

27. *El Paso Daily Times,* 26 August 1898, p. 3, col. 4.

28. Ibid., 4 September 1898, p. 2, col. 1.

29. Ibid., 26 August 1898, p. 3, col. 4.

30. Ibid., 28 August 1898, p. 2, col. 2.

31. Ibid., 26 August 1898, p. 3, col. 4.

32. Ibid.

33. Ibid., 31 August 1898, p. 4, col. 3.

34. Ibid.

35. William A. Keleher, *The Fabulous Frontier: Twelve New Mexico Items* (Santa Fe: The Rydal Press, 1945), 240-58.

36. *El Paso Daily Times,* 4 September 1898, p. 3, col. 2.

37. Keleher, *The Fabulous Frontier,* 259.

38. *El Paso Daily Times,* 3 September 1898, p. 3, col. 3.

39. Stephen Fox, *John Muir and His Legacy: The American Conservation Movement* (Boston: Little, Brown, and Company, 1981), 108; also see John F. Reiger, *American Sportsmen and the Origins of Conservation,* rev. ed. (Norman: University of Oklahoma Press, 1986).

40. Ibid., 103.

41. Alfred Runte, *National Parks: The American Experience,* 2nd ed. (Lincoln: University of Nebraska Press, 1987), 83.

42. *El Paso Daily Times,* 4 September 1898, p. 3, col. 2.

43. W. H. B. Kent and R. V. R. Reynolds, "A Favorable Report on the Proposed Sacramento Forest Reserve, Territory of New Mexico," 1906, U.S. Department of Agriculture, U.S. Forest Service library file 1680, Alamogordo, typescript.

44. Patricia M. Spoerl, "A Brief History of the Early Years of the Lincoln National Forest," February 1981, U.S. Forest Service files, Alamogordo (typescript).

45. *Congressional Record,* 62d Cong., 2d sess., 1912, vol. 48, 5729.

46. Ibid., 5855.

47. *Alamogordo News-Advertiser,* 24 October 1913, p. 1, col. 1-3.

48. David H. Stratton, "Albert B. Fall," in *New Mexico Past and Present,* ed. Richard N. Ellis (Albuquerque: University of New Mexico Press, 1971), 217-8.

49. *Congressional Record,* 63d Cong., 2d sess., 1914, vol. 51, pt. 3, 2290.

50. Ibid., 64th Cong., 1st sess., 1916, vol. 3, pt. 4, 314. *Journal of the Senate,* 64th Cong., 1st sess., 1916, 78.

51. *Congressional Record,* 63d Cong., 2d sess., 1914, vol. 51, pt. 3, 2290; see also ibid., 64th Cong., 1st sess., 1916, vol. 3, pt. 4, 314; Thomas L. Altherr, "The Pajarito or Cliff Dwellers' National Park Proposal," *New Mexico Historical Review* 7 (July 1985): 288-9. Hal Rothman, Bandelier National Monument: An Administrative History.

52. *Santa Fe New Mexican,* 6 December 1921, p. 2, col. 1.

53. Howard P. Chudacoff, *The Evolution of American Urban Society,* 2d ed. (Englewood Cliffs, N.J.: Prentice-Hall, 1981), 40.

54. *Otero County Advertiser,* 13 April 1907, p. 1, col. 2.

55. *Alamogordo News,* 17 August 1907, p. 2, col. 2.

56. *Alamogordo News-Advertiser,* 15 August 1913, p. 1, col. 7.

57. *Proceedings of the First National Park Conference* (Washington, D.C.: Government Printing Office, 1912), 1.

58. *Department of the Interior Reports,* 1 (Washington, D.C.: Government Printing Office, 1914), 88.

59. Ibid.

60. *Statutes at Large of the United States of America,* vol. 39, pt. 1, *Resolutions, 1917* (Washington, D.C.: Government Printing Office, 1917), 535-6.

61. Robert Shankland, *Steve Mather of the National Parks* (New York: Alfred A. Knopf, 1951), 106.

62. David M. Kennedy, *Over Here: The First World War and Society* (Oxford: Oxford University Press, 1980), 45.

63. *Reports of the Department of the Interior* (Washington, D.C.: Government Printing Office, 1920), 14.

64. Ibid., 15.

65. Stratton, "Albert B. Fall," 219; *Congressional Record,* 67th Cong., 1st sess., 1921, vol. 61, pt. 1, 7.

66. *Congressional Record,* 63d Cong., 2d sess., 1917, vol. 51, pt. 4, 3318.

67. *Congressional Record,* 64th Cong., 2d sess., 1917, vol. 54, pt. 1, 272.

68. Stratton, "Albert B. Fall," 218.

69. *Congressional Record,* 66th Cong., 1st sess., 1919, vol. 58, pt. 5, 4284.

70. *Rio Grande Republic,* 10 March 1921, p. 2, col. 1.

71. *Congressional Record,* 66th Cong., 2d sess., 1920, vol. 59, pt. 7, 6495.

72. *Congressional Record,* 64th Cong., 2d sess., 1917, vol. 54, pt. 3, 2471; see also Davis Darrell Joyce, "The Senate Career of Albert B. Fall," Master's thesis, New Mexico State University, 1963, 87.

73. John Ise, *Our National Park Policy: A Critical History* (Baltimore: Johns Hopkins University Press, 1961), 296.

74. *Southern All-Year National Park,* brochure, 23 January 1922, Merritt C. Mechem Papers, New Mexico Records Center and Archives, Santa Fe.

75. *Report of the Secretary of the Interior* (Washington, D.C.: Government Printing Office, 1921), 110.

76. *Alamogordo News,* 3 February 1921, p. 1, col. 3.

77. Ibid., 20 October 1921, p. 1, col. 4; 20 October 1921, p. 5, col. 1; 3 November 1921, p. 1, col. 6; 27 October 1921, p. 1, col. 4; 27 October 1921, p. 2, col. 2.

78. Ibid., 21 November 1921, p. 1, col. 4.

79. *Southern All-Year National Park,* brochure, 23 January 1922, Mechem Papers.

80. *Alamogordo News,* 17 November 1921, p. 1, col. 4; 17 November 1921, p. 2, col. 2.

81. *Santa Fe New Mexican,* 5 October 1922, p. 2, col. 1-3.

82. Ibid., 10 November 1921, p. 1, col. 4.

83. H. H. Brook to Governor Mechem, 17 March 1922, Mechem Papers.

84. Harry L. Kent Papers, General Files, September 1921-August 1922, box 1-9, 13 January 1922, Rio Grande Historical Collections/Hobson-Huntsinger University Archives, New Mexico State University, Las Cruces.

85. Ibid., 19 January 1922.

86. *Alamogordo News,* 4 May 1922, p. 2, col. 3.

87. Shankland, *Steve Mather of the National Parks,* 222.

88. H. H. Brook to Governor Mechem, 10 February 1922, Mechem Papers. The All-Year National Park Bill was also known as Bursum-Hudspeth Bill.

89. *Journal of the Senate,* 67th Cong., 2d sess., 1922, 211.

90. *Congressional Record,* 67th Cong., 2d sess., 1922, vol. 62, pt. 10, 30 June-29 July 1922, 10064.

91. Ibid., 10063

92. Ibid.

93. Ibid., 10065. Neither the *Congressional Record* nor the *Journal of the Senate* identified the senators in attendance or recorded the Senate's voting pattern on the park measure.

94. Ibid., 10064.

95. *Alamogordo News,* 24 November 1921, p. 1, col. 5.

96. William Boone Douglass to Governor Mechem, 4 May 1921, Mechem Papers.

97. *Congressional Record,* 62d Cong., 1st sess., 1912, vol. 51, pt. 4, 314.

98. *Santa Fe New Mexican,* 28 September 1922, p. 2, col. 1-4.

99. Ibid., 7 December 1922, p. 4, col. 5-6; ibid., 16 November 1922, p. 5, col. 1-2; see also *Alamogordo News,* 24 November 1921, p. 1, col. 5.

100. National Park Association Bulletin, 28, 7 June 1922.

101. Ibid., 30, 8 November 1922, 1.

102. Ibid., 29, 26 July 1922, 4.

103. National Park Association Bulletin, 32, 7 February 1923.

104. Nestor Montoya to H. H. Brook, 15 July 1922, White Sands National Monument (WSNM) library, historical file 1922.

105. Robert Sterling Yard, "New Mexico Aflame Against Two Bills," *Outlook* 133 (January-May 1923): 124-25.

106. David Hodges Stratton, "Albert B. Fall and the Teapot Dome Affair," Ph.D. diss., University of Colorado, 1955, 94.

107. Shankland, *Steve Mather of the National Parks,* 223.

108. Stratton, "Albert B. Fall and the Teapot Dome Affair," 2.

109. Donald C. Swain, *Wilderness Defender: Horace M. Albright and Conservation* (Chicago: University of Chicago Press, 1970), 147.

110. Horace M. Albright as told to Robert Cahn, *The Birth of the National Park Service: The Founding Years, 1913-33* (Salt Lake City: Howe Brothers, 1985), 135.

Chapter 5

1. Hal Rothman, *Preserving Different Pasts: The American National Monuments* (Urbana and Chicago: University of Illinois Press, 1989), xiv.

2. Tom Charles, *Story of the Great White Sands* (Alamogordo: publisher unknown, ca. 1939), 6-7.

3. Tom Charles to E. H. Simons, 30 July 1931, Tom Charles Family Papers, MS 18, The Rio Grande Historical Collections/Hobson-Huntsinger University Archives, New Mexico State University, Las Cruces.

4. *Rio Grande Republican,* 11 February 1882, p. 4, col. 2.

5. A. J. Fountain, "Report of Col. A. J. Fountain, Commissioner Doña Ana County," in *Aztlan: The History, Resources, and Attractions of New Mexico* (Boston: D. Lothrop and Company, 1885), 40.

6. *New Mexico,* Bureau of Immigration, 1893, 235, 242.

7. *Report of the Department of the Interior, Governor of New Mexico,* 57th Cong., 1st sess., 1901, pt. 3, 478-79.

8. Ibid., 479.

9. Fayette Alexander Jones, *New Mexico Mines and Minerals* (Santa Fe: The New Mexican Printing Company, 1904), 235.

10. Ibid.

11. *Las Cruces Thirty-four,* 16 March 1906, p. 1, col. 6.

12. *Alamogordo News,* 15 November 1906, p. 2, col. 2.

13. Ibid., 14 December 1907, p. 4, col. 2; *Otero County Advertiser,* 30 November 1907, Supplement.

14. Ibid., 8 August 1908, p. 2, col. 1.

15. Ibid.

16. George Perry Grimsley, "Gypsum and Gypsum Products," *U.S. Geological Survey, Mineral Resources* (Washington, D.C.: Government Printing Office, 1905), 1044.

17. A. E. Koehler, Jr., *New Mexico—the Land of Opportunity: Official Data on the Resources and Industries of New Mexico the Sunshine State* (Albuquerque: Press of the Albuquerque Morning Journal, 1915), 86.

18. *Rio Grande Republican,* 3 March 1916, p. 1, col. 4.

19. *Alamogordo News,* 14 July 1921, p. 1, col. 6 (Great Sulphur Company); ibid., 19 June 1924, p. 4, col. 2 (United Gypsum Company); ibid., 19 October 1922, p. 1, col. 6 (Gypsum Products Company).

20. Ibid., 18 February 1932, p. 1, col. 2.

21. Tom Charles to Arthur Seligman, 19 March 1932, WSNM library, historical file 1932.

22. Tom Charles, *Story of the Great White Sands,* 6-7.

23. Ibid., 7.

24. Tom Charles correspondence file, WSNM library, historical file 1930.

25. R. G. Herron to president of the Las Cruces Commercial Club, 17 March 1926, WSNM library, historical file 1920.

26. Senate, *Report of the Secretary of War,* 31st Cong., 1st sess., 1850, S. Exec. Doc. 64, 14.

27. Paul Edwards, ed., *The Encyclopedia of Philosophy,* vol. 1 (New York: Macmillan Publishing Company, and the Free Press, 1967), 282.

28. Tom Charles to A. B. Fall, 6 November 1925, Tom Charles Family Papers, MS 18, box 1, folder 2, The Rio Grande Historical Collections/Hobson-Huntsinger University Archives, New Mexico State University, Las Cruces.

29. Numa Frenger to Tom Charles, 23 March 1926, Tom Charles Family Papers, MS 18, box 1, folder 2. Frenger served as secretary-treasurer of New Mexico A&M, secretary of Las Cruces Chamber of Commerce, vice-president of Elephant Butte Water Users Association of New Mexico, and served as a judge.

30. Tom Charles to Numa Frenger, 24 March 1926, Tom Charles Family Papers, MS 18, box 1, folder 2.

31. *Alamogordo News,* 18 January 1934, p. 1, col. 3.

32. Tom Charles to A. B. Fall, circa 1926, Tom Charles Family Papers, MS 18, box 1, file 7.

33. Sam Bratton to Ray Lyman Wilbur, 13 January 1930, WSNM library, historical file 1930.

34. Bronson Cutting to Ray Lyman Wilbur, 7 February 1930, National Archives (NA), Record Group (RG) 48, Washington, D.C., file 12-1, part 1, 16 January 1930-3 November 1936.

35. Ibid.

36. Copy of Executive Order 5276, 7 February 1930, "Withdrawal of Public Lands for Classification—New Mexico," NA, RG 48, file 12-1, part 1, 16 January 1930-3 November 1936.

37. Thomas Boles to Horace Albright, 2 February 1930, NA, RG 48, file 12-1, part 1, 16 January 1930-3 November 1936.

38. Richard Dillon to Ray Lyman Wilbur, 24 March 1930, NA, RG 48, file 12-1, part 1, 16 January 1930-3 November 1936.

39. Tom Charles to Dennis Chavez, 27 June 1931, Tom Charles Family Papers, MS 18, box 1, file 7.

40. Tom Charles to Claude Simpson, 30 July 1931, ibid.

41. Tom Charles to Dennis Chavez, 27 June 1931, ibid.

42. Tom Charles to W. D. Bryars, 22 May 1931, WSNM library historical file, 1931.

43. Ibid.

44. William A. Hawkins to Tom Charles, 16 July 1931, WSNM library, historical file 1931.

45. Numa Frenger to Tom Charles, 23 March 1926, Tom Charles Family Papers, MS 18, box 1, folder 2.

46. Arno B. Cammerer to Horace Albright, 8 February 1932, NA, RG 48, file 12-1, part 1, 16 January 1930-3 November 1936.

47. Horace Albright to Ray Lyman Wilbur, March 1930, NA, RG 79, New Mexico Monuments.

48. Thomas Boles to Tom Charles, 5 May 1931, WSNM library, historical file 1931.

49. J. S. B. Woolford to Tom Charles, 25 July 1931, WSNM library, historical file 1931.

50. Thomas Boles to E. H. Simons, 24 September 1931, WSNM library, historical file 1931.

51. Rothman, *Preserving Different Pasts,* 155-7.

52. "Great Sand Dunes National Monument" information sheet. NPS information at Great Sand Dunes National Monument, Colorado. Toll forwarded a favorable monument recommendation to Albright. Because of Toll's strong support and Albright's endorsement, Interior Secretary Wilbur persuaded Hoover to proclaim Great Sand Dunes National Monument on 17 March 1932.

53. Roger Toll to Tom Charles, 2 February 1932; also see Roger Toll to director, "White Sands Inspection Report," 29 January 1932, both in WSNM library, historical file 1932.

54. Tom Charles to Arthur Seligman, 20 February 1932. Ibid.

55. Roger Toll to Tom Charles, 30 December 1932. Ibid.

56. Arthur Seligman to Ray Lyman Wilbur, 28 April 1931. Ibid.

57. Tom Charles to Arthur Seligman, 7 February 1931. Ibid.

58. Roger Toll to Tom Charles, 26 January 1932. Ibid.

59. Roger Toll to Tom Charles, 2 February 1932. Ibid.

60. Tom Charles to Bronson Cutting, 27 March 1931. Ibid.

61. J. S. B. Wolford to Thomas Boles, 1 July 1931, Tom Charles Family Papers, MS 18, box 1, file 3.

62. G. D. Macy, "Highway Construction," *New Mexico* (February 1934): 18.

63. W. R. Eccles to Tom Charles, 5 April 1932, Tom Charles Family Papers, MS 18, box 1, file 2.

64. Charles Wilhelm (draft by Tom Charles) to W. R. Eccles, 29 February 1932, ibid.

65. Ibid.

66. Roger Toll to Tom Charles, 29 August 1932, ibid.

67. Horace M. Albright to Tom Charles, 17 May 1932, WSNM library, historical file 1932.

68. J. F. Hinkle to Tom Charles, 21 May 1932, ibid. For additional information about "other lands" within parks see Temple, Barker & Sloane, Inc., "Mineral Ownership and Development Activity in and Around the National Parks," 22 February 1985, WSNM Library.

69. J. F. Hinkle to Tom Charles, 4 February 1932, ibid.

70. Arno B. Cammerer to Dennis Chavez, 12 July 1932, ibid.

71. Ibid.

72. Ibid.

73. J. F. Hinkle to Arno B. Cammerer, 25 July 1932, ibid.

74. Ray Lyman Wilbur to Herbert Hoover, 16 January 1933, NA, RG 48, file 12-1, part 1, 16 January 1930-3 November 1936.

75. Western Union Telegram, 27 January 1933, WSNM library copy.

76. Horace M. Albright to Tom Charles, 26 January 1933, WSNM library, historical file 1933.

77. *Alamogordo News,* 2 February 1933, p. 1, col. 6-7.

78. Ibid., 2 February 1933, p. 2, col. 1.

79. Department of Interior, *Annual Report of the Secretary of the Interior 1933* (Washington, D.C.: Government Printing Office, 1933), 164-165.

80. Harris Gaylord Warren, *Herbert Hoover and the Great Depression* (London: Oxford University Press, 1959), 65.

81. Ray Lyman Wilbur and Arthur Mastick Hyde, *The Hoover Policies* (New York: Charles Scribner's Sons, 1937), 229.

82. Herbert Hoover, *The Memoirs of Herbert Hoover: The Cabinet and the Presidency 1920-1933* (New York: The Macmillan Company, 1952), 241; see also *Annual Report of the Secretary of the Interior 1933,* 159-162. The White Sands entry into the monument ranks on 18 January 1933 coincides with the inclusion of three other midnight monument proclamations: Black Canyon of the Gunnison (2 March 1933), Death Valley (11 February 1933), and Grand Canyon (22 December 1932) national monuments.

83. Edgar Eugene Robinson and Paul Carroll Edwards, eds., *The Memoirs of Ray Lyman Wilbur 1875-1949* (Stanford: Stanford University Press, 1960), 431.

84. Ibid., 432.

85. *Annual Report of the Secretary of the Interior 1933,* 159-62.

86. Robinson and Edwards, eds., *The Memoirs of Ray Lyman Wilbur,* 432.

87. U.S., *The Statutes at Large,* "Concurrent Resolutions, Recent Treaties, Executive Proclamations and Agreements, Proposed Amendments to the Constitution and Twentieth Amendment to the Constitution," vol. 47 in two parts (December 1931 to March 1933), 2552.

88. Tom Charles, *The Story of the Great White Sands,* 2.

89. John Ise, *Our National Park Policy: A Critical History* (Baltimore: Johns Hopkins University Press, 1961), 354.

90. Alfred Runte, *National Parks: The American Experience,* 2d ed. (Lincoln: University of Nebraska Press, 1987), 49.

91. Mrs. Tom (Bula) Charles, *Tales of the Tularosa* (Alamogordo: Pass to the North, 1953), 50-1.

92. Pinkley's first comment concerning Tom's Gyp Outfit appears in *Southwestern National Monuments Monthly Report,* November 1933, WSNM library.

Chapter 6

1. Mrs. Tom (Bula Ward) Charles, *Tales of the Tularosa* (Alamogordo: Pass to the North, 1953), 53.

2. Frank Pinkley to Arno B. Cammerer, *Southwestern National Monuments Monthly Reports—January Supplement,* January 1933-June 1933, WSNM library. Following the National Park Service administration realignment on 1 August 1937, Pinkley's Southwestern National Monuments were assigned to Region III; White Sands National Monument remained within the Southwestern National Monuments until 1 July 1953, when it was placed directly under the administrative control of Region III. Currently, WSNM is assigned to the National Park Service's Southwest Region.

3. Hal Rothman, *Preserving Different Pasts: The American National Monuments* (Urbana and Chicago: University of Illinois Press, 1989), 89-116.

4. Ibid., 163.

5. Ibid., 112.

6. C. W. Morgan, ed., *Alamogordo News,* 18 January 1934, p. 1, col. 3; also see Rothman, *Preserving Different Pasts,* 113. Rothman adds that from the National Park Service viewpoint the custodians' vigilance or "guardianship," of national monuments, that is, protecting the natural resources from insensitive tourists and vandals, was equally important.

7. Freeman Tilden, *The National Parks: What They Mean to You and Me* (New York: Alfred A. Knopf, 1951), 256.

8. *Southwestern National Monuments Monthly Report,* 1 October 1933-30 June 1934, WSNM library.

9. "Custodian (Part-Time) Personnel Form," National Archives (NA), Record Group (RG) 79, box 2424, file WSNM-New Mexico.

10. Walter P. Taylor to Frank Pinkley, 22 May 1933, ibid; the first individuals to apply were C. C. Merchant of Alamogordo, Harry A. Davis of El Paso, and Chester E. Anderson of Roy, New Mexico. Davis and Merchant dispatched inquiries to Sen. Sam Bratton, and Anderson applied to Sen. Bronson Cutting during February 1933. C. C. Merchant to Sam Bratton, 10 February 1933; Harry A. Davis to Sam Bratton (ca.) February 1933; and Chester E. Anderson to Bronson Cutting, 10 February 1933, all in ibid.

11. *Alamogordo News,* 2 February 1933, p. 2, col. 1; and 10 August 1933, p. 2, col. 1.

12. Tom Charles, *Story of The Great White Sands* (Alamogordo: publisher unknown, ca. 1939), 1-4.

13. *Alamogordo News,* 23 June 1932, p. 1, col. 3.

14. Arthur E. Demaray to Frank Pinkley, 26 July 1933, NA, RG 79, box 2424, file WSNM-New Mexico.

15. Arthur E. Demaray to Frank Pinkley, 26 July 1933, ibid.

16. *Southwestern National Monuments Monthly Report,* October 1933-June 1934, WSNM library.

17. Chief, Division of Appointments to Tom Charles, July 1934, NA, RG 79, box 2424, file WSNM-New Mexico; Guy W. Numbers to Tom Charles, 12 November 1936, ibid.

18. Tom Charles to Arno B. Cammerer, 18 April 1934, ibid.

19. Frank Pinkley to Tom Charles, 22 May 1936, ibid.

20. Frank Pinkley to Tom Charles, 21 July 1934, WSNM library historical file, 1934; also see Tom Charles, *Story of the Great White Sands,* 3; Bula Charles, *Tales of the Tularosa,* 54; and John Ise, *Our National Park Policy: A Critical History* (Baltimore: Johns Hopkins Press, 1961), 346 and 359-63.

21. Horace M. Albright to Ferris Shelton, 11 May 1933, NA, RG 79, box 2424, file WSNM-New Mexico; also see Ronald A. Foresta, *America's National Parks and Their Keepers* (Washington, D.C.: Resources for the Future, Inc., 1984), 45.

22. *Alamogordo News,* 7 December 1933, p. 1, col. 5 and 7. The Civilian Conservation Corps assigned 103 men and 2 women to White Sands National Monument. Shortly thereafter Civil Works Administration laborers replaced them. Also see John C. Paige, *The Civilian Conservation Corps and the National Park Service, 1933-1942: An Administrative History* (National Park Service: Department of the Interior, 1985).

23. *Southwestern National Monuments Monthly Report,* December 1933, WSNM library; also see copy of Civil Works Program—Statistical Summary, April 1934, NA, RG 79, box 2424, file WSNM-New Mexico; and *Southwestern National Monuments Monthly Report,* 1934. The final cost of the road construction into the dunes, begun in December 1933, was $28,281.36. Following the completion of Civil Works Administration and Public Works Administration projects in 1934, the Federal Emergency Relief Administration provided funds for various WSNM clean-up projects.

24. Ibid., August 1933.

25. Ibid.

26. Ibid., 16 July 1936.

27. Ibid., August 1933.

28. Copy of White Sands National Monument, 1939, Information Sheet, NA, RG 79, box 2427, file 208-01.3.

29. *Alamogordo News,* 3 May 1934, p. 1, col. 6 and 7.

30. Ibid; also see Mrs. Ben (Louise Charles) Rutz, "Uncle Sam's Newest Play Ground," *New Mexico* 6 (June 1934): 15.

31. *Alamogordo News,* 3 May 1934, p. 1, col. 6 and 7. Unfortunately Arthur Seligman died in 1933.

32. W. H. Hutchinson, ed., *A Bar Cross Man: The Life and Personal Writings of Eugene Manlove Rhodes* (Norman: University of Oklahoma Press, 1956), 376.

33. *Alamogordo News,* 3 May 1934, p. 1, col. 6.

34. Ibid.

35. Ibid., p. 2, col. 2.

36. Horace M. Albright to Tom Charles, 7 January 1939, NA, RG 79, box 2429, file WSNM-New Mexico.

37. *Southwestern National Monuments Monthly Report,* November 1933, WSNM library.

38. R. T. Spence to G. M. Wootton, 7 February 1936, Charles Family Papers, The Rio Grande Historical Collections/Hobson-Huntsinger University Archives, New Mexico State University Library, Las Cruces.

39. Stephen Kemp, "Parkland Follies," *National Parks* 60 (March-April 1986): 26-27; and Alfred Runte, *National Parks: The American Experience,* 2d ed., rev. (Lincoln: University of Nebraska Press, 1987), 155-79.

40. *Alamogordo News,* 4 August 1932, p. 3, col. 4.

41. Frank Pinkley to Tom Charles, 22 December 1933, WSNM library, historical file 1933.

42. Tom Charles to Frank Pinkley, 3 February 1936, NA, RG 79, box 2424, file WSNM-New Mexico.

43. *Southwestern National Monuments Monthly Report,* December 1935, WSNM library.

44. Ibid., September 1938.

45. Tom Charles to Frank Pinkley, 25 April 1934, WSNM library, historical file 1934.

46. Demaray to Harold L. Ickes, 9 October 1934, ibid.

47. Thomas Alan Sullivan, comp., *Proclamations and Orders Relating to the National Park Service* (Washington, D.C.: Government Printing Office, 1947), 320.

48. Leon Metz, *Pat Garrett: The Story of a Western Lawman* (Norman: University of Oklahoma Press, 1974), 278; also see Senate, *White Sands Missile Range, New Mexico,* 98th Cong., 1st sess., 1983, S. Hrg. 98-730.

49. Tom Charles to Frank Pinkley, 13 June 1939, WSNM library, historical file 1939.

50. Hugh Miller to Tom Charles, 15 June 1939, ibid.

51. Peter L. Eidenbach and Mark Wimberly, "Archaeological Reconnaissance in White Sands National Monument," 1980, 17.

52. G. A. Moskey to Frank Pinkley, 7 January 1937, WSNM library, historical file 1937; Frank Pinkley to Tom Charles, 14 January 1937, ibid; also see Frank Worden to Tom Charles, 29 October 1937, ibid.

53. Frank Pinkley to Herbert Maier, 8 November 1937, ibid.

54. Copy of "National Park Service Federal Acreages as of December 31, 1957 for Use in Compiling Annual Report to Government Service Agency as of June 30, 1958 on Federal Real Property Holding Region," NA, RG 79, box 2424, file WSNM-New Mexico.

55. Copy of "Land Ownership Record," deeds 1-11, ibid.

56. Volney J. Westley to Dave Clark, 17 December 1965, WSNM library, file D-18; also see Senate, *White Sands Missile Range, New Mexico,* 98th Cong., 1st sess., 1983, S. Hrg. 98-730.

57. John Turney to Regional Director, 30 August 1968, WSNM library, file L-1429.

58. Department of Interior, "Non-Metals-1909," *U.S. Geological Survey—Mineral Resources of the United States,* pt. 2 (Washington, D.C.: Government Printing Office, 1911), 377.

59. Douglas McKay to President Dwight D. Eisenhower, 21 February 1953, NA, RG 79, box 3851, Central Classified files-WSNM.

60. Copy of "Proclamation 3024, Adding Lands to the White Sands National Monument, New Mexico," 27 June 1953, WSNM library.

61. *Superintendents' Monthly Narrative,* 8 August 1961, WSNM library.

62. Hugh M. Miller to Tom Charles, 27 September 1937, WSNM library, historical file 1937.

63. Copy of J. L. Lawson and U.S. Government Dog Canyon Agreement, 9 September 1938, WSNM library, land agreement file; also see John H. Diehl, "White Sands National Monument Dog Canyon Water Supply Report," June 1938, WSNM library, historical file 1938. John H. Diehl, regional National Park Service engineer, predicted that laying the necessary fifteen miles of water pipes from Dog Canyon to WSNM would cost the federal government $31,500.

64. Hugh Bozarth to John Mack Gosdin, 9 September 1968, WSNM library, historical file A-88; also see "White Sands National Monument Master Plan-1965," WSNM library. Throughout 1939 the NPS unsuccessfully negotiated with concerned ranchers to acquire water pipeline easements from the mountain stream to the headquarters and residential area.

65. *Superintendents' Monthly Narrative,* 7 June 1966, WSNM library.

66. Ibid., 2 October 1964.

67. Ibid.

68. Information from Oliver Lee Memorial State Park.

69. *Southwestern National Monuments Monthly Report,* September 1935, WSNM library.

70. Ibid., September 1939.

71. Ibid.

72. White Sands National Monument flyer (1934) found in NA, RG 79, box 2424, file WSNM-New Mexico.

Chapter 7

1. *Alamogordo News,* clipping from 1939-40, WSNM folder, Alamogordo Public Library. Faris ignored Charles's dune drives.

2. *Otero County Advertiser,* 25 April 1908, p. 3, col. 3.

3. *Alamogordo News,* 9 March 1929, p. 1, col. 6.

4. Tom Charles Family Papers, 1925-42, box 1, folder 2, 25 March 1941, The Rio Grande Historical Collections/Hobson-Huntsinger University Archives, New Mexico State University, Las Cruces.

5. *Superintendents' Monthly Narrative,* 1941-67, WSNM library.

6. Mrs. Albert B. (Emma Morgan) Fall to Horace M. Albright, 23 May 1933, NA, RG 79, box 2424, file WSNM-New Mexico.

7. Horace M. Albright to Mrs. Albert B. Fall, 5 June 1933, ibid.

8. Hillory A. Tolson to Tom Charles, 20 March 1940, NA, RG 79, box 2430, Central Classified file 1933-49, file 901, "White Sands Privileges."

9. *Alamogordo News,* 11 February 1943, p. 1, col. 3.

10. Ibid., 1 April 1943, p. 1, col. 2; Johnwill delivered the eulogy calling Charles a "swell Boss, a friend, a co-worker, and a wonderful park operator." *Superintendents' Monthly Narrative,* 24 April 1943, WSNM library.

11. Tom Charles Family Papers, newspaper clipping, 19 November 1943. In May 1943, the Alamogordo Chamber of Commerce requested that the National Park Service place a commemorative plaque at the monument honoring Tom Charles as the "Father of White Sands National Monument." Acting Superintendent Charles A. Richey, of the Southwestern National Monuments, wrote to the chamber advising them that it was not National Park Service policy to erect memorials; however, he suggested contacting the state highway department and proposing to them that a portion of the road from WSNM to Alamogordo be named the "Tom Charles Parkway." There was no action by the Chamber of Commerce or state highway department to implement Richey's suggestion. Charles A. Richey to Alamogordo Chamber of Commerce, 8 May 1943, NA, RG 79, box 2428, file WSNM-New Mexico; with Lillian Bagwell, interview with author, Alamogordo, 27 May 1987. When I asked Lillian Bagwell, former secretary and manager of the Alamogordo Chamber of Commerce, if she had knowledge of Richey's idea she stated that no one in the organization ever discussed the issue.

12. *Superintendents' Monthly Narrative,* 24 April 1943, WSNM library.

13. Ibid., January 1964.

14. *Southwestern National Monuments Annual Report,* 1936, 1937, 1938, 1939, WSNM library.

15. Ibid., September 1938.

16. *Superintendents' Monthly Narrative,* 24 November 1948.

17. Rothman, *Preserving Different Pasts,* 188.

18. *Superintendents' Monthly Narrative,* 1941-61, WSNM library.

19. Ibid., 2 September 1954.

20. *Missile Ranger,* 16 February 1990, p. 8, col. 3-8. I registered for the Lake Lucero trip in April 1987. I have had the opportunity to visit most areas within WSNM, and the experience gained from visiting the gypsum dune source completed my understanding of the geological processes involved in dune formations at WSNM.

21. Rothman, *Preserving Different Pasts,* 173.

22. Isabelle F. Story, ed., *Glimpses of Our National Parks* (Washington, D.C.: Government Printing Office, 1934), 6.

23. *Southwestern National Monuments Monthly Report,* November 1934, WSNM library.

24. Ibid.

25. Ibid.

26. Ibid., 1937; ibid., 1938.

27. Ibid., July 1940.

28. Conrad L. Wirth, *Parks, Politics, and the People* (Norman: University of Oklahoma Press, 1980), 237.

29. Ibid.

30. Roy E. Appleman, *Mission 66 for the National Park System* (Washington, D.C.: Government Printing Office, 1956), introductory page.

31. Ibid., 115. The tentative costs for Mission 66 totaled $786,545,600.

32. *Superintendents' Monthly Narrative,* 3 August 1960, WSNM library.

33. Donald Dayton to Daniel Beard, 22 June 1965, WSNM library, file D-18.

34. *White Sands National Monument Master Plan-1965,* WSNM library, 3.

35. *Southwestern National Monuments Monthly Report,* September 1934, WSNM library.

36. "National Park Service Statistical Abstract," 1979, Department of the Interior, National Park Service, Denver, Colorado.

37. *Superintendents' Monthly Narrative,* 23 December 1942, WSNM library.

38. Donald Dayton to Daniel Beard, 22 June 1965, WSNM library, file D-18.

39. Ibid. I can recall visiting the museum during the 1960s and seeing the numerous historical exhibits on display. The prehistoric, Apache, Spanish, Mexican, and American (especially Indian and cavalry clashes) appeared to overshadow the presentations on geology and natural history.

40. Ibid.

41. *Southwestern National Monuments Monthly Report,* 24 May 1937, WSNM library.

42. Johnwill Faris to Alamogordo Chamber of Commerce, 18 April 1958, WSNM library, historical file, A-8215.

43. Tom Charles, "The Nation's Sand Pile," *New Mexico* 15, no. 3 (March 1937): 10; Mrs. Ben Rutz, "Uncle Sam's Newest Play Ground," 15.

44. Aldo Leopold, *A Sand County Almanac: With Essays on Conservation from Round River* (New York: Oxford University Press, Inc., 1949; reprint, New York: Ballantine Books, 1984); Joseph Wood Krutch, *The Desert Year* (New York: William Sloane Associates, 1951); and *The Voice of the Desert: A Naturalist's Interpretation* (New York: William Sloane Associates, 1954); and Conrad Richter, *The Mountain on the Desert: A Philosophical Journey* (New York: Alfred A. Knopf, 1955).

45. Erik Reed to Hugh Miller, 3 January 1956, WSNM library, historical file A-8215.

46. "Art Exhibit Commemorating Establishment Day," January 1960, lists of artists and titles, WSNM library, historical file 1960.

47. Johnwill Faris to Hugh Miller, 25 January 1960, WSNM library, historical file A-8215.

48. *Superintendents' Monthly Narrative,* 1948-55, WSNM library.

49. Hugh M. Miller to Johnwill Faris, 21 April 1958, Southwest Regional Office (SWRO), National Park Service (NPS), White Sands National Monument (WHSA), file A-8215.

50. *Southwestern National Monuments Monthly Report,* 23 April 1936, WSNM library.

51. *White Sands National Monument Master Plan—1965,* WSNM library.

Chapter 8

1. C. L. Sonnichsen, *Tularosa: Last of the Frontier West* (New York: The Devin-Adair Company, 1960), 3.

2. Erik Bergaust, *Werner von Braun* (Washington, D.C.: National Space Institute, 1976), 91-6.

3. Newton B. Drury to Oscar L. Chapman, 10 February 1949, National Archives (NA), Record Group (RG) 79, box 2430, Central Classified file 1933-49.

4. Roscoe E. Bell to Arthur E. Demaray, NA, RG 48, 2 April 1951, file 2-68, New Mexico, Part 4, 1931-53; also see Ibid. The military emphasized the Tularosa Basin's attributes

> considerations of weather, visibility, access to large industrial areas, economical accessibility to urban communities, areas of instrumentation, areas for recovery of experimental apparatus, proportion of public domain available, minimum interference with local activities, necessary intelligence security, strategical location, cost of equipment and facilities already in place, cost of relocation, proximity to location of Army security forces, and initial and projected cost to the United States.

5. T. A. Walters to H. A. Woodring, 18 May 1937, NA, RG 48, file 2-68, New Mexico, 1937-53.

6. H. A. Woodring to T. A. Walters, 25 May 1937, ibid.

7. Marvin A. Kreidberg and Merton G. Henry, "History of Military Mobilization in the United States Army 1775-1945," *Department of the Army Pamphlet #20-212* (Washington, D.C.: Government Printing Office, 1955), 581.

8. *Alamogordo News,* 6 November 1941, p. 1, col. 5; also see Senate, *White Sands Missile Range, New Mexico,* 98th Cong., 1st sess., S. Hrg. 98-730.

9. *Alamogordo News,* 5 February 1942, p. 1, col. 4.

10. Ibid., 25 October 1941, p. 1, col. 5. I am uncertain of precisely what was implied by natural targets, unless they were referring to the mesquite or yucca plants!

11. *El Paso Times,* 6 March 1989, p. 2A, col. 1-6 and p. 1, col. 2-3; see Edward Abbey's, *Fire on the Mountain* (Albuquerque: University of New Mexico Press, 1962), for a fictional account of this "legal thievery."

12. *Las Cruces Bulletin,* 26 June 1991, p. A-4, col. 1-2.

13. *Alamogordo News,* 6 November 1941, p. 1, col. 5.

14. Jeanne Culbertson, "The Effect of Holloman Air Force Base on Alamogordo," Master's thesis, New Mexico State University, 1972, 16.

15. Ibid., 29.

16. Copy of Executive Order 9029, 20 January 1942, NA, RG 48, file 2-68, New Mexico, 1931-53.

17. Ibid.

18. *Superintendents' Monthly Narrative,* 25 October 1948, WSNM library.

19. George Fitzpatrick, "Bombing Range Negotiations Progress," *New Mexico* 1 (January 1942): 39.

20. Sonnichsen, *Tularosa,* 276.

21. Culbertson, "The Effect of Holloman Air Force Base on Alamogordo," 26.

22. *Superintendents' Monthly Narrative,* 1 March 1946, WSNM library.

23. *Missile Ranger,* 4 July 1985, p. 9, col. 1. A young aviator, 2d Lt. Max H. Condron, died while attempting an evening landing on the airstrip on 3 December 1942. Subsequently his fellow pilots called the airstrip Condron Field and in July 1945 the military officially designated it Condron Field.

24. *Wind and Sand,* 16 March 1950, p. 8, col. 2. The army's buildup in the Tularosa Basin was known as the Ordcit Project.

25. *Superintendents' Monthly Narrative,* 23 May 1945, WSNM library.

26. Oscar L. Chapman to Robert Patterson, 6 March 1946, NA, RG 48, Part 3, box 2-68, New Mexico Reservations for Military and Naval Purposes.

27. Copy of Special Use Permit Authorizing Intermittent Use of White Sands National Monument, New Mexico, by the War Department for Military Purposes, ibid.

28. Ibid.

29. Interviews with WSNM Chief Ranger Robert Schumerth and Ranger Dave Evans, at WSNM 5 March 1987.

30. Ibid.

31. Hillory Tolson to Roscoe E. Bell, 29 July 1948, NA, RG 48, file 2-46.

32. Newton Drury to Secretary of the Interior, 10 February 1949, NA, RG 48, file 12-46.

33. *Missile Ranger,* 4 July 1980, p. 1, col. 4.

34. Ibid., 4 July 1985, p. 20.

35. *Wind and Sand,* 16 March 1950, p. 8, col. 2.

36. *Missile Ranger,* 4 July 1980, p. 30, col. 1 and 4 July 1985, p. 4, col. 1.

37. Culbertson, "The Effect of Holloman Air Force Base on Alamogordo," 60.

38. *Las Cruces Sun-News,* 4 July 1948, p. 1, col. 4.

39. Ibid., 2 August 1948, p. 1, cols. 7 and 8. The Department of Defense spokesmen were Gen. John L. Homer, representing Defense Secretary Kenneth Royall; Major General White; Brig. Gen. Philip G. Blackmore, who was White Sands Proving Ground commander; Navy Capt. W. A. Gorry, and Lt. Col. H. B. Hudlbury, representing the army's research and development branch; and Air Force Col. P. F. Helmick, from Alamogordo (Holloman) Air Base.

40. Ibid., 9 July 1948, p. 1, col. 6.

41. Gregg Herken, *The Winning Weapon: The Atomic Bomb in the Cold War 1945-1950* (New York: Vintage Books, 1982), 18.

42. *Las Cruces Sun-News,* 4 August 1948, p. 1, col. 3.

43. Ibid., 1 August 1948, p. 1, col. 7.

44. Roscoe E. Bell to Acting Secretary of Interior C. Girard Davidson, 19 January 1949, NA, RG 48, file 12-46.

45. Roscoe E. Bell to Julius Krug, 24 February 1949, NA, RG 48, box 2-68, New Mexico Reservations for Military and Naval Purposes.

46. Ibid.

47. *Superintendents' Monthly Narrative,* 23 April 1945, WSNM library.

48. Roscoe E. Bell to Julius Krug, 5 January 1949, NA, RG 48, file 2-68.

49. Ibid., 24 February 1949.

50. Newton Drury to Julius Krug, 10 February 1949, NA, RG 48, file 12-46.

51. *Superintendents' Monthly Narrative,* 23 June 1949, WSNM library.

52. Ibid., 12 May, 19 May, 31 May, and 24 July 1946.

53. Ibid., 2 June 1949.

54. Roscoe E. Bell to Oscar L. Chapman, 2 April 1951, NA, RG 48, file 2-68, New Mexico, Part 4.

55. *El Paso Times,* 6 March 1989, p. 1, col. 2; also see Ibid., p. 2, col. 6. McDonald defiantly remarks that he will "take no more promises." Despite compensation rejections by the U.S. Court of Claims, New Mexico Congressman Joe Skeen and U.S. Sen. Pete Domenici plan to present a compensation bill to Congress confident that the federal government would accept its "responsibility." Recently the reasoning has been that if the United States can compensate interned Japanese-Americans and their descendants, then surely we should do no less for the ranchers.

56. Fred A. Seaton to Neil H. McElroy, 11 March 1958, NA, RG 48, file 2-68.

57. *Superintendents' Monthly Narrative,* 8 May 1961, WSNM library.

58. Ibid., 3 November 1961.

59. WSNM Information letter, 30 October 1961, WSNM library, historical file unnumbered.

60. *Superintendents' Monthly Narrative,* 5 February 1962, WSNM library.

61. Ibid.

62. Cyrus Vance to Stewart L. Udall, 20 February 1963, WSNM library, historical file unnumbered.

63. Ibid.

64. *Superintendents' Monthly Narrative,* 8 April 1963, WSNM library.

65. John A. Carver, Jr., to Cyrus Vance, 24 May 1963, WSNM library, historical file unnumbered.

66. Eugene H. Merrill to John A. Carver, Jr., 29 June 1963, ibid.

67. Copy of "Request for Use of White Sands National Monument—Meeting of 3 July 1963," ibid.

68. Ibid.

69. Forrest M. Benson, Jr., to J. M. Carpenter, 8 October 1963, Southwest Regional Office (SWRO), National Park Service (NPS), library, White Sands National Monument (WHSA) file A-19.

70. Ibid.

71. Hugh P. Beattie to J. M. Carpenter, 12 October 1963, SWRO, NPS, library, WHSA file A-19.

72. J. M. Carpenter to Conrad L. Wirth, 16 October 1963, SWRO, NPS, library, WHSA file A-19.

73. Copy of "Special Use Permit-1963" in WSNM library, historical file unnumbered.

74. *Superintendents' Monthly Narrative,* 11 May 1964, WSNM library.

75. Ibid., 12 June 1964.

76. Copy of "Master Special Use Agreement—1977" and "Memorandum of Understanding—1986," ibid.

77. *Alamogordo News,* 28 January 1943, p. 1, col. 6.

78. Hugh Miller to Johnwill Faris, 21 April 1958, WSNM library, historical file 1958.

79. Hugh Miller to Bob Hoffman, 8 May 1958, ibid.

80. Editorial, *National Parks* 63 (March-April 1989): 10-1. Kathryn Kahler, "Airborne Views," *National Parks* 11 (March-April 1986): 18; also see Kenneth W. King, David L. Carver, and David M. Worley, "Vibration Investigation of the Museum Building at White Sands National Monument, New Mexico," Open-File Report 88-544, U.S. Geological Survey, 1988.

81. Richard Benzinger to White Sands Missile Range environmental officer, 25 May 1984, WSNM library, Holloman AFB file.

82. Joe A. Whiteley to commander, Holloman AFB, 22 June 1984, ibid.

83. Walter T. Worthington to Donald Harper, 17 September 1985, WSNM library, Holloman AFB/Government Department Agencies file A-94.

84. Donald Harper to Regional Director, 7 May 1986, ibid.

85. James F. Record to Donald Harper, 10 June 1986, ibid.

86. Donald Harper to James Record, 29 April 1987, ibid.

87. *Annual Report of the Secretary of Interior 1945* (Washington, D.C.: Government Printing Office, 1945), 208.

88. Dyan Zaslowsky, *These American Lands: Parks, Wilderness, and the Public Lands* (New York: Henry Holt and Company, 1986), 32; and *Colorado Prospector,* July 1985, 16. Reprint newspaper columns of various years. This facsimile is found at Great Sand Dunes National Monument, Colorado.

89. Niles Fulwyler to White Sands Missile Range personnel—open letter, 5 August 1985, in author's possession.

Chapter 9

1. Bill Devall and George Sessions, *Deep Ecology: Living As If Nature Mattered* (Layton, Utah: Gibbs M. Smith, Inc., 1985), 110.

2. Frederick Jackson Turner, *The Frontier in American History* (New York: Henry Holt and Company, 1920), 269.

3. Francis Jennings, *The Invasion of America: Indians, Colonialism, and the Cant of Conquest* (New York: W. W. Norton and Company, 1976), 15-31.

4. Craig W. Allin, *The Politics of Wilderness Preservation* (Westport, Conn.: Greenwood Press, 1982), 18-43; also see Richard A. Bartlett, *Nature's Yellowstone* (Tucson: University of Arizona Press, 1974); and *Yellowstone: A Wilderness Besieged* (Tucson: University of Arizona Press, 1985).

5. Roderick Nash, *Wilderness and the American Mind,* 3d ed. (New Haven, Conn.: Yale University Press, 1982), 162.

6. Ibid., 180-1.

7. Aldo Leopold, *A Sand County Almanac: With Essays on Conservation from Round River* (New York: Oxford University Press, 1949; reprint, New York: Ballantine Books, 1984), 141.

8. Stephen Fox, "We Want No Straddlers," *Wilderness* 48 (Winter, 1984): 5-15.

9. Nash, *Wilderness and the American Mind,* 209-19.

10. Ibid., 219.

11. George T. Frampton, Jr., "Wilderness," *Wilderness* 52 (Winter 1988): 2.

12. Ibid. The Wilderness Act of 1964 directed the secretary of the interior to assume the responsibility for recommending to the president appropriate wilderness designations and protection plans for congressional review. The Interior Department identified its holdings for public use as natural, recreational, and historical areas, and within these three categories five classifications of use, ranging from "intensive" to "primitive," were delineated.

13. Allin, *The Politics of Wilderness Preservation,* 146-9.

14. Ibid., 149.

15. Roderick Nash, "Path to Preservation," *Wilderness* 48 (Summer 1984): 5.

16. Ibid., 11.

17. Allin, *The Politics of Wilderness Preservation,* 161.

18. Ibid., 196-7.

19. Marcus Aurelius, *The Meditations,* trans. George Long, Great Books of the Western World, vol. 12 (Chicago: Encyclopedia Britannica, Inc., 1952), 277.

20. Nash, *Wilderness and the American Mind,* 257.

21. *Earth Day—The Beginning,* compiled and edited by the National Staff of Environmental Action (New York: Bantam Books, 1970), preface.

22. Nash, *Wilderness and the American Mind,* 271.

23. Corry McDonald, *Wilderness: A New Mexico Legacy* (Santa Fe: Sunstone Press, 1985), 33.

24. "Great Sand Dunes National Monument Wilderness Recommendation," September 1972; "Great Sand Dunes National Monument Master Plan," July 1977, Great Sand Dunes National Monument library.

25. McDonald, *Wilderness,* 103.

26. Barry Mackintosh, *The National Parks: Shaping the System* (Washington, D.C.: National Park Service, 1985), 68-91.

27. Edward Abbey, *Desert Solitaire: A Season in the Wilderness* (New York: Ballantine Books, 1968), 264.

28. "White Sands Wilderness Recommendation," August 1972, WSNM library, Wilderness file.

29. Ibid.

30. Copy of "Wilderness Act—Public Law 88-5," 3 September 1964.

31. John Turney, interview with author, Alamogordo, New Mexico, 30 May 1987.

32. Ibid.

33. Ibid.

34. *Alamogordo Daily News,* 2 April 1972, p. 1, col. 4, and p. 8, col. 4.

35. Ibid., 2 April 1972, p. 1, cols. 3 and 4.

36. Ibid., 21 April 1972, p. 1, col. 2.

37. Ibid., 9 April 1972, p. 1, col. 2.

38. Ibid., 19 May 1972, p. 3, col. 1.

39. Ibid.

40. "Otero County Planning Commission Meeting"—25 April 1972, Otero County Courthouse, County book 1.

41. Clifton G. McDonald to John Turney, 1 May 1972 and Resolution 1972, 7, WSNM library, Wilderness file.

42. *Alamogordo Daily News,* 2 April 1972, p. 8, col. 6.

43. "WSNM Wilderness Study Plan"—1972, WSNM library.

44. *Alamogordo Daily News,* 21 April 1972, p. 4, col. 2.

45. Frank Kowski to George Hartzog, 6 April 1972, Southwest Regional Office (SWRO), National Park Service (NPS), library, WHSA (White Sands National Monument) file A-44-D.

46. Ibid.

47. E. H. deSaussure to John Turney, 1 May 1972, WSNM library, Wilderness file.

48. Ibid.

49. "WSNM Wilderness Study Plan"—1972.

50. George Hartzog in "White Sands Wilderness Recommendation," August 1972.

51. John Turney, interview.

52. John A. McComb to Curtis Bohlen, 28 August 1973, SWRO, NPS, library, (WHSA) file L48-LOC; Harry B. Crandell to Curtis Bohlen, 29 January 1973, ibid., WHSA file L30-D; and Phillenore D. Howard to Curtis Bohlen, 10 September 1973, ibid., WHSA file L48-LOC.

53. Curtis Bohlen to Harry B. Crandell, 20 March 1973, SWRO library, WHSA file L-48.

54. Ibid.

55. Ibid.

56. Curtis Bohlen to John A. McComb, 18 October 1973, ibid.

57. Richard C. Olson, ed., "The Wilderness System," *The Living Wilderness* 33 (Winter 1974-75): 44.

58. Edward Abbey, *Fire on the Mountain* (1962 and reprint, Albuquerque: University of New Mexico Press, 1989), 109.

Chapter 10

1. Tom Charles, *Story of the Great White Sands* (Alamogordo: publisher unknown, ca. 1939), 13.

2. Rothman, *Preserving Different Pasts,* 89-118; also see Harold L. Ickes, *The Secret Diary of Harold L. Ickes: The First Thousand Days 1933-1936* (New York: Simon and Schuster, 1953), 22-4; Graham White and John Mase, *Harold Ickes of the New Deal: His Private Life and Public Career* (Cambridge, Mass.: Harvard University Press, 1985), 105; Barry MacKintosh, "Harold L. Ickes and the National Park Service," *Journal of Forest History* (April 1985): 78.

3. *El Paso Times,* 9 December 1986, p. 1B, col. 3. The Southwest Regional headquarters in Santa Fe reports that from January-October 1986, WSNM visitors numbered 606,750 compared to Carlsbad Cavern's 693,200 visitors.

4. Erna Fergusson, *Our Southwest* (New York: Alfred A. Knopf, 1952), 143; Edgar C. McMechen, "Saharas of America," *Travel* 61, no. 2 (June 1933): 7; Fred W. Emerson, "Uncle Sam's Biggest Sand Pile," *Nature Magazine* 30, 4 (October 1937): 217; Tom Charles, "The Nation's Sand Pile," *New Mexico* 15, no. 3 (March 1937): 10; Mrs. Ben Rutz (Louise Charles), "Uncle Sam's Newest Play Ground," *New Mexico* 6 (June 1934): 15; Nell Murbarger, "The Great White Sands," *Natural History* 59, no. 4 (April 1950): 228; also see Robert Sterling Yard, *The Book of the National Parks* (New York: Charles Scribner's Sons, 1933), 385; Patricia Nelson Limerick, *Desert Passages: Encounters with the American Deserts* (Albuquerque: University of New Mexico Press, 1985), 4. In 1933 Robert Sterling Yard, executive secretary of the National Park Association, implored his readers, in *The Book of the National Parks,* to visit the Southwestern spectacles. Predating Edward Abbey's appeal for the visitor to abandon his four-wheeled, air-conditioned vehicle in exchange for intimacy with the world of nature, Yard urged visitors to "live a little with the desert."

Experiencing the desert, he wrote, "will enthrall your senses; it will possess you. And once possessed, you are charmed for life." Half a century later, Patricia Nelson Limerick added this idea in *Desert Passages:* "if you have seen one desert, you have not seen them all." In addition see, Pamela Roberson, "Dune Scape," *New Mexico Magazine* 63, no. 5 (May 1985): 58. White Sands National Monument's unique ecosystem and its breathtaking gypsum dunes have not been ignored by artists or photographers. The gypsum dune field was one of the featured landscapes, which included Monument Valley and the Grand Canyon, in the 1987 Miramar Productions video, *Desert Vision: The Magical Southwest,* and was included in noted landscape photographer David Muench's "Nature's America" gallery poster series during the late 1980s. Also, in 1985, photographer Pamela Roberson discovered to her delight WSNM's unique landscapes.

5. *Missile Ranger,* 28 June 1991, p. 1, col. 1-3.

6. *Southwestern Monument's Monthly Report,* October 1936, WSNM library.

BIBLIOGRAPHY

Manuscript Collections

Administration Office. U.S. Forest Service. Alamogordo, N.M.

Charles, Tom, Family. Papers. The Rio Grande Historical Collections/Hobson-Huntsinger University Archives, New Mexico State University, Las Cruces, N.M.

Fall, Albert Bacon Papers. The Rio Grande Historical Collections/Hobson-Huntsinger University Archives, New Mexico State University, Las Cruces, N.M.

Great Sand Dunes National Monument (GSDNM), library. Colorado.

Kent, Harry L. Papers. The Rio Grande Historical Collections/Hobson-Huntsinger University Archives, New Mexico State University, Las Cruces, N.M.

Mechem, Merritt C. Papers. New Mexico Records Center and Archives, Santa Fe, N.M.

National Archives, Record Group 48, White Sands National Monument and New Mexico military and naval reservations.

National Archives, Record Group 79, White Sands National Monument, New Mexico.

Otero County Courthouse. Alamogordo, N.M.

Park library. Mesa Verde National Park, Colo.

Southwest Regional Office (SWRO), National Park Service (NPS), library. Santa Fe, N.M.

White Sands National Monument (WSNM), library. New Mexico.

Bibliography

Government Documents

Adams, George I. "Geology, Technology, and Statistics of Gypsum." *U.S. Geological Survey 223.* Washington, D.C.: Government Printing Office, 1904.

Albright, Horace M. *Glimpses of Our National Monuments.* Washington, D.C.: Government Printing Office, 1929.

Appleman, Roy E. *Mission 66 for the National Park System.* Washington, D.C.: Government Printing Office, 1956.

Bachman, George O. "Paleotectonic Investigations of the Pennsylvanian System in the United States Part I, Regional Analyses of the Pennsylvanian System—New Mexico." *Geological Survey Professional Paper 853.* Washington, D.C.: Government Printing Office, 1975.

Bailey, Vernon. "Mammals of New Mexico." *United States Department of Agriculture, North American Fauna No. 53.* Washington, D.C.: Government Printing Office, 1931.

Darton, Nelson H. "Red Beds and Associated Formations in New Mexico." *U.S. Geological Survey Bulletin 794.* Washington, D.C.: Government Printing Office, 1928.

Derr, Phillip S. et al. "Soil Survey of Otero Area, New Mexico." *U.S. Department of Agriculture, Soil Conservation Service.* Washington, D.C.: Government Printing Office, 1981.

Graton, L. C. "The Alamogordo Desert." *U.S. Geological Survey Professional Paper 68.* Washington, D.C.: Government Printing Office, 1910.

Grimsley, George Perry. "Gypsum and Gypsum Products." *U.S. Geological Survey, Mineral Resources.* Washington, D.C.: Government Printing Office, 1905.

Herrick, H. N. "Gypsum Deposits in New Mexico." *U.S. Geological Survey Bulletin 223.* Washington, D.C.: Government Printing Office, 1904.

Keyes, C. R. "Geology and Underground-Water Conditions of the Jornado del Muerto, New Mexico." *U.S. Geological Survey Water-Supply Paper 123.* Washington, D.C.: Government Printing Office, 1905.

King, Kenneth W., David L. Carver, and David M. Worley. "Vibration Investigation of the Museum Building at White Sands National Monument, New Mexico." Open-File Report 88–544, U.S. Geological Survey, 1988.

Bibliography

Kreidberg, Marvin A., and Merton G. Henry. "History of Military Mobilization in the United States Army 1775-1945." *Department of the Army Pamphlet #20-212.* Washington, D.C.: Government Printing Office, 1955.

McKee, Edwin D., and John R. Douglass. "Growth and Movement of Dunes at White Sands National Monument, New Mexico." *U.S. Geological Survey Professional Paper 750-D.* Washington, D.C.: Government Printing Office, 1971.

————, ed. "A Study of Global Sand Seas." *Geological Survey Professional Paper 1052.* Washington, D.C.: Government Printing Office, 1979.

McKee, Edwin D., and Richard J. Moiola. "Geometry and Growth of the White Sands Dune Field, New Mexico." *U.S. Geological Research* 3, no. 1 (January-February 1975).

McLean, J. S. "Saline Ground-Water Resources of the Tularosa Basin, New Mexico." *U.S. Geological Survey 561.* Washington, D.C.: Government Printing Office, 1970.

Mather, Stephen T. *General Information Regarding the National Monuments.* Washington, D.C.: Government Printing, Office, 1917.

Meinzer, O. E., and R. F. Hare. "Geology and Water Resources of Tularosa Basin, New Mexico." *U.S. Geological Survey Water-Supply Paper 343.* Washington, D.C.: Government Printing Office, 1915.

Neher, R. E. "Soils and Vegetation Inventory of White Sands Missile Range." *U.S. Department of Agriculture, Soil Conservation Service, West Region.* Washington, D.C.: Government Printing Office, 1970.

Otero County, New Mexico. *Inventory of the County Archives of New Mexico* (1939). Typescript.

Otero County, New Mexico. *Otero County Planning Commission* (1972).

Otero County, New Mexico. *Otero County Marriage Records* (not dated), books 1 and 2.

Richardson, G. B. "Report of a Reconnaissance in trans-Pecos Texas." *U.S. Geological Survey 166.* Washington, D.C.: Government Printing Office, 1909.

Slichter, C. S. "Observations on the Groundwaters of Rio Grande Valley." *U.S. Geological Survey Water-Supply Paper 141.* Washington, D.C.: Government Printing Office, 1905.

Sullivan, Thomas Alan, *Proclamations and Orders Relating to the National Park Service.* Washington, D.C.: Government Printing Office, 1947.

Bibliography

U.S. Congress. Senate. *Notes of a Military Reconnoissance.* S. Exec. Doc. 7, 30th Cong., 1st sess., 1848.

U.S. Congress. Senate. *Report and Map of the Examination of New Mexico.* S. Exec. Doc. 23, 30th Cong., 1st sess., 1848.

U.S. Congress. Senate. *Treaty Between United States and Mexico.* S. Exec. Doc. 52, 30th Cong., 1st sess., 1848.

U.S. Congress. Senate. *Report of the Secretary of War.* S. Exec. Doc. 64, 31st Cong., 1st sess., 1850.

U.S. Congress. Senate. *Reports of the Secretary of War with Reconnaissances of Routes from San Antonio to El Paso.* S. Exec. Doc. 64, 31st Cong., 1st sess., 1850.

U.S. Congress. Senate. 59th Cong., 1st sess., 1906. *Congressional Record,* vol. 40, pt. 8.

U.S. Congress. Senate. 62d Cong., 1st sess., 1912. *Congressional Record,* vol. 51, pt. 4.

U.S. Congress. Senate. 62d Cong., 2d sess., 1912. *Congressional Record,* vol. 48.

U.S. Congress. Senate. 63d Cong., 2d sess., 1914. *Congressional Record,* vol. 51, pt. 3.

U.S. Congress. Senate. 64th Cong., 1st sess., 1916. *Congressional Record,* vol. 3, pt. 4.

U.S. Congress. Senate. 64th Cong., 2d sess., 1917. *Congressional Record,* vol. 54, pt. 1.

U.S. Congress. Senate. 66th Cong., 1st sess., 1919. *Congressional Record,* vol. 58, pt. 5.

U.S. Congress. Senate. 66th Cong., 2d sess., 1920. *Congressional Record,* vol. 59, pt. 7.

U.S. Congress. Senate. 67th Cong., 1st sess., 1921. *Congressional Record,* vol. 61, pt. 1, 7.

U.S. Congress. Senate. 67th Cong., 2d sess., 1922. *Congressional Record,* vol. 62, pt. 10.

U.S. Congress. Senate. *Journal of the Senate.* 64th Cong., 1st sess., 1916.

U.S. Congress. Senate. *Journal of the Senate.* 67th Cong., 2d sess., 1922.

U.S. Congress, Senate. *White Sands Missile Range, New Mexico.* 98th Cong., 1st sess., 1984, S. Hrg. 98-730.

Bibliography

U.S. Department of Interior. *Annual Report of the Secretary of the Interior 1933.* Washington, D.C.: Government Printing Office, 1933.

U.S. Department of Interior. *Annual Report of the Secretary of the Interior 1945.* Washington, D.C.: Government Printing Office, 1945.

U.S. Department of Interior. Bureau of Ethnology. *8th Annual Report 1886-7.* Washington, D.C.: Government Printing Office, 1891.

U.S. Department of Interior. "National Park Service Statistical Abstract." National Park Service, Denver, Colorado, 1979.

U.S. Department of Interior. "Non-Metals-1909." *U.S. Geological Survey—Mineral Resources of the United States.* Washington, D.C.: Government Printing Office, 1911.

U.S. Department of Interior. *Proceedings of the First National Park Conference.* Washington, D.C.: Government Printing Office, 1912.

U.S. Department of Interior. *Report of the Department of the Interior. Governor of New Mexico.* 57th Cong., 1st sess, 1901, pt. 10.

U.S. Department of Interior. *Report of the Secretary of the Interior.* Washington, D.C.: Government Printing Office, 1921.

U.S. *Statutes at Large of the United States America,* vol. 34, pt. 1 (December 1905-March 1907). "Concurrent Resolutions of the Two Houses of Congress and Recent Treaties, Convention, and Executive Proclamations," 1907.

U.S. *Statutes at Large of the United States of America,* vol. 39, pt. 1. *Resolutions,* 1917. Washington, D.C.: Government Printing Office, 1917.

U.S. *Statutes at Large of the United States of America.* "Concurrent Resolutions, Recent Treaties, Executive Proclamations and Agreements, Proposed Amendments to the Constitution and Twentieth Amendment to the Constitution." Vol. 47 in two parts (December 1931 to March 1933).

Wilkins, D. S. "Geohydrology of the Southwest Alluvial Basins, Aquifer-Systems Analysis, Parts of Colorado, New Mexico, and Texas." *U.S. Geological Survey Water—Resources Investigations Report 84-4224.* Washington, D.C.: Government Printing Office, 1986.

Books

Bibliography

Abbey, Edward. *Fire on the Mountain*. Albuquerque: University of New Mexico Press, 1962. Reprint, 1989.

——— *Desert Solitaire: A Season in the Wilderness*. New York: Ballantine Books, 1968.

———. *The Journey Home: Some Words in Defense of the American West*. New York: E. P. Dutton, 1977.

Agnew, S. C. *Garrisons of the Regular U.S. Army: New Mexico 1846-1899*. Santa Fe: Press of the Territorian, 1971.

Albright, Horace M., as told to Robert Cahn. *The Birth of the National Park Service: The Founding Years, 1913-33*. Salt Lake City: Howe Brothers, 1985.

Allin, Craig W. *The Politics of Wilderness Preservation*. Westport, Conn.: Greenwood Press, 1982.

Atkinson, Richard. *White Sands: Wind, Sand and Time*. Globe: Southwest Parks and Monuments Association, 1977.

Aurelius, Marcus. *The Meditations*. Translated by George Long. Great Books of the Western World. Vol. 12. Chicago: Encyclopedia Britannica, Inc., 1952.

Austin, Mary. *Land of Little Rain*. Boston: Houghton Mifflin and Company, 1903.

Bagnold, R. A. *The Physics of Blown Sand and Desert Dunes*. Reprint. London: Chapman and Hall, 1971.

Ball, Eve. *Indeh: An Apache Odyssey*. Provo, Utah: Brigham Young University Press, 1980.

———. *In the Days of Victorio: Recollections of a Warm Springs Apache*. Tucson: University of Arizona Press, 1970.

Bancroft, H. H. *History of Arizona and New Mexico: Works of Bancroft*. Vol. 17. San Francisco: The History Company, 1889.

Bartlett, John Russell. *Personal Narrative of Explorations and Incidents*. Vol. 2. New York: S. Appleton and Company, 1854.

Bartlett, Richard A. *Great Surveys of the American West*. Norman: University of Oklahoma Press, 1962.

———. *Nature's Yellowstone*. Tucson: University of Arizona Press, 1974.

226

Bibliography

————. *Yellowstone: A Wilderness Besieged.* Tucson: University of Arizona Press, 1985.

Bergaust, Erik. *Werner von Braun.* Washington, D.C.: National Space Institute, 1976.

Bergon, Frank, ed. *The Wilderness Reader.* New York: New American Library, 1980.

Bolton, Herbert E. "Coronado in Perspective." *New Mexico Past and Present.* Edited by Richard Ellis. Albuquerque: University of New Mexico Press, 1971.

Bowden, Charles. *Blue Desert.* Tucson: University of Arizona Press, 1986.

Bowers, Janice Emily. *Seasons of the Wind: A Naturalist's Look at the Plant Life of Southwestern Sand Dunes.* Flagstaff, Ariz.: Northland Press, 1986.

Brower, David R., ed. *Wildlands in Our Civilization.* San Francisco: Sierra Club, 1964.

Burroughs, John. *Pepacton.* Boston: Houghton, Mifflin and Company, 1881.

Byrne, Frank. *Earth and Man.* Dubuque, Iowa: William C. Brown Company, 1974.

Calvin, Ross. *Sky Determines: An Interpretation of the Southwest.* New York: The Macmillan Company, 1934.

Cazeau, Charles J., ed. *Physical Geology: Principles, Processes, and Problems.* New York: Harper and Row Publishers, 1976.

Charles, Mrs. Tom (Bula). *Tales of the Tularosa.* Alamogordo: Pass to the North, 1953.

Charles, Mrs. Tom (Bula). *More Tales of the Tularosa.* Alamogordo: Bennett Printing Company, 1961.

Charles, Tom. *Story of the Great White Sands.* Alamogordo: publisher unknown, ca. 1939.

Chudacoff, Howard P. *The Evolution of American Urban Society.* 2d ed. Englewood Cliffs, N.J.: Prentice-Hall, 1981.

Devall, Bill, and George Sessions. *Deep Ecology: Living As If Nature Mattered.* Layton, Utah: Gibbs M. Smith, Inc., 1985.

Dick-Peddie, William A. "Vegetation of Southern New Mexico." In *Arid Lands in Perspective,* edited by W. O. McGinnies and B. J. Goldman. Tucson: University of Arizona Press, 1969.

Bibliography

Dodge, Natt D. *The Natural History of White Sands National Monument.* Globe, Arizona: Southwest Parks and Monuments Association, 1971.

Edwards, Paul, ed. *The Encyclopedia of Philosophy.* Vol. 1. New York: Macmillan Publishing Company and the Free Press, 1967.

Eidenbach, Peter L., and Mark L. Wimberly. *Future Past: The Research Prospectus.* Tularosa: Human Systems Research, 1977.

Feltner, William, and John L. McCarty, comps. *New Mexico in Verse.* Dalhart, Tex.: Dalhart Publishing Company, 1935.

Fergusson, Erna. *Our Southwest.* New York: Alfred A. Knopf, 1952.

Fletcher, Colin. *The Man Who Walked Through Time.* New York: Alfred A. Knopf, 1967.

Flores, Dan L., ed. *Jefferson and Southwestern Exploration: The Freeman and Custis Accounts of the Red River Expedition of 1806.* Norman: University of Oklahoma Press, 1984.

Flores, Dan, and Amy Gormley Winton. *Canyon Visions: Photographs and Pastels of the Texas Plains.* Lubbock: Texas Tech University Press, 1989.

Foresta, Ronald A. *America's National Parks and Their Keepers.* Washington, D.C.: Resources for the Future, Inc., 1984.

Fountain, A. J. "Report of Col. A. J. Fountain, Commissioner Dona Ana County." In *Aztlan: The History, Resources, and Attractions of New Mexico.* Boston: D. Lothrop and Company, 1885.

Fox, Stephen. *John Muir and his Legacy: The American Conservation Movement.* Boston: Little, Brown, and Company, 1981.

Giammattei, Victor Michael, and Nanci Greer Reichert. *Art of a Vanished Race: The Mimbres Classic Black on White.* Woodland, California: Dillon-Tyler, 1975.

Gibson, A. M. *The Life and Death of Colonel Albert Jennings Fountain.* Norman: University of Oklahoma Press, 1965.

Goetzmann, William H. *New Lands, New Men: America and the Second Great Age of Discovery.* New York: Penguin Books, 1986.

228

Bibliography

————. *Army Exploration in the American West 1803-1863*. New Haven, Conn.: Yale University Press, 1959. Reprint. Lincoln: University of Nebraska Press, 1979.

————. *Exploration and Empire: The Explorer and the Scientist in the Winning of the American West*. New York: Alfred A. Knopf, 1966.

Gregg, Josiah. *Commerce of the Prairies*. Edited by Max L. Moorhead. Norman: University of Oklahoma Press, 1954.

Hallenbeck, Cleve. *Journey and Route of Cabeza de Baca*. Port Washington, NY: Kennifat Press, 1940. Reissue, 1971.

Hamblin, Kenneth. *The Earth's Dynamic Systems*. New York: Macmillan Publishing Company, 1985.

Hammond, George P., and Edward H. Howes, eds. *Overland to California on the Southwestern Trail 1849: Diary of Robert Eccleston*. Berkeley: University of California Press, 1950.

Harris, David V. *The Geologic Story of the National Parks and Monuments*. 2d ed. Fort Collins: Colorado State University Foundation Press, 1978.

Heitman, Francis B. *Historical Register and Dictionary of the United States Army*. Washington, D.C.: Government Printing Office, 1903. Reprint. Urbana: University of Illinois Press, 1965.

Herken, Gregg. *The Winning Weapon: The Atomic Bomb in the Cold War 1945-1950*. New York: Vintage Books, 1982.

Hewett, Edgar L. *Ancient Life in the American Southwest*. Indianapolis: The Bobbs-Merrill Company, 1930.

Hoover, Herbert. *The Memoirs of Herbert Hoover: The Cabinet and the Presidency 1920-1933*. New York: The Macmillan Company, 1952.

Hunt, Charles B. *Physiography of the United States*. San Francisco: W. H. Freeman and Company, 1967.

Hutchinson, W. H., ed. *A Bar Cross Man: The Life and Personal Writings of Eugene Manlove Rhodes*. Norman: University of Oklahoma Press, 1956.

Ickes, Harold L. *The Secret Diary of Harold L. Ickes: The First Thousand Days 1933-1936*. New York: Simon and Schuster, 1953.

229

Bibliography

The Imperial Dictionary of The English Language. Rev. ed., s.v. "national" and "monument." New York: The Century Company, 1883.

Ise, John. *Our National Park Policy: A Critical History.* Baltimore: Johns Hopkins University Press, 1961.

Jameson, John R. *Big Bend on the Rio Grande: Biography of a National Park: 1540-1795.* New York: Peter Lang Publishing, Inc., 1987.

Jennings, Francis. *The Invasion of America: Indians, Colonialism, and the Cant of Conquest.* New York: W. W. Norton and Company, 1976.

Jewett, Roberta A., and Kent G. Lightfoot. "The Shift to Sedentary Life: A Consideration of the Occupation of Early Mogollon Pithouse Villages." In *Mogollon Variability,* edited by Charlotte Benson and Steadman Upham. Las Cruces: New Mexico State University, University Museum, 1986.

Jicha, Henry L., Jr., and Christina Lochman-Balk. *Lexicon of New Mexico Geologic Names: Precambrian through Paleozoic.* Socorro: New Mexico School of Mines and Mineral Resources, 1958.

John, Elizabeth A. H. *Storms Brewed in Other Men's Worlds: The Confrontation of Indians, Spanish, and French in the Southwest.* College Station: Texas A&M University Press, 1975.

Jones, Fayette Alexander. *New Mexico Mines and Minerals.* Santa Fe: The New Mexican Printing Company, 1904.

Keleher, William A. *The Fabulous Frontier: Twelve New Mexico Items.* Santa Fe: The Rydal Press, 1945.

Kennedy, David M. *Over Here: The First World War and Society.* Oxford: Oxford University Press, 1980.

Koehler, A. E., Jr. *New Mexico—the Land of Opportunity: Official Data on the Resources and Industries of New Mexico the Sunshine State.* Albuquerque: Press of the Albuquerque Morning Journal, 1915.

Krutch, Joseph Wood. *The Desert Year.* New York: William Sloane Associates, 1951.

———. *The Voice of the Desert: A Naturalist's Interpretation.* New York: William Sloane Associates, 1954.

Bibliography

Leopold, Aldo. *A Sand County Almanac: With Essays on Conservation from Round River.* New York: Oxford University Press, Inc., 1949. Reprint. New York: Ballantine Books, 1984.

Ligon, J. Stockley. *Wild Life of New Mexico: Its Conservation and Management.* Santa Fe: Santa Fe New Mexican Publishing Corp., 1927.

Limerick, Patricia Nelson. *Desert Passages: Encounters with the American Deserts.* Albuquerque: University of New Mexico Press, 1985.

————. *The Legacy of Conquest: The Unbroken Past of the American West.* New York: W. W. Norton & Company, 1987.

Lipe, William D. "The Southwest." In *Ancient Native Americans,* edited by Jesse D. Jennings. San Francisco: W. H. Freeman and Company, 1978.

McDonald, Corry. *Wilderness: A New Mexico Legacy.* Santa Fe: Sunstone Press, 1985.

Mackintosh, Barry. *The National Parks: Shaping the System.* Washington, D.C.: National Park Service, 1985.

MacMahon, James A., ed. *The Audubon Society Nature Guides: Deserts.* New York: Alfred A. Knopf, 1985.

Metz, Leon. *Pat Garrett: The Story of a Western Lawman.* Norman: University of Oklahoma Press, 1974.

Nabhan, Gary Paul. *Gathering the Desert.* Tucson: University of Arizona Press, 1985.

National Staff of Environmental Action. *Earth Day—The Beginning.* New York: Bantam Books, 1970.

Nash, Roderick. *Wilderness and the American Mind.* 3d ed. New Haven, Conn.: Yale University Press, 1982.

————, ed. *American Environmentalism: Readings in Conservation History.* 3d ed. New York: McGraw-Hill, 1990.

New Mexico. Bureau of Immigration, 1893.

Opler, Morris Edward. *An Apache Life-Way: The Economic, Social, and Religious Institutions of the Chiricahua Indians.* Chicago: University of Chicago Press, 1941.

Bibliography

————. "Mescalero Apache." In *Southwest Handbook of North American Indians*. Vol. 10, edited by Alfonso Ortiz. Washington, D.C.: Smithsonian Institution, 1983.

Ortega, Joaquin. *The Intangible Resources of New Mexico*. Santa Fe: Archaeological Institute of America, 1945.

Paige, John C. *The Civilian Conservation Corps and the National Park Service, 1933-1942: An Administrative History*. Washington, D.C.: National Park Service, Department of the Interior, 1985.

Powell, John Wesley. *Report on the Lands of the Arid Region*. Washington, D.C.: Government Printing Office, 1879.

Prucha, Francis Paul. *The Sword of the Republic: The United States Army on the Frontier, 1783-1846*. Bloomington: Indiana University Press, 1969.

Reid, Jefferson, and David E. Doyel, eds. *Emily W. Haury's Prehistory of the American Southwest*. Tucson: University of Arizona Press, 1986.

Reiger, John F. *American Sportsmen and the Origins of Conservation*. Rev. ed. Norman: University of Oklahoma Press, 1986.

Reilly, Carroll L. *The Frontier People*. Albuquerque: University of New Mexico Press, 1987.

Reinech, H-E, and I. B. Singh. *Depositional Sedimentary Environments*. New York: Springer-Verlag, 1973.

Rhodes, Eugene Manlove. *Bransford of Rainbow Range*. New York: H. K. Fly, 1920.

————. *Good Men and True*. New York: H. K. Fly, 1920.

————. *Once in the Saddle and Paso Por Aqui*. Boston: Houghton Mifflin Company, 1927.

————. *Beyond the Desert*. New York: Grosset and Dunlap, 1934.

Richter, Conrad. *The Mountain on the Desert: A Philosophical Journey*. New York: Alfred A. Knopf, 1955.

Righter, Robert W. *Crucible for Conservation: The Creation of Grand Teton National Park*. Boulder: Colorado Associated University Press, 1982.

Bibliography

Robinson, Edgar Eugene, and Paul Carroll Edwards, eds. *The Memoirs of Ray Lyman Wilbur 1875-1949.* Stanford: Stanford University Press, 1960.

Rothman, Hal. *Preserving Different Pasts: The American National Monuments.* Urbana and Chicago: University of Illinois Press, 1989.

Runte, Alfred. *National Parks: The American Experience.* 2d ed., rev. Lincoln: University of Nebraska Press, 1987.

Rutz, Louise Charles. "Early Days in New Mexico with the Charles Family." In *Otero County Pioneer Family Histories.* Alamogordo: Tularosa Basin Historical Society, 1981.

Sandeen, William. "Geology of the Tularosa Basin, New Mexico." In *New Mexico Geological Society Guidebook of Southeastern New Mexico.* Santa Fe: New Mexico Geological Society, 1954.

Sax, Joseph L. *Mountains without Handrails: Reflections on the National Parks.* Ann Arbor: University of Michigan Press, 1980.

Schrepfer, Susan R. *The Fight to Save the Redwoods: A History of Environmental Reform, 1917-1978.* Madison: University of Wisconsin Press, 1983.

Schroeder, Albert H. *Apache Indians.* New York: Garland Publishing, Inc., 1974.

Seager, William R. *Geology of Organ Mountains and Southern San Andres Mountains, New Mexico.* Socorro: New Mexico Institute of Mining and Technology, 1981.

Shankland, Robert. *Steve Mather of the National Parks.* New York: Alfred A. Knopf, 1951.

Shreve, Forrest. *Vegetation of the Sonoran Desert.* Washington, D.C.: Carnegie Institution of Washington Publications 591, 1951.

Sonnichsen, C. L. *The Mescalero Apaches.* Norman: University of Oklahoma Press, 1958.

————. *Tularosa: Last of the Frontier West.* New York: The Devin-Adair Company, 1960.

————. *El Paso Salt War.* El Paso: Texas Western Press, 1961.

Stratton, David H. "Albert B. Fall." In *New Mexico Past and Present,* edited by Richard N. Ellis. Albuquerque: University of New Mexico Press, 1971.

Story, Isabelle F., ed. *Glimpses of Our National Parks.* Washington, D.C.: Government Printing Office, 1934.

Bibliography

Swain, Donald C. *Wilderness Defender: Horace M. Albright and Conservation.* Chicago: University of Chicago Press, 1970.

Talmage, Sterling B., and Thomas P. Wootton. *The Non-Metallic Mineral Resources of New Mexico and Their Economic Features.* Socorro: State Bureau of Mines and Mineral Resources, 1937.

Tilden, Freeman. *The National Parks: What They Mean to You and Me.* New York: Alfred A. Knopf, 1951.

Trowbridge, A. C., ed. *Dictionary of Geological Terms.* New York: Dolphin Books, 1962.

Turner, Frederick Jackson. *The Frontier in American History.* New York: Henry Holt and Company, 1920.

Twitchell, Ralph Emerson. *History of the Military Occupation of the Territory of New Mexico from 1846-1851.* Denver: The Smith-Brooks Company, 1909.

———. *The Leading Facts of New Mexican History.* Vol. 3. Cedar Rapids, Iowa: The Torch Press, 1917.

Van Dyke, John C. *The Desert: Further Studies in Natural Appearances.* New York: Charles Scribner's Sons, 1904.

Warren, Harris Gaylord. *Herbert Hoover and the Great Depression.* London: Oxford University Press, 1959.

Weber, David J. *The Mexican Frontier 1821-1846: The American Southwest Under Mexico.* Albuquerque: University of New Mexico Press, 1982.

Weber, Robert H., and Frank E. Kottlowski. *Gypsum Resources of New Mexico.* Socorro: New Mexico Bureau of Mines and Mineral Resources, 1959.

White, Graham, and John Mase. *Harold Ickes of the New Deal: His Private Life and Public Career.* Cambridge, Mass.: Harvard University Press, 1985.

Wilbur, Ray Lyman, and Arthur Mastick Hyde. *The Hoover Policies.* New York: Charles Scribner's Sons, 1937.

Wirth, Conrad L. *Parks, Politics, and the People.* Norman: University of Oklahoma Press, 1980.

Bibliography

Wooton, E. O., and Paul C. Standley. *Flora of New Mexico*. Washington, D.C.: Government Printing Office, 1915.

Worster, Donald, ed. *The Ends of the Earth: Perspectives on Modern Environmental History*. New York: Cambridge University Press, 1988.

Wright, George M., Joseph S. Dixon, and Ben H. Thompson. *Fauna of the National Park Service of the United States*. Washington, D.C.: Government Printing Office, 1933.

Yard, Robert Sterling. *The Book of the National Parks*. New York: Charles Scribner's Sons, 1933.

Zaslowsky, Dyan. *These American Lands: Parks, Wilderness, and the Public Lands*. New York: Henry Holt and Company, 1986.

Articles

Albright, Horace M. "Research in the National Parks." *Scientific Monthly* 36 (January-June 1933): 483-501.

Altherr, Thomas L. "The Pajarito or Cliff Dweller's National Park Proposal, 1900-1920." *New Mexico Historical Review* 60 (July 1985): 271-94.

Bender, A. B. "Government Explorations in the Territory of New Mexico 1846-1859." *New Mexico Historical Review* 9, no. 1 (January 1934): 1-32.

Benson, Seth B. "Concealing Coloration Among Some Rodents of the Southwestern United States." *University of California Publications in Zoology* 40 (1933): 1-70.

Botkin, Charles W. "The White Sands National Monument." *Pan American Geologist* 60 (1933): 304-5.

Bowers, Janice E. "Plant Geography of Southwestern Sand Dunes." *Desert Plants* 6 (Summer 1984): 31-54.

Brady, F. W. "The White Sands." *Mines and Minerals* 25, nos. 1-4 (1905): 529-30.

Brown, David E. "Chihuahuan Desert Scrub." *Desert Plants* 4 (1982): 169-79.

———. "Return of the Natives." *Wilderness* 52 (Winter 1988): 49.

Burbank, Jim. "Fate of Mexican Wolf Has People Howling." *New Mexico* 68 (February 1990): 52-7.

Bibliography

Charles, Tom. "The Nation's Sand Pile." *New Mexico* 15, 3 (March 1937): 10-1.

Cockerell, T. D. A., and Fabian Garcia. "Preliminary Note on the Growth of Plants in Gypsum." *Science* 8 (July-December 1898): 119-21.

Editorial. *National Parks* 63 (March-April 1989): 10-1.

Emerson, Fred W. "An Ecological Reconnaissance in the White Sands, New Mexico." *Ecology* 16, no. 2 (April 1935): 226-33.

————. "Uncle Sam's Biggest Sand Pile." *Nature Magazine* 30, 4 (October 1937): 217-9.

Fitzpatrick, George. "Bombing Range Negotiations Progress." *New Mexico* 1 (January 1942): 39-40.

Fletcher, Milford. "Through Darkest New Mexico with Tongue in Cheek or the Exotic African Oryx." *Park Service* 6 (Winter 1986): 25.

Fox, Stephen. "We Want No Straddlers." *Wilderness* 48 (Winter 1984): 4-19.

Frampton, George T., Jr. "Wilderness." *Wilderness* 52 (Winter 1988): 2.

Harrington, M. W. "Lost Rivers." *Science* 6 (1885): 265-6.

Hays, Samuel P. "The Environmental Movement." *Journal of Forest History* 25, 4 (October 1981): 219-21.

Herrick, C. L. "The Geology of the White Sands of New Mexico." *New Mexico University Bulletins* 1 and 2 (1900): 1-15.

————. "Lake Otero, An Ancient Salt Lake Basin in Southeastern New Mexico." *American Geologist* 34 (1904): 174-89.

Hill, R. T. "The Texas-New Mexican Region." *Geological Society American Bulletin* 3 (1891): 85-100.

Hinton, Harwood P. "John Simpson Chisum, 1877-84." *New Mexico Historical Review* 31, no. 3 (July 1956): 177-205.

Kahler, Kathryn. "Airborne Views." *National Parks* 11 (March-April 1986): 16-9.

Kemp, Stephen. "Parkland Follies." *National Parks* 60 (March-April 1986): 26-7.

Bibliography

MacBride, Thomas H. "The Alamogordo Desert." *Science* 21 (January 1905): 90-7.

McKee, Edwin D. "Structures of Dunes at White Sands National Monument, New Mexico." Special Issue 7. *Sedimentology* 1 (1966): 1-69.

Mackintosh, Barry. "Harold L. Ickes and the National Park Service." *Journal of Forest History* 29 (April 1985): 78-84.

McMechen, Edgar C. "Saharas of America." *Travel* 61, no. 2 (June 1933): 7-11.

Macy, G. D. "Highway Construction." *New Mexico* (February 1934): 18.

Murbarger, Nell. "The Great White Sands." *Natural History* 59, 4 (April 1950): 228-35.

Nash, Roderick. "Path to Preservation." *Wilderness* 48 (Summer 1984): 5-11.

Olson, Richard C., ed. "The Wilderness System." *The Living Wilderness* 33 (Winter 1974-5): 41-6.

Packard, A. S., Jr., and F. W. Putnam, eds. "Salt Lake Plain in New Mexico." *American Naturalist* 4 (1870): 695-6.

Quammen, David. "Yin and Yang in the Tularosa Basin." *Audubon* 87 (January 1985): 61-8.

Reid, William H., and Gail R. Patrick. "Gemsbok (Oryx gazella) in White Sands National Monument." *The Southwestern Naturalist* 28 (18 February 1983): 97-9.

Righter, Robert W. "National Monuments to National Parks: The Use of the Antiquities Act of 1906." *The Western Historical Quarterly* 20 (August 1989): 281-301.

Roberson, Pamela. "Dune Scape." *New Mexico* 63 (May 1985): 58-67.

Runte, Alfred. "Origins and Paradox of the American Experience." *Journal of Forest History* 21 (April 1977): 65-75.

Ruthven, Alexander G. "A Collection of Reptiles and Amphibians from Southern New Mexico and Arizona." *American Museum of Natural History Bulletin* 23 (1907): 483-603.

Rutz, Mrs. Ben (Louise Charles). "Uncle Sam's Newest Play Ground." *New Mexico* 6 (June 1934): 15-6.

Science 21, no. 187 (29 July 1898): 119.

Science 21, no. 525 (1905): 90.

Sellars, Richard W. "National Parks: Worthless Lands or Competing Land Values," *Journal of Forest History* 27 (July 1983): 130-45.

Shields, Lora Mangum. "Zonation of Vegetation Within the Tularosa Basin, New Mexico." *The Southwestern Naturalist* 1 (April 1956): 49-68.

Stone, R. O. "Desert Glossary." *Earth Science Review* 3 (1967): 211-68.

Waterfall, U. T. "Observations on the Desert Gypsum Flora of Southwestern Texas and Adjacent New Mexico." *The American Midland Naturalist* 36 (1946): 456-66.

Whitfield, Charles J. and Hugh L. Anderson. "Secondary Succession in the Desert Plains Grassland." *Ecology* 19 (April 1938): 171-80.

Wright, R. A., and J. H. Honea. "Aspects of Desertification in Southern New Mexico, U.S.A.: Soil Properties of a Mesquite Duneland and a Former Grassland." *Journal of Arid Environment* 11 (1986): 139-45.

Yard, Robert Sterling. "New Mexico Aflame Against Two Bills." *Outlook* 133 (January-May 1923): 124-5.

Dissertations and Theses

Allmendinger, Roger J. "Hydrologic Control over the Origin of Gypsum at Lake Lucero, White Sands National Monument, New Mexico." Master's thesis, New Mexico Institute of Mining and Technology, 1971.

Bundy, Roy E. "Color Variation in Two Species of Lizards: *Phrynosoma modestum* and *Holbrookia maculata* Subspecies." Ph.D. diss., University of Wisconsin, 1955.

Culbertson, Jeanne. "The Effect of Holloman Air Force Base on Alamogordo." Master's thesis, New Mexico State University, 1972.

Joyce, Davis Darrell. "The Senate Career of Albert B. Fall." Master's thesis, New Mexico State University, 1963.

Lozano, Rogelio. "The Distribution and Ecology of Two *Echinocereus triglochidiatus* Populations in White Sands National Monument, New Mexico." Master's thesis, University of Texas at El Paso, 1979.

Bibliography

McFarland, Craig. "Habitat Partitioning Among Three Species of Lizards from White Sands National Monument, New Mexico." Master's thesis, University of Wisconsin, 1969.

Meyer, Delbert Eugene. "Studies on Background Color Selection in Two Species of Lizards: *Halbrookia maculata* subspecies and *Phrynosoma modestum.*" Ph.D. diss., University of Wisconsin, 1959.

Schaffner, Edward Ray. "Flora of the White Sands National Monument of New Mexico." Master's thesis, New Mexico Agriculture and Mechanic College, 1948.

Seligmann, Gustav Leonard Jr. "The El Paso and Northeastern Railroad System and Its Economic Influence in New Mexico." Master's thesis, New Mexico State University, 1958.

Sholly, Robert H. "Alamogordo, New Mexico: A Case Study in the Dynamics of Western Town Growth." Master's thesis, University of Texas at El Paso, 1971.

Stratton, David Hodges. "A. B. Fall and the Teapot Dome Affair." Ph.D. diss., University of Colorado, 1955.

Unpublished Sources

Bednarz, James C., "The Mexican Wolf: Biology, History, and Prospects for Reestablishment in New Mexico," *Endangered Species Report 18,* U.S. Fish and Wildlife Service, 1988. WSNM Library

---. "An Evaluation of the Ecological Potential of White Sands Missile Range to Support a Reintroduced Population of Mexican Wolves," *Endangered Species Report 19,* U.S. Fish and Wildlife Service, 1989. WSNM Library.

Borell, Adrey E. "Birds of White Sands National Monument," 1938. Typescript. SWRO Library.

Bugbee, Robert E. "Notes On Animal Occurrence and Activity in the White Sands National Monument, New Mexico," 1942. Typescript. SWRO Library.

Charles, William Kamp. "The Davies-Charles Family in the U.S.A.," 1960. Typescript. Tom Charles Family Papers.

Dice, Lee R. "Mammal Distribution in New Mexico," 1927. Typescript. SWRO Library.

Diehl, John H. "White Sands National Monument Dog Canyon Water Supply Report," 1938. Typescript. WSNM Library.

Bibliography

Eidenbach, Peter L., and Mark L. Wimberly. "Archaeological Reconnaissance in White Sands National Monument," 1980. WSNM Library.

"Great Sand Dunes National Monument Wilderness Recommendation," September 1972. Great Sand Dunes NM Library.

"Great Sand Dunes National Monument Master Plan," July 1977. GSDNM Library.

Hartzog, George. "White Sands Wilderness Recommendation," August 1972. WSNM Library.

Heil, Kenneth D., and Steven Brack. "The Rare and Sensitive Cacti of White Sands National Monument." Contract Report for the National Park Service by Ecosphere Environmental Services, New Mexico, 1985. WSNM Library.

Hendrickson, Peter D., ed. "An Administrative History of the White Sands National Monument," 1973. Typescript. WSNM Library.

Historical information obtained from the Alamogordo Chamber of Commerce Museum of History.

Historical information obtained from the Great Sand Dunes National Monument.

Historical information obtained from the Oliver Lee Memorial State Park.

Kent, H. B., and R. V. R. Reynolds. "A Favorable Report on the Proposed Sacramento Forest Reserve, Territory of New Mexico," 1906. U.S. Department of Agriculture, U.S. Forest Service library file 1680, Alamogordo. Typescript.

Kunzmann, Michael R., et al., "Tamarisk Control in Southwestern United States." Proceedings of Tamarisk Conference, Special Report No. 9, 1989. WSNM Library.

McDougall, W. B. "Some Wildlife Problems at White Sands National Monument," 1939. Typescript. SWRO Library.

———. "Wildlife Project at White Sands National Monument," Special Report, 1939. SWRO Library.

National Park Association Bulletin, 1922, 1923. Governor Merritt C. Mechem Papers.

Petticord, David V. "White Sands National Monument Information Letter," 1971. Typescript. WSNM Library.

Bibliography

Pinkley, Edna Townsley. "A National Monuments Enthusiast Riding Her Hobby," ca. 1937. Mesa Verde National Park Library.

Pinkley, Frank. "Southwestern National Monuments," excerpt from National Park Service meeting in Santa Fe, ca. 1939. Mesa Verde National Park Library.

"Plants and Animals of the White Sands: A Discussion of Dunes Ecology, 1983." National Park Service, WSNM library.

"Preliminary Draft Resources Management Plan and Environment Assessment for White Sands National Monument," 1981. Typescript. WSNM Library.

Reed, Erik F. "Special Report," 1937. Typescript. WSNM Library.

Region III Quarterly (January 1940). SWRO Library.

Reid, William H. Untitled report, examining the saltcedar in White Sands National Monument, undated. Typescript. WSNM Library.

————. "Final Report: White Sands National Monument Natural Resources and Ecosystem Analysis," 1980. WSNM Library.

Southwestern National Monuments Monthly Report (1933-40). WSNM Library.

Spoerl, Patricia M. "A Brief History of the Early Years on the Lincoln National Forest," February 1981. U.S. Forest Service file, Alamogordo. Typescript.

Stuart, Trace, and Mary Sullivan. "Archaeological Clearance Survey of Approximately 15 Miles of Fence Line at White Sands National Monument," Report 594, New Mexico State University, August 1984. New Mexico State University Library.

Sumner, Lowell. "White Sands National Monument Science Studies Plan," 1969. WSNM Library.

Superintendents' Monthly Narratives (January 1941-June 1967). WSNM Library.

Temple, Barker & Sloane, Inc. "Mineral Ownership and Development Activity in and Around the National Parks," 22 February 1985. WSNM Library.

Vandiver, Vincent W. "White Sands Geological Report." Southwestern Monuments Special Report 3, National Park Service, May 1936. Typescript. WSNM Library.

Bibliography

Wenger, Gilbert, and William Featherstone. "Historical Sketch of White Sands National Monument," 1955. Typescript. WSNM Library.

White Sands National Monument library historical files. Typescript.

White Sands National Monument Master Plan 1965 and *1976.* WSNM Library.

Wimberly, Mark L., and Peter L. Eidenbach. "Preliminary Reconnaissance of Archaeological Potential of White Sands National Monument," 1973. WSNM Library.

Newspapers

Alamogordo Daily News (New Mexico)
Alamogordo News (New Mexico)
Alamogordo News-Advertiser (New Mexico)
Albuquerque Journal (New Mexico)
El Paso Daily Times (Texas)
El Paso Times (Texas)
Las Cruces Bulletin (New Mexico)
Las Cruces Sun-News (New Mexico)
Las Cruces Thirty-Four (New Mexico)
Otero County Advertiser (Alamogordo, New Mexico)
Rio Grande Republican (Las Cruces, New Mexico)
Santa Fe New Mexican (New Mexico)
Tularosa Valley Tribune (New Mexico)
Missile Ranger (White Sands Missile Range, New Mexico)
Wind and Sand (White Sands Missile Range, New Mexico)

Interviews

Bagwell, Lillian. Interview with author. Alamogordo, New Mexico, 27 May 1987. While interviewing former secretary of Alamogordo Chamber of Commerce Lillian Bagwell in 1987, she informed the author that the historical files of the commercial club and chamber of commerce were destroyed during the early 1950s. She stated that her attempts to save the documents proved futile because her boss wanted to lighten the office's administrative holdings. At the time, the chamber of commerce was relocating to its present location at White Sands Boulevard.

Charles, Ralph. Letter to author, 19 September 1986.

Murray, Morgan. Telephone conversation with author, Alamogordo, New Mexico, 4 June 1987.

Bibliography

Rutz, Louise Charles. Letter to author, 7 September 1986.

———. Interview with author. Placitas, New Mexico, 11 September 1990.

Schumerth, Robert, and Dave Evans. Interviews with author. White Sands National Monument, 5, 15 and 17 March 1987.

Turney, John. Interview with author. Alamogordo, New Mexico, 30 May 1987.

INDEX

Index

Index

Index

Index

Index

Index

Index

Index

Index

256

Index

Index

Index

Index

Index

Index

Index

Index

Index

Index

Index

Index

Index

White Sands was designed by Harold Augustus
and composed on a Macintosh IIci and AST 386 computer,
using QuarkExpress 3.1 and Pagemaker 4.0 with Ganjon from the Adobe
Library. Maps in this publication were rendered on FreeHand 3.0 and the
cover was designed using Adobe Illustrator 3.2.
Text was outputted on a Linotronic L300 by Subia Corporation.
It was printed and bound by Thomson-Shore, Inc.,
on 50 lb Natural Offset